"For police and emergency personnel responding to calls for service where human tragedy is often observed firsthand, I can think of no better book than this. In addition to addressing the complex problems associated with observation and participation in critical trauma and highly emotional stress situations, Dr. Conn also provides tools for building individual and personal resilience for police and emergency personnel. Nothing could be more important than safe-guarding our first responders in a world too often marred by mass shootings, spree killings, and terrorist attacks. I highly recommend this book. It is a great read for police officers and emergency personnel everywhere!"

Robert W. Taylor, PhD, professor of criminology and public affairs at the University of Texas at Dallas

"Dr. Conn does an excellent job integrating current research with best practices to provide a comprehensive understanding of key factors in professional resilience for police and other first responders."

Jeff Morley, PhD, registered psychologist and retired RCMP officer

Increasing Resilience in Police and Emergency Personnel

Increasing Resilience in Police and Emergency Personnel illuminates the psychological, emotional, behavioral, and spiritual impact of police work on police officers, administrators, emergency communicators, and their families. Author Stephanie Conn, a clinician and researcher as well as a former police officer and dispatcher, debunks myths about weakness and offers practical strategies in plain language for police employees and their families struggling with traumatic stress and burnout. Sections of each chapter also offer guidance for frequently overlooked roles such as police administrators and civilian police employees. Using real-world anecdotes and exercises, this book provides strengths-based guidance to help navigate the many complex and sometimes difficult effects of police and emergency work.

Stephanie M. Conn, PhD, is a former police officer, as well as the daughter and wife of police officers, and currently works as a therapist in private practice, specializing in police stress, trauma, work–life balance, coping, and resilience. She began as a dispatcher/call-taker before becoming an officer with the Fort Worth Police Department and then earning her doctorate in counseling psychology. She has presented widely to emergency responders, sharing wisdom gained from her police experience, research, and therapy practice.

Increasing Resilience in Police and Emergency Personnel

Strengthening Your Mental Armor

STEPHANIE M. CONN

Routledge
Taylor & Francis Group

NEW YORK AND LONDON

First published 2018
by Routledge
711 Third Avenue, New York, NY 10017

and by Routledge
2 Park Square, Milton Park, Abingdon, Oxon, OX14 4RN

Routledge is an imprint of the Taylor & Francis Group, an informa business

Library of Congress Cataloging-in-Publication Data
A catalog record for this title has been requested

ISBN: 978-1-138-64367-3 (hbk)
ISBN: 978-1-138-64368-0 (pbk)
ISBN: 978-1-315-56339-8 (ebk)

Typeset in Goudy
by Florence Production Ltd, Stoodleigh, Devon, UK

*I would like to dedicate this book to my dad, Donald Fairrel.
Dad, you were always an inspiration to me; a symbol of strength
and nobility; a model for working hard, making sacrifices, and doing
the right thing. I know you sacrificed a lot to try to be the best
officer and leader you could while also trying to be the best husband
and father. While you weren't always home for dinner, I always
felt you were with me in mind and heart. Thank you for your
support as a father and your service as a police officer.*

Stephie

Contents

Preface

The objective of this book is to identify the psychological, emotional, behavioral, and spiritual impact of police work and to offer guidance to mitigate the detrimental effects by promoting resilience. The book comprises six chapters, with each chapter further divided into sections relating to four key groups: the police officer, the police administrator, the emergency communicator, and the police family member. The chapter topic will be discussed as it relates to each of these groups, with some unavoidable overlaps. You may be tempted to skip sections, reading only the sections for your identified group. I urge you to read these sections as well. There might be something you take away from these sections that would help you understand others. You might even takeaway something for yourself. Each chapter will end with a summary of the key points, or takeaways, for the topic discussed. Think of these as takeaways as tools you can put in your duty bag. You might not need them all the time but, when you need them, you NEED them.

As a cop-turned-psychologist, former emergency communicator, daughter and wife of police officers, I share a multifaceted perspective on the impact of police work. As a positive psychologist and researcher, I'm able to see past the pathology-based themes of other writings to provide proven strategies for mitigating and, in some cases, even preventing the negative impact of police work. Periodically, I will share brief excerpts or stories from my formal and informal research on police stress, coping, and identity processes; from my observations and experiences as a police officer/communicator; and from stories shared with me by other police I personally know.

Acknowledgments

I would like to acknowledge all of the women and men who participated in my research over the years for sharing their wisdom, experience, and insights to help me understand their resiliency processes. Without these insights, this book would not be possible. I also want to acknowledge the contributions of the many people I have worked with over the years in various capacities: fellow officers, dispatchers, call-takers, peer team members, chaplains, mental health professionals, and clients. I have learned so much from the lived experiences of others who have, little by little, added to both my knowledge and admiration of those in this noble profession.

I would also like to acknowledge the support of my husband, Perry. We have been a team since we first met, with you on one side of the radio and me on the other. I could not have done this without your support. You've inspired me, believed in me, and pushed me to push myself. You've been a mirror, reflecting when I've been resilient, and when I've neglected my own resilience. I love you for that and for the wonderful man you are.

> Man is capable of changing the world for the better if possible, and of changing himself for the better if necessary.
>
> (Frankl, 2006, p. 131)

REFERENCE

Frankl, V. E. (2006). *Man's search for meaning*. Boston, MA: Beacon Press.

Chapter 1

Are Police Resilient?

> For what then matters is to bear witness to the uniquely human potential at its best, which is to transform a personal tragedy into a triumph, to turn one's predicament into a human achievement. When we are no longer able to change a situation—just think of an incurable disease such as inoperable cancer—we are challenged to change ourselves.
>
> (Frankl, 2006, p. 112)

The preceding quote epitomizes resilience as it reflects acknowledging and accepting our limits as human beings and working within these confines to be our best selves. This optimistic stance on human potential underpins the information offered in this book, with specific suggestions for its application to a variety of life circumstances. This optimism is central to achieving resilience and reducing suffering. But I'm getting ahead of myself. First, let's talk about what we mean by "resilience."

RESILIENCE—A STATE OR A TRAIT?

So, what is resilience? Is it something we have? Something we are born with? Something we develop? If we develop resilience, how do you go about doing that? Why do some develop it while others don't? I think it's important that I acknowledge these questions and make a point to tackle each of them in this book. I invite you to think about your questions and preconceptions about resiliency and consider how your responses might influence your actual resiliency.

First, resilience is the ability to bounce back from adversity. "Back" doesn't mean that things will be restored to exactly as they were before. We can never have back what was, whether it was good or bad. People and situations are constantly evolving, so we have to consider a "bounce back" more in terms of restoration of our ability to function. How well we are able to function is a combination of factors such as how we are doing emotionally, physically, spiritually, and psychologically in various domains of our lives like work, family, and social lives. As you likely know, functioning is a rather complex concept with many moving parts.

Optimal functioning in each of these domains is difficult to achieve. Life is messy. There will be times when you excel in one domain and another one will suffer for it. Other times, one domain will demand more of you, which will cause you to neglect others. A prime example of this in police work is when there is a critical police incident such as a shooting or a non-operational (organizational) stressor like a promotional process. These events will place extra demands and stress on you, limiting the amount of time and mental energy you have to participate in other life roles. Accept this reality and embrace the temporary shift in priorities. If you notice that you are always spending your time on one domain at the expense of others, a change is likely needed. The neglect of other domains may or may not be intentional, but the effect is the same. Focusing too much on work weakens family and health. Focusing too much on family isn't good for one's career. Balance is key to succeeding in all areas of life. Therefore, part of "bouncing back" following an event means re-establishing balance in your life.

This, of course, assumes that there was a balance to begin with. It assumes that, prior to an event, you were in a state of optimal wellness. This is sometimes not the case. I have worked with individuals who have cited workplace "emergencies" as consuming all of their family time, only to discover that they were this way with every job they ever had, leading me to believe that this is a way of life, not an environmental reality. This way of life might be due to the individual's addiction to work, addiction to drama, struggle to plan ahead because they are constantly putting out fires, or struggling to say "no" to others. These are some of the lifestyle patterns that contribute to suffering, making individuals *more* vulnerable to negative reactions to critical incidents and organizational stressors than those who have maintained a healthy lifestyle.

Other times, the chronicity of imbalance between life roles is due to being compromised in some way. Balance, like resilience, takes mental and physical energy, planning, and awareness. For those struggling with mental health issues such as depression, anxiety, or post-traumatic stress disorder (PTSD), it may seem impossible to muster up the energy to make a course correction to achieve life role balance. Making matters worse, many people struggle with mental health issues for ungodly amounts of time before acknowledging there is a problem, much less doing anything about it. I cannot count how many clients who have told me that they have struggled with their difficulty for *years* before getting help. There are many reasons for this and I will discuss them at length in Chapter 5.

Overwhelmingly, experts agree that resilience isn't something you have or don't have. It's neither a state nor a trait, but a *process*. Like officer safety, physical fitness, or sobriety, it's something that requires a daily commitment and actions in furtherance of this commitment. This should be fairly obvious, given that the objective of this book is to provide strategies for increasing resilience. Yes, some people have inherited temperaments that make them more adaptive to adversity. For instance, research shows that those with negative emotional states such as anxiety, depression, and anger have a higher risk of developing PTSD (Clark, 2005). Conversely, those with more positive emotionality tend to fare better (Clark, 2005). Don't worry though, temperament can only take you so far. If you weren't endowed with an ideal temperament, you can still be resilient.

To be clear, being resilient does not mean that you won't develop a mental health issue such as PTSD. What it does mean is that you are better able to recover from it than if you were not resilient in the first place. This proposition sounds strange to some police employees I've spoken with. They don't outright contest it, but there seems to be a look that says, "If a person were resilient, wouldn't they prevent themselves from developing PTSD, depression, or marital difficulty in the first place?" My response to this question would be an unequivocal "no." At times, there are circumstances which are so profoundly impactful, interrupting the body's defense mechanisms and normal coping activities, rendering an individual vulnerable to psychological injury. I'll discuss this at length in Chapter 2 but will offer an overview here to illustrate my point. Take, for example, a very traumatic event such as seeing a murdered child. The emotional part of the brain, the amygdala, will likely override the information-processing portion of the brain, the hippocampus, interrupting the individual's ability to process the information so that healing can occur. As a result, the brain will mistakenly believe that the event is not over because it didn't store the memory properly. The brain will send reminders of the event such as intrusive images and nightmares because it is designed to keep warning its host (you) of perceived danger until it registers that the event is over and the danger is gone. These reminders come from the primitive part of the brain and have evolutionary value. This is a prime example of the event being so horrific that the normal brain processes are being interrupted, and an evolutionary-based system, designed to enhance survival, wreaks havoc on the individual. A normally resilient individual may not be able to offset the physiological chain of events that I just described. However, a resilient person would take measures to promote healing from the psychological injury. A less resilient person would take measures to avoid or mask the signals coming from the brain, hoping that they would simply stop if they're ignored. There are many ways individuals ignore these signals of danger from the brain such as drinking, sleeping, "retail therapy," risk-taking, and so forth.

POLICE: RESILIENT OR PLAGUED BY TRAUMA AND DENIAL?

Over the last few years, we have become increasingly aware of the impact of chronic stress and trauma on first responders. Due to anti-stigma campaigns and the courage of many first responders to speak about their experiences, we have been talking about mental health issues more now than we ever have. Overall, this is a welcome shift, and I hope it continues until the stigma is finally lifted. Despite the benefits, there could be unintended negative consequences to all of this talk. Are you still there? Bear with me and I will explain what I mean.

Some of the discussions about PTSD and other mental health issues in first responder's work have been framed in a way that makes them sound as if it is inevitable that you will develop them. I don't doubt that the reason for the strength of these discussions is owed to decades of these issues being downplayed or ignored by others. I recognize that, currently, these issues are *still* being downplayed and ignored, placing the onus of proving a work-related injury on persons who are already suffering. However, these discussions, and some of the organizational responses, may be unintentionally inflating the perceived incidence rates for these difficulties. Organizational practices that send a pathology-based message (Do this debriefing/training to avoid getting PTSD) are a disservice to police officers who would otherwise be well with their own coping and wellness strategies. Psychological research may also be adding to the perception of police officers being unwell, since research with police populations, similar to the general population, has largely been disorder-focused and deficit-based, highlighting difficulties in police officers instead of their strengths. It offers us a skewed view of police officers, their coping skills, and their potential to be resilient. The media also perpetuates the notion that police officers are not doing well. Consider the nature of news headlines. Which headline do you think would grab more attention: "PTSD rates in police are escalating" or "Only a small percentage of police officers have PTSD"? The last headline isn't nearly as exciting as the first one. Exciting headlines sell.

The majority of first responders do not develop PTSD or other mental health disorders. This holds true even after recognizing that mental health issues are underreported in policing. Recent research (including my own) shows that police officers are taking measures to cope better and have healthier lifestyles. Many folks have come to my office, having read about a mental health difficulty, oftentimes informed by Dr Google, and believe that they have one disorder or another. Oftentimes, their "symptoms" are normal responses to abnormal events and will go away on their own or with some small changes in thinking or coping styles. Unfortunately, I think this trend of "What's wrong with me?" is exacerbated by insurance companies who require a diagnosis before they will reimburse for counseling.

With regard to mental health training and debriefings offered by police organizations, don't throw out the baby with the bathwater. These practices are still helpful to many officers by empowering them with information that normalizes their responses and connects them to resources if they decide they need them. It's the manner in which they are introduced that makes all the difference in the world. When I offer organizational training and I am speaking with officers and call-takers about reactions to traumatic events, I am cautious not to propose that PTSD or other mental health issues are inevitable. Instead, I alert them to the idea that they *could* develop PTSD, depression, or burnout, given an abundance of risk factors combined with the absence of protective factors. There isn't a magical formula as to which risk and protective factors evolve into PTSD. It is a highly complex and individual situation. Risk factors include lack of social support, history of traumatic events, the perception of threat to life during the incident, coping styles, and even genetic susceptibility. Aside of the absence of risk factors, some protective factors include the presence of social support, positive personalities, and an overall satisfaction with life. It's the officers' resilience, coupled with support, which will allow them to heal. It requires making the decision that you will take care of yourself and then doing it *continuously*.

The truth of the matter is that police are actually quite resilient. Statistically, police officers are on par with or, in some instances, slightly above the general population in terms of rates of mental health issues. Even when they have been found to be generously above the general population, it is still a minority of officers. The percentage of police officers afflicted by anxiety and depression is mixed and is oftentimes confounded by statistics for PTSD since those with PTSD seem to have a higher risk of developing depression. PTSD rates in active duty police officers vary from 7 to 19 percent (Carlier, Lamberts, & Gersons, 1997; McCaslin et al., 2006; Neylan et al., 2005). One study of first responders responding to the attack on the World Trade Center found that 8.8 percent of the first responders likely had depression, while 11.1 percent likely had PTSD, based on self-administered symptom questionnaires (Stellman et al., 2008). Although these statistics are higher than the general population statistics (6.7 percent of Americans have depression [Anxiety and Depression Association of America, 2016], while 7–8 percent have PTSD [U.S. Department of Veteran Affairs, 2016]), it is important to note that at least 91 percent of first responders did NOT have depression nor did almost 89 percent have PTSD after their exposure to the terrorist attacks and the subsequent loss of lives, including the lives of their co-workers. Even if many of the first responders underreported their symptoms, there would still be a substantial number of them who remained healthy. Let's look at a few reasons why police are such resilient people.

I think it's fair to say that people who decide to go into a stressful, dangerous profession have a personality or at least the attitude of being tough. I have had many people say to me when I was a police officer: "I don't know how you do it. I could never do that job." They would go on to speak about being too afraid to chase bad guys or deal with conflicts on a daily basis. So those who choose this job already possess courage and determination to manage difficult situations. Burke (2009) studied the reasons why individuals entered policing and found four primary reasons: 1) a family history of policing, 2) attraction to the power of the position, 3) prior experience with police (sometimes as a crime victim), and 4) desire to help people. In short, they believe in their ability to exercise control over situations, right the wrongs, and be helpful to others. When the expectations are realistic, because they're aware of the limitations of the police role, they will likely experience less stress. Their prior traumatizations, addressed with adaptive coping, may be a protective factor, in that they have developed and practiced coping with adversity. When they have an exaggerated view of their ability to control outcomes, they're more likely to suffer and question their abilities, increasing their risk of traumatic stress. I'll revisit the impact of prior traumatizations later in this chapter.

The second layer of "resilience screening" is the pre-screening background and psychological evaluation. This process weeds out many of those who are not suitable and able to be resilient on the job, including those whose assumptions about their ability to handle the job are misguided. Important indicators of coping, well-being, and interpersonal skills are assessed.

The next layer involves the training that police receive which promotes their coping and sense of self-efficacy. Training in stress management, crisis intervention, and work–life balance offers police the skills to manage the difficulties in their jobs. These courses are more recent additions to the police academy curriculum. So, many police did not have this during their initial training but, rather, as part of their continued education training. In fact, I have heard from officers that they did not absorb the stress management training during the academy because they were so gung ho to learn about more exciting topics like weapons, drugs, car chases, and takedowns. They revisited the training material later when it was needed for guidance on what to do and who to contact when stress levels were high or they were otherwise struggling. This leads me to the next piece of evidence supporting the resilience of police: they are action-oriented. If there is a problem, they want to "fix" it. This can also be problematic in that they may not seek or allow support from others in "fixing" difficulties, but I will discuss that in the last chapter.

I conducted three research studies with police officers, inquiring of how they cope with their exposure to secondary traumatic stress, their decision to delay retirement, and how they maintained work–life balance. In each of these studies, I found that officers were quite innovative and determined to do what was best for them. In fact, many people said that I would have trouble recruiting for the study on work–life balance because I wouldn't find officers who maintained balance, given the difficulties in shiftwork and an unpredictable work environment. I got more participants than I needed!! Officers across the United States and Canada had a lot to say about how they were promoting their resilience by finding small ways to maintain work–life balance. This is not to say that they did not have difficulties. They did. Yet they managed to be resilient and adapt to their circumstances. I discuss this study as well as the study with police officers who are delaying their retirement in depth in Chapter 4 when I discuss non-operational stressors. The study on coping with exposure to secondary traumatic stress is discussed in Chapter 3.

So, let's recap: people who voluntarily approach conflicts are screened and determined to be psychologically fit for the job, have experience with and possibly even training for adaptive coping, and those who are innovative, action-oriented, problem-solvers to make resilient police. Let's look at some of the challenges to police resilience.

Common Challenges to Resilience for Police Officers

Some challenges for police officers are unique (daily exposure to threat of harm, traumatization of others, work hours), while others occur across professional groups (mental health issues, work–life balance, relationship difficulties, and substance abuse). Each of these will be discussed at length in the chapter on critical police incidents (Chapter 2) and when I discuss secondary traumatic stress (Chapter 3) and non-operational stressors (Chapter 4). For now, I'll provide an overview of them, as they relate to the topic of this chapter, the resilience of police.

Mental Health Issues

Police are fallible human beings, just like everyone else. As such, they sometimes experience mental health issues. Anxiety is the most common mental health condition, affecting 40 million Americans (18 percent of the population) (Kessler, Chiu, Demler, & Walters, 2005). In the United States, depression is the leading cause of disability for persons between the age of 15 and 44. It affects 15 million American adults (6.7 percent) (Anxiety and Depression Association of America, 2016).

Some mental health conditions have a genetic predisposition to them. Yet, having the gene isn't always enough to produce the disorder. It sometimes requires something in the person's environment to activate it. In fact, the social environment is believed to affect a person's predisposition for certain ailments in four ways: 1) it can trigger the disposition, 2) it can compensate for it, 3) it can prevent certain behaviors due to environmental controls, and 4) it can enhance adaptive processes (Shanahan & Hofer, 2005). For example, a genetic predisposition to depression can be activated by chronic exposure to traumatic events (as is the case in police work). Similarly, a genetic predisposition to depression may not evolve into depression if a person is financially secure, has a loving and supportive family, a strong social network, and a job they love where they received in-service training on stress management. In short, it's complicated. You can't just blame a person's family biology for their mental health issues.

Post-Traumatic Stress Disorder

To meet the diagnostic criteria for PTSD, one has to be exposed to actual or threatened death; serious injury; sexual violence either directly, witness it occurring to another, learn about it having occurred to a close friend or loved one; and/or experience repeated exposure to aversive details of the traumatic event as a first responder collecting human remains or being exposed to details of child abuse. These events are considered Criterion A events that must happen to explain the symptoms that follow. These are the symptoms that follow: one or more intrusion symptoms (distressing memories, dreams, flashbacks, re-experiencing/reactions when exposed to environmental cues/reminders), one or more kinds of avoidance behavior (try to avoid memories; thoughts; feelings about the event and/or people, places, activities, objects, situations), two or more negative alterations in mood and cognitions associated with the event (amnesia; persistent, exaggerated negative beliefs about the self, others, the world; persistent, distorted blame of self/others; persistent negative emotional states; diminished interest/participation in activities; detachment from others; difficulty having positive emotions), and two or more symptoms of reactivity and physical arousal (irritable, reckless/self-destructive behavior, hypervigilance, exaggerated startle response, difficulty with concentration and/or sleep). These symptoms have to last for at least a month, cause significant distress or impairment in various forms of functioning, and not be attributed to other reasons like a head injury or substance use (American Psychiatric Association, 2013). So, it's a very detailed set of criteria that have to be met in order to receive this diagnosis. However, it's easy to see that even having half of these symptoms would be very difficult.

As I cited earlier, the incident rates for PTSD in policing closely align with those in the general population. However, when active-duty police have PTSD and have to continue to face traumatic events, it's infinitely worse. They can't escape the places and situations that activate flashbacks or intrusive thoughts, memories, and images. Having flashbacks while on the job compromises their safety and the safety of others. Even the fear of having a flashback or re-experiencing episode is enough to interfere with safe functioning.

Anxiety and Depression: Bigger Concerns for Police

PTSD draws the majority of attention despite findings that suggest that generalized anxiety disorder or major depressive disorder is more likely to develop following trauma exposure (Bryant, O'Donnell, Creamer, McFarlane, Clark, & Silove, 2010). Developing PTSD from a traumatic event also predicted having depression and anxiety but not the reverse (Ginzburg, Ein-Dor, & Solomon, 2009). However, diagnosis of PTSD, depression, and anxiety doesn't usually happen, even if individuals meet diagnostic criteria for all three disorders. Typically, only one disorder will be diagnosed. This isn't good since each disorder calls for specific treatment. Only treating anxiety when PTSD and depression are also occurring results in minimal relief for the individual. I've seen this quite a bit in my practice when individuals have gone to therapists not trained in trauma. Fortunately, these individuals hadn't given up on getting help.

Anxiety

It's very difficult to find incident rates of anxiety in police. Despite being the most common mental health condition, it's shadowed by research on PTSD in police. Given that police are, in fact, people, we can assume that they experience anxiety like the rest of the world. The officers I know worry about the same stuff as everybody else: their financial situations, health, relationships, public speaking, traffic, and so forth. Studies have found that police have the same level of mental health issues as supermarket employees and bankers (van der Velden, Rademaker, Vermetten, Portengen, Yzermans, & Grievink, 2012).

However, there are also some police-specific situations that cause anxiety. In a nutshell, anxiety is fear relating to "Three Cs": certainty (lack of), control, and comfort. Police face uncertainty every day. This is expected. What police *don't* expect to have to deal with is the uncertainty in the police organization. This also taps into the second "C," control. Police anxiety is less about danger on the streets and more about their lack of control of the organizational hassles such as shiftwork, overtime, court appearances, and promotional opportunities. Police oftentimes don't feel like they have any influence over their work environment. They get stuck on calls for long periods of time. They get called in on their day off. The last "C," comfort, is also difficult to achieve in police work. The work is routinely physically and emotionally uncomfortable because police work long hours; wear restrictive, heavy gear; and get stuck in emotionally draining, sometimes awkward, situations.

Depression

Some research has shown that police officers have higher rates of depression than the general population (Violanti & Drylie, 2008). Yes, pre-employment screening might reduce the chance that a person currently experiencing debilitating depression will be hired by a police agency, but it is no assurance that this person will *never* experience depression. That is like saying that they passed the physical examination when they were hired so they should be expected to never develop *any* health problems. That logic is ludicrous.

In fact, there are more officers suffering from depression than the more visible and publicized PTSD. Despite the prevalence of depression in police officers, there appears to be a hesitancy to accept this medical condition as legitimate. After all, people who suffer from depression appear to have nothing to be depressed about. For instance, they have their jobs, family, friends, money, and health. This line of thinking only compounds the angst and shame felt by officers with depression. They *know* that they oftentimes don't have these *reasons*, yet they still have depression.

Some believe that being depressed means that you are weak; that you can't handle the job. I don't think I've heard an over-simplification so brutally unfair. First, depression is a medical condition that is genetically inherited. Second, this inherited gene interacts with the person's environment to produce (or not produce) depressive thoughts, feelings, and behavior. Beyond the inheritance of depressive genes, there are many other factors involved in producing depression such as thyroid levels, sleep deprivation, side effects of many medications, and exposure to light (or lack thereof on night shift). None of these sound like character flaws or weaknesses to me.

The stigma of depression adds insult to injury. Unfortunately, mental health issues are oftentimes regarded by others as a "just" disease in that others say, or at least think, "You *just* can't cope. You *just* feel sorry for yourself . . . you *just* . . . you *just* . . ." (Howard & Crandall, 2007, pp. 1–2). The word "just" divides people, preventing understanding and compassion, worsening the prognosis for individuals with mental health issues. One police officer who suffered from traumatic stress shared her story with me, with permission to share here. She told me of using her undercover skills to hide her pain and suffering. In fact, her undercover skills were so practiced and perfected that she fooled everyone around her. Her pain was deep undercover and only *she* knew her truth. She hid her suffering because mental health issues continue to be stigmatized, especially in the policing profession.

So how does a psychologically healthy individual enter the policing profession and develop depression? Let's consider the typical police officer's environment. Every day, police officers are called to deal with negative events and be in contact with negative people. As discussed earlier, when police officers have a genetic predisposition to depression and are chronically exposed to negative events and people, it's to be expected that depression might occur. It doesn't mean that the depression is permanent, nor does it imply that it will be so severe that he/she cannot continue working. It simply means that the police officer will have to seek treatment for the chemical imbalance that occurs, as well as the problematic thinking and behaving that keep it going.

Even without a genetic predisposition to depression, chronic exposure to negative events can shift a police officer's positive worldview to a negative one. A large-scale study has shown that 70 percent of police officers working in high stress environments reported depressive symptoms (Gershon, Barocas, Canton, Li, & Vlahov, 2009). To be clear, these are *symptoms*, not a full-blown depressive disorder. There is a significant difference between these two. There are many names for this occurrence and just as many theories to explain it such as vicarious traumatization, burnout, cynicism, and moral distress. Whatever name you use, depressive thoughts, feelings, and behaviors oftentimes accompany each of these. It is hard to imagine that the world is a positive place when you are only ever called to deal with it when it's not. Police officers see the worst in people and may lose their faith in mankind. I'd be depressed if I lost my faith in mankind. The narrative in your head might sound something like this: "People treat people horribly. The world is going down the drain. I can't do anything about it but I am expected to." Does this sound familiar? Organizational stressors are oftentimes the bigger culprit when it comes to the police officer's change in worldview. Policies, procedures, unsupportive supervisors or co-workers tend to worsen officers' views of mankind even more than the "bad guys" do because they don't expect to face so many organizational hassles.

Additionally, officers may develop depression from the same life events that non-officers face such as loss and health decline. Yet, police may suffer more with these concerns, given their increased reluctance to seek professional help. Even if they do decide to seek help, shiftwork oftentimes complicates officers' ability to attend therapy appointments or participate in activities that can alleviate depression. This paints a dismal picture of the capacity of police to be resilient. Fear not. It isn't hopeless. Many officers have taken measures to lift their mood and counter the negative effects from the job. We'll talk more about this in Chapter 4.

Spiritual Impact of Police Work

The impact of stress on the spirituality of police officers is often overlooked. Using a broad definition of spirituality, it encompasses concepts of meaning-making, a sense of purpose, and connectedness with others (Smith & Charles, 2010). Officers report changes in their spiritual beliefs after entering the policing profession (Carlier, 1999; Carlier et al., 1997; Marshall, 2003). In a study of officers on cumulative career traumatic stress, 53 percent of officers reported that their faith or religious beliefs had changed due to the job (Marshall).

Many enter the policing profession with idealistic hopes of helping others, referring to police work as a "calling" only to find that some members of the community do not support them for the job they are doing. Police work changes the "soul" of police officers as they repeatedly face human suffering, deception, and violence. Officers report changes in their spiritual beliefs after entering the policing profession (Carlier, 1999; Carlier et al., 1997). Some officers' spiritual beliefs help them make meaning out of the tragedies they face. The continuing ability to make meanings out of these events is deemed critical to the officers' psychological well-being (Pearlman & Saakvitne, 1995).

A sense of connectedness is another important component of spirituality that may be threatened by the stress of police work. Officers report a need to feel connected to members of their community. However, a trend toward isolating from the non-police community may compromise this facet of spirituality.

Substance Abuse

Some police officers mask their pain with substances such as alcohol and drugs and with "process" addictions such as Internet, spending, and staying very busy. Although not unique to policing, there does appear to be some evidence that police are particularly vulnerable to substance abuse (Ballenger et al., 2010). Drinking is promoted by the police culture to help officers deal with the stresses from the job (Violanti, 2003). We referred to it as "choir practice" in my department. It was both a social event and a means to unwind after a long, hard shift. In fact, police culture so strongly promotes drinking among officers as a means of "fitting in" that officers have reported believing that officers who did *not* drink were considered suspicious or unsociable by other officers (Davey, Obst, & Sheehan, 2001).

We have all seen the headlines reporting the story of a police officer abusing alcohol or drugs. It seems like something that happens to other people and very little is reported about how the officer arrived at this place in life. It is such a contradictory story. It's like an obese personal trainer or a hairstylist with bad hair. It doesn't make sense. Yet, substance abuse in policing has a long history. I think back to when my department asked me many years ago to offer training on alcohol abuse awareness after a series of alcohol-related offenses had been committed by our officers. I was shocked by what I learned. I learned that officers, my fellow officers, were very good at hiding their substance abuse. It only came to light when it was so bad that it could no longer be ignored: when it seriously affected their attendance, or resulted in their arrest.

Substance abuse may start out as social drinking with fellow officers to relax after a shift. It can be the insidious escalation of prescription drugs once taken legitimately for back pain. Many people who abuse substances can do so while still appearing functional to most observers. Making matters worse is the fact that many of the observers are co-workers who are reluctant to say anything to the officer or others due to a code of silence. It might feel like a betrayal to express concern about a fellow officer's substance abuse. Yet, anonymous help is available and will be discussed in Chapter 5.

Relationship Difficulties

As with other issues discussed up to this point, police officers are not exempt from the issues that affect non-police individuals. They also have relationship strains stemming from differences in parenting styles; communication difficulties; differing views of how to interact with extended family, how to balance work and family, financial strains, and so forth. The nature of police work also lumps on some additional strains such as shiftwork and traumatic stress. Yet, as for the state of resilience in police officers, relationship difficulties are no more problematic for them than non-police individuals. The contention that police officers have high divorce rates is a myth. In fact, research shows that they have a *lower* divorce rate when compared to other professions (Honig, 2007; McCoy & Aamodt, 2010). Personally, I know several police families who have remained intact (and happy) for decades, despite the strains of the job. Police officers and their families might even be *more* resilient because they have sometimes been prepared for the strains of the job. What other profession has family nights, peer support teams, and support groups for their employees' families? I can only think of other first responder professions such as fire and ambulance services. Do you suppose lawyers have family nights for spouses of lawyers to meet to talk about the strain of long hours and demanding work? I have never heard of such a thing.

Suicide

Suicide by any person is incredibly tragic, but there is something particularly tragic about a police suicide. Police officers are oftentimes viewed as the strongest, most stoic members of the society. This is the problem. The image of the police officer as being invulnerable seems to be absorbed by officers themselves. The conflict between public image and inner feelings of vulnerability can be excruciating. Police suicide devastates the lives of so many people. We must make every effort as a law enforcement family to get informed, care for and support each other, and speak up about mental health issues before it's too late. The latest studies show that police suicides have declined in the last few years. In 2016, there were 108 documented police suicides, down from 141 in 2008 (Badge of Life, 2016). However, more officers died by suicide than by gunfire or traffic accidents COMBINED (97). One suicide is one too many. It's important to understand why the helpers are struggling to help themselves.

As a male-dominated profession, it is important to consider the influence of male socialization. This can even be applied to women who work in this historically "male" profession. Think about some of the things people say to little boys (and girls too) when they are growing up—"Don't cry," "Stop crying," "Crying is for babies," "If you don't have something nice to say, don't say anything," and the list goes on and on. We've been taught to shut down and deny how we feel if it is a "negative" emotion. We might make other people uncomfortable because they don't know what to do for us or they feel they can't offer what we need. Add to these historical teachings about what we are supposed to be doing with our "negative" emotions, the messages we might get from our employer and co-workers (whether it is intended or not)—"He/She's off work mad" and "He/She's screwed. They're never going to get that promotion now." This traps officers into feeling they can't talk about their difficulties. They believe that the only choice is to suck it up until they can't do it any longer. I will discuss warning signs and strategies to support persons considering suicide in Chapter 3.

Work–Life Conflict

Like other professions, police oftentimes struggle to maintain balance between their work and their home lives. The conflict between work and home is based upon three categories of conflict: 1) time-based, where each domain competes with the other for limited time; 2) strain-based, where the strain in one role affects the individual's ability to perform other roles; and 3) behavior-based, where there is a conflict between incompatible behaviors in competing roles. Time-based conflict is self-explanatory, but I will provide examples of strain- and behavior-based conflicts. A common strain-based conflict in policing is the stress officers feel from work, whether it's due to a heavy call load, heavy case load, promotional exams, or politics. This stress interferes with their ability to be present and positive when interacting with family and friends outside of work. Emotionally, they may be depleted or angry about work matters. Police spouses have told me of personality changes where their loved one has become irritable and easily angered. Behavior-based conflict in policing might be the use of the police officer role, to include managing the direction of a conversation (interrogation) when speaking with their loved ones. In this case, they are in a different mindset, which would require a mental shift to their home-life roles like parent or spouse.

In work–life conflict, it appears that family life suffers the most. Research shows that family significantly interferes with work for about 10 percent of people, while 25 percent report high levels of work interfering with family (Duxbury & Higgins, 2003). Police are overloaded at their job and there are dire consequences for their health and home. One study on police found that they averaged at least 10 hours of overtime per week, oftentimes unpaid (Duxbury, 2007). Understaffing is a common complaint in police agencies, as it places more demands on officers to get the work done. Making matters worse, agency budgetary constraints means they are donating their time. This overtime interferes with family, as work demands are placed ahead of family demands (Duxbury, 2007). The study also found that just over half of the police employees reported high levels of stress, while one-third would be considered as high risk for burnout. Their physical and mental health was suffering due to high levels of workload.

The Gender Factor: Resilience in Women in Policing

Women in policing may have additional strains that hamper their ability to be resilient. I've spoken with women in policing who have self-identified as "double failures," believing that they are failing as police and as mothers. Despite much of the changes in household responsibilities and childcare, women continue to have more demands from home than their male counterparts (Duxbury, 2007). As a result, many work less overtime than their male counterparts. This can hamper their career advancement, as they are not perceived to be as dedicated to their job. Women struggle to give 100 percent of themselves to their work AND their family.

Women also have a higher prevalence rate of PTSD than men (Kessler, Sonnega, Bromet, Hughes, & Nelson, 1995). This is, in part, due to having higher levels of exposure to events, such as sexual assault, that lead to PTSD. Additionally, women are more likely to develop PTSD once exposed to a trauma. It's not clear why this is the case. Possibly, it's the personal nature of the traumatic event. Given that women have higher rates of exposure to the most impactful traumas and a heightened risk of PTSD once exposed, women are more than twice as likely as males to develop PTSD (Kessler et al., 1995). In interviewing sexual assault victims, they have to suppress their own emotions while trying to manage the emotions of the victim, referred to as "emotional labor" (Hochschild, 1983), to complete the investigation. However, female police officers are more likely than males to use constructive coping such as talking to significant others or relying on their faith, reducing the likelihood that they would develop mental health concerns such as depression (He, Zhao, & Archbold, 2002).

An additional factor interfering with the resilience of women in policing is the organizational culture. Women in policing are sometimes subjected to harassment, sexual and otherwise, and challenges to their abilities as officers. Although I think this is improving, women still have to prove their worth alongside their male counterparts in this profession. Support from co-workers and the organization is a key determinant of a person's ability to be resilient in the workplace. It has practical (promotional, assistance on calls) and mental (sense of belonging and acceptance) consequences for women's resilience in the workplace. I found that organizational and supervisory support was a key factor in what helped officers manage their exposure to traumatic stress as well as maintaining work–life balance (Conn, Amundson, Borgen, & Butterfield, 2015; Conn & Butterfield, 2013).

POLICE ADMINISTRATORS

As a police administrator, you have to be concerned with your own resilience as well as fostering the resilience of your subordinate officers. One of the best ways to promote the resilience in others is to model it. Modeling resilient behaviors is more compelling than anything you can ever tell or teach another. People learn best by observing. They also believe what they see you *do* more than what you say. I remember asking a large audience of police officers who their role models were, and after a moment of silence, I heard snickering coming from the back of the room. I asked what was so funny and they informed me that it was far easier to think about who was *not* their role model; who was a disaster at managing their life. They took these disastrous examples and decided they didn't want to turn out like that. In my research on work–life balance and in multiple conversations with police officers, I learned that police look at others as examples of masters and disasters in coping. Officers identified examples of fellow officers who were terrible examples of balance, complete with wrecked health, disintegrating marriages, and financial ruin. Although it was helpful for them to see what they did *not* want to be like, it didn't necessarily give them the best direction as to what they should be doing or could be doing to promote their resilience. This is why effective leaders have the opportunity (and responsibility) to model resilient behavior.

I was reminded by a police leader at a resilience conference that police leaders are humans too. This often gets forgotten because they bear the brunt of line officers' angst with the organization. Yet, they have to deal with their own angst with those above them. Administrators have far more organizational pressures on them than most line officers. They face political pressure, fiscal constraints, and longer hours, which may include being available 24/7 by phone or email. Police management oftentimes work even more hours than their subordinates, increasing from 49 to 57 hours per week between 2001 and 2003, much of which is unpaid (Duxbury & Higgins, 2003).

Messages of Resilience: Shaping the Self-Fulfilling Prophecy

Police administrators wield a lot of power in shaping the culture of a police agency. They convey powerful messages about job expectations and employees' abilities to be resilient. For instance, I have listened to police administrators inadvertently be *de-motivational* speakers when they talked about the inevitable incapacitation of their employees due to the strain of the job. They sometimes talk about job strain in a way that implies that police don't stand a chance to be resilient. I cringe when I hear these talks because, for better or for worse, believing is seeing. If we believe that we are not doing well, then we interpret information to support this belief. On the other hand, if we believe that we are resilient, we will see the evidence of that. I'll share two stories that demonstrate this.

A few years ago, I heard hostage survivor, Amanda Lindhout, speak at a trauma conference. Standing before an auditorium full of mental health and trauma experts from around the world, Amanda told her story of being held captive in Somalia for 14 months by a Hizbul Islam fundamentalist group. Amanda held onto one of the strongest determinants of resilience: hope. She had hope that she would be rescued from these unimaginable circumstances. This hope fueled her will to live, to persevere when it would have been easier to give up.

The power of self-fulfilling beliefs can be seen in the writings of Viktor Frankl. Frankl was held in concentration camps in Auschwitz during World War II. He recounted in his book, *Man's Search for Meaning*, that he maintained a sense of purpose and appreciated the smallest amount of freedom he enjoyed during his encampment: his ability to choose how he would respond to the situation. Frankl also noticed that those who had a task to complete upon their release were more apt to survive. They longed to fulfill this purpose. This forward-directed orientation, feeling that one has more to do in life, can contribute greatly to your resilience in the face of adversity.

Viktor Frankl gave a speech to a group of counseling students about having an overly optimistic view of mankind. Frankl suggested the students presuppose man's greatness. He urged them to "overestimate" others so that these others might be able to rise to meet this overestimation. Frankl warned that if you simply viewed others as they *are* instead of what they *could be*, you could actually contribute to them not fulfilling their potential. An everyday example of this can be seen with children. When we speak of them and to them in regard to what they are capable of, they come to believe it as well. They strive to be their best self.

These overestimations become a self-fulfilling prophecy so long as they're not wildly unreachable goals or they're severely lacking in resources and supports to achieve them. I fully believe in the power of having an overly optimistic view of others. I meet many people in my work as a psychologist and most people are accustomed to focusing on their deficits and the negative aspects of matters. I find that this narrow focus negates each person's and each situation's potential. When I share my recognition of my clients' strengths, they are pleasantly surprised to recognize this in themselves. They don't always have this reaction. Other times, they deny or downplay their strengths. They are not accustomed to acknowledging their positive qualities because they mistakenly believe that it means that they will not change other aspects of their life. There is a strong "all-or-nothing" sentiment about their qualities as people. They believe that they are either good at life or they're not. The fact that they're in my office suggests that they believe they're NOT good at life.

As a police administrator, you have the ability to cultivate your officers' belief in their abilities to fulfill their purpose. A very interesting body of research suggests that expecting more from others actually results in more effort and, consequently, more goals accomplished. It's referred to as the Rosenthal effect, or expectancy effect, and has been used by teachers in their work with students. Students excel when their teachers expect more from them and provide adequate support to achieve. The same could be said of police employees. So, no matter which leadership model you follow, you can promote the resilience of your subordinate officers if you convey your belief in their potential; including their potential to be resilient.

Leadership Style

It's beyond the scope of this book to review recommended leadership models. There are many other books dedicated to this topic. My main objective is to promote resilience in police, which includes police in administrative positions. Another objective is to offer guidance on leadership styles that promote the resilience of police employees. This is important because a large body of research shows that the organizational hassles have a stronger impact on officer health than traumatic stress (Brough, 2002; Hart, Wearing, & Headey, 1995). When I interviewed police about what helped and what hindered their coping with exposure to traumatic stress, 50 percent identified a supportive work environment as helping them cope, while 60 percent identified unsupportive work environments as a hindrance (Conn & Butterfield, 2013). That means that, for some, their work environment was seen as both helpful AND hindering. Work environment included supportive supervisors who demonstrated care for their officers, provided resources, and were approachable if the officer was having a problem. They could tell the supervisor that they were not coping well with something and it would be taken seriously. Leadership, like resilience, is a process. It isn't something one has or doesn't have. It is the process of motivating and supporting others (Vroom & Jago, 2007).

Several large-scale studies of the Royal Canadian Mounted Police led Linda Duxbury (2007) to conclude ". . . you cannot be a leader if you have no followers—no matter your position in the hierarchy. Similarly, you can be a leader at any level of the organization" (p. 80). Furthermore, Duxbury suggested key differences between leaders and managers. Managers have subordinates, focus on the work, and are risk-avoidant, while leaders have followers, focus on people, and see risk as necessary and leading to opportunities (Duxbury). I agree with her contentions. Police employees need leaders. They need people that they are willing to follow, who they know believe in them and care about their well-being. The biggest risk in police culture tends to be change. Yet, change is inevitable. Being risk-averse in policing seems like an oxymoron but, unfortunately, some administrators (and line folks) fear and resist change. They regard it as a threat to the system they know; the "way it's always been." The more committed your officers are to their job, the more likely they are to resist organizational change. That's just the way it is. It's a good thing that they are committed in most respects besides the change element. Leaders are able to motivate their followers to accept change because they have a history of focusing on the well-being of their followers.

Trauma Histories—Friend or Foe of Resilience?

Some believe that having a traumatic history improves individuals' ability to handle adversity because they have been there; done that. They have had to overcome their challenges and would not be overwhelmed by adversity. It's not their first rodeo, so to speak. They know they've made it through before and they know what they're made of. Others propose that having traumatic histories disadvantages people in handling adversity because of the mounting strain on the person and their social system. The accumulation of traumas can also have a multiplicative effect on the person's distress. It is difficult to know what to believe, given that there is research that supports both contentions.

I think it's easier to understand the subjective nature of traumatic events using a model proposed by Anderson, Goodman, and Schlossberg (2011). They proposed that people's ability to cope with situations depends on four factors, the "4 S's System": situation, self, support, and strategies. One's ability to cope is a matter of assets and deficits. There are certain aspects of the situation that make it easier (an asset) or harder (a deficit). For instance, unexpected situations are usually harder to deal with. Events brought on by one's actions differ from those brought about by others. Officer-involved shootings where the bad guy forces a suicide-by-cop situation affects people in different ways. For some, it's easier to deal with it because the bad guy left them no choice. It was going to be the bad guy or the officer. That's a "no-brainer." For others, feeling like they didn't have another choice but to shoot the bad guy is problematic. Whether it is problematic varies based on the remaining three factors: self, support, and strategies. The self in the situation includes gender, age, life experiences, personality, and so forth. Continuing with the suicide-by-cop situation, an officer with a history of officer-involved-shootings, ability to relate to the person shot (e.g., same age as their child), who is already struggling with a health condition, may have a harder time than another officer without these complicating factors. Folding in the support variable, an officer who has a supportive significant other at home when they leave their shift will fare better than one who doesn't. Lastly, the strategies the officer uses to deal with the event also affect the impact of the event. Coping can be constructive or destructive. As stated in the section on gender, research shows that women are more apt to use constructive coping than men, making their strategies more likely to be an asset than a liability (He et al., 2002). Adaptive coping entails directly approaching the problem, while maladaptive coping is doing things to avoid it, such as drinking; distracting oneself; or avoiding places, people, or situations.

The majority of police recruits have experienced at least one traumatic event prior to entering policing (Buchanan, Stephens, & Long, 2001; Burke, 2009; Huddleston, Paton, & Stephens, 2006). One body of research suggests that having prior traumas or adversity can be a protective factor, if the stress from the events is mild to moderate. Based on animal studies, researchers believe that having prior success in mastering adversity actually changes the brain, called neuroplasticity. This change, in turn, serves to protect against the stress in future adversity (Southwick & Charney, 2012).

On the other hand, having a series of stressful or traumatic events can contribute to changes in the brain that make it more difficult to deal with adversity, also regarded as neuroplasticity. This is more likely the case when the adversity is beyond mild to moderate and is repeatedly experienced (Feder, Nestler, & Charney, 2009). The individual's brain changes to make the individual more likely to have an exaggerated response to future stressors. So, it seems that prior trauma can be a friend or a foe, depending on how it was experienced in terms of intensity, chronicity, and whether one coped well enough to consider it a mastery experience. I see this in my daily work with clients. Some clients learned how to cope with their traumas and grew more confident in their abilities. Even though they were struggling with something, they have the experience that says they can handle it. They have come to know who they can count on and who they can't. I've also seen those who haven't dealt with the old traumas. The story they're telling themselves is quite different. They tell themselves that they can't handle ANYTHING. They see ongoing difficulties as proof of that. They have developed unhealthy coping habits, including avoidance, which have taken a rigid hold of their lives.

CIVILIAN POLICE EMPLOYEES

Research on civilian police employee resilience is sorely lacking. They are oftentimes overlooked because they are a much less visible police employee. This is true of civilian police employees such as dispatchers, call-takers, crime scene technicians, translators, and victim service workers. I was a dispatcher for 3 years before becoming an officer. It was a stressful job. There were many times when I felt powerless to help the caller while worrying about the officers who were responding. I always created a picture of the caller and others at the scene, as they described what was happening.

What we know is civilian police employees have many of the same stressors that sworn officers have. They struggle with shiftwork, over-time, and critical incidents just like officers do. However, dispatchers, call-takers, and other civilian employees tend to get less training, support, and respect than sworn police officers. Studies have shown that inadequate training tends to contribute to higher levels of burnout (Newman, Mastracci, & Guy, 2005). Having less support than their sworn counterparts also seems to correlate to higher levels of burnout (McCarty & Skogan, 2012). Police officers tend to feel more camaraderie than civilian employees do, which is a buffer for burnout.

Research shows that 18–24 percent of dispatchers likely meet diagnostic criteria for PTSD (Pierce & Lilly, 2012). The more years of experience, the more likely the person has the disorder. This is believed to be due to the accumulation of traumatic incidents, which is sometimes called "delayed-onset PTSD." The symptoms mirror those of sworn officers, with hypervigilance being the most common. This is interesting, given that dispatchers and call-takers do not work in the field where their safety is actually threatened. Yet, they are able to connect to the threat over the phone and radio in such a way as to be traumatized. This is clearly recognized in the revision to diagnostic criteria for PTSD in the latest version of the *Diagnostic and Statistical Manual*: "Experiencing repeated or extreme exposure to aversive details of the traumatic event(s) (e.g., first responders collecting human remains; police officers repeatedly exposed to details of child abuse)" (American Psychiatric Association, 2013, p. 271). Dispatchers, call-takers, and many other civilian police employees are exposed to aversive details of traumatic events on a daily basis. The types of events that contribute to PTSD are similar to those seen in sworn officers. Namely, calls relating to children are the hardest and most traumatizing incidents to deal with.

POLICE FAMILY MEMBERS

Police employees are not the only ones affected by police work. It extends to their home life, affecting their loved ones. Families are affected by the organizational hassles of the job—shiftwork, overtime, policies, and promotional processes—by their secondary exposure to traumatic events, and the shifts in family dynamics when the police employee is affected by his or her work. Despite this, many police families have taken measures to weather the difficulties that come with this work. Throughout the book, I'll be sharing research on what helps family members to cope with these difficulties.

The resilience of police family members appears to be related to the resilience of officers themselves. Trauma experts explain this using the concept of "assortative mating," which refers to the tendency of individuals to choose partners with similar personalities (Merikangas, Bromet, & Spiker, 1983; Sherlock, Verweij, Murphy, Heath, Martin, & Zietsch, 2016). For instance, an individual who struggles to cope adaptively and maintain healthy habits is likely to be partnered with a person with similar struggles. They are more compatible than a couple where one person has maladaptive coping mechanisms and the other one has adaptive ones. Another variation of this is co-dependency. With co-dependency, significant others of the traumatized police employees believe it's their job to "fix" the afflicted loved one. It goes without saying that this is not a healthy dynamic. I'll speak more about this "overfunctioner-underfunctioner" dynamic in Chapter 2.

In addition to similar assortative mating, research has shown that there is a "contagion effect" between police and their significant others (Crothers, 1995; Larson & Almeida, 1999; Miller, 2007). This means that the significant other feels what the police employee feels. In therapy, we are warned against this, as it takes away from the person feeling the emotion and interferes with our ability to be helpful to the person. Instead, it's best to understand how the other person feels without succumbing to the feelings as well. I would argue this holds true for family members who are trying to support the police employee. Absorbing their feelings prevents them from offering support in the moment and can be traumatizing for them. This is referred to as secondary traumatic stress disorder (STSD), compassion fatigue (Figley, 1995) or vicarious traumatization (McCann & Pearlman, 1990). I'll speak further about STSD in Chapter 2 when I discuss critical police incidents. The contagion effect can affect the resilience of police family members, if they don't take steps to deal with it.

Spouses and Significant Others

As a wife of a police officer, I can also attest to the shared strain from the organizational hazards of the work such as shiftwork, court on days off, work during holidays, and public scrutiny. When they signed up to do police work, you agreed to these hassles, whether you knew it or not!

Studies have shown that spouses and partners of officers experiencing PTSD symptoms experienced secondary stress symptoms that mirrored those PTSD symptoms (Dwyer, 2005; Hirshfeld, 2005). Higher levels of PTSD symptoms in first responders have indicated higher levels of secondary trauma in first responder wives (Dwyer). Additionally, the more job stresses the officer experiences, the higher levels of hypervigilance for both the officer and the spouse (Roberts & Levenson, 2001). Secondary traumatization has led spouses to avoid the source of the trauma, the officers (McCann & Pearlman, 1990). Secondary trauma of first responder wives has been strongly correlated to psychological distress, depression, anxiety (Dwyer; Hirshfeld, 2005), and increased levels of alcohol consumption (Hirshfeld, 2005). Research shows that therapists have been traumatized by exposure to traumatic experiences (Figley, 1995). Therefore, family members may be at higher risk for traumatization because of their emotional connection to the first responder and their daily exposure to the first responder and because family members are not mental health professionals with professional support to effectively deal with their exposure.

Children of Police

Children of police are likely the most overlooked group when it comes to the impact of policing. Based on their ages, many people assume that children are unaware of what is happening with the police parent unless it is something extreme such as a line of duty death. Yet, children of police are affected by the work and would benefit from targeted support to be resilient. In addition to witnessing and being affected by the police parent's mood, stress levels, and shiftwork, children of police are oftentimes parented differently than non-police children. Police parents tend to "police" their children because they are aware of the dangers in the world and want to protect their children from them. My father was a police officer for my entire childhood. I know he ran the criminal histories of the family members of the people I dated or hung out with because he always asked me for their full names. When children are younger, the hypervigilance of the police parent contributes to the child's anxiety and exaggerated fear of strangers. Just like spouses, children are susceptible to emotional contagion, absorbing the stress, anger, and sadness that the police member feels.

Children are also affected by the spillover of police work into the home. I saw, firsthand, how police work was present in conversations about my dad's day while sitting at our kitchen table and interrupted sleep with a callout in the middle of the night. It was a living room full of cops, talking about cases, politics, and bad guys (including those on the street, in the police station, and in municipal government). I could hear many of these conversations from my bedroom down the hall. In fairness, I think these experiences helped me to be prepared for doing the job years later, but I also think that it can detract from family life. In fact, a few months before my dad passed away, he apologized for this, stating that he wished he had done things a little differently. He had put work ahead of family for many years and there were consequences to this choice, in terms of family and health.

MY TWO-CENTS ON RESILIENCE

I've been interested in resilience for a very long time. I've seen my share of struggles, as a police officer and as a psychologist. When I was studying the resilience of officers in maintaining their non-police identities, I wasn't exactly the picture of balance myself. I was burning the candle at both ends doing research; providing therapy; teaching at two universities; and trying to be a wife, a friend, and to get some exercise, as time allowed. I remember going for a physical evaluation following a car accident. When the doctor was interviewing me about my life and how I was functioning post-accident, my life seemed like a paradox. I was studying work–life balance and resilience, but I had a life that was anything but balanced. Yet, despite this imbalance, I was functioning very well. The doctor asked me how I could be so resilient. I thought about it for a moment. My response emerged with conviction: I *decided* that I was a resilient person and then I did what I imagined was the most resilient thing to do, again and again. Not being resilient was not an option. I would struggle, but I would know that the struggle was in furtherance of something that was important to me—

my work, my research, my health, my relationship. They were all worth the effort. I was living according to one of my favorite quotes by Friedrich Nietzsche: "*He who has a why to live for can bear almost any how.*" I was connected to the point of all that I was doing. I wasn't regarding it as something I *had* to do, that was forced on me by someone else. I also knew that this imbalance was temporary. Knowing this can make a big difference. One of my graduate students, who had made a similar declaration of resilience, explained it so clearly and succinctly during one of my class discussions on resilience: she did not *have to* do all that was on her plate in terms of work, school, family, and friends; she *got to* do it. It was a privilege, even a blessing, to have so much meaningful work and people in her life. I felt the same way but just hadn't put this mental construct into words just yet.

You can choose not to do the job. After all, there are other jobs out there. Reconnecting to the reasons why you got into the work in the first place might help you adjust to the difficulties that come with it. Maybe you got into policing to help people, to have challenging work, or to be outside instead of being cooped up in an office. Notice and appreciate that this is what you're getting to do. Don't let the difficulties overshadow these key parts of your work. The same goes for family. Yes, you may feel you *have* to run your kids around on days off. Again, notice and appreciate that you are choosing to support your kids who are active, developing little people. You are getting to be a part of that development when you take them to practice. Even household tasks that feel like burdens on your day(s) off are products of your choice to have a clean, functional home. When you are connected to purpose in your life, and see your choices in it, you will be more resilient.

TOOLS FOR YOUR DUTY BAG

- Like officer safety, resilience is a process that requires a daily commitment.
- You may not bounce "back" following an event, because you can never go back. You can, however, return to healthy functioning.
- Police that develop PTSD or depression can still be resilient but may take longer to recover.
- The majority of police employees are quite resilient, managing daily exposure to traumatic events and organizational hassles.
- Prior traumas can be either a protective factor or a risk factor, depending on if adaptive or maladaptive coping was used, as well as the intensity and duration of the traumatic event.
- Police leaders can contribute to the resilience of officers by promoting their belief in their ability to be resilient.
- Civilian police employees have the same challenges to resilience such as exposure to trauma and shiftwork but tend to have fewer sources of support than sworn members.
- Family members of police are affected by the traumatic experiences as well as the organizational hassles of police.

REFERENCES

American Psychiatric Association. (2013). *Diagnostic and statistical manual of mental disorders: DSM5*. Washington, DC: American Psychiatric Association.

Anderson, M., Goodman, J., & Schlossberg, N. (2011). *Counseling adults in transition: Linking Schlossberg's theory with practice in a diverse world* (4th ed.). New York: Springer Publishing Company.

Anxiety and Depression Association of America. (2016). *Facts & statistics*. Retrieved January 8, 2017, from www.adaa.org/about-adaa/press-room/facts-statistics.

Badge of Life (2016). Police suicide studies. Retrieved online from www.badgeoflife.com/police-suicide-studies/.

Ballenger, J. F., Best, S. R., Metzler, T. J., Wasserman, D. A., Mohr, D. C., Liberman, . . . Marmar, C. R. (2010). Patterns and predictors of alcohol use in male and female urban police officers. *The American Journal on Addictions, 20,* 21–29.

Brough, P. (2002). Female police officers' work experiences, job satisfaction and psychological well-being. *Psychology of Women Section Review, 4,* 3–15.

Bryant, R. A., O'Donnell, M. L., Creamer, M., McFarlane, A. C., Clark, C. R., & Silove, D. (2010). The psychiatric sequelae of traumatic injury. *American Journal of Psychiatry, 167,* 312–320.

Buchanan, G., Stephens, C. V., & Long, N. (2001). Traumatic experiences of new recruits and serving police officers. *Australasian Journal of Trauma and Disaster Studies*. Retrieved from http://trauma.massey.ac.nz/issues/2001-2/buchanan.htm.

Burke, K. J. (2009). *Adjusting to life "on the beat": A longitudinal examination of adaptation to the police profession*. Unpublished PhD thesis, University of Tasmania, Tasmania, Australia.

Carlier, I. V. E. (1999). Finding meaning in police traumas. In J. M. Violanti & D. Paton (Eds.), *Police trauma: Psychological aftermath of civilian combat* (pp. 227–233). Springfield, IL: Charles C. Thomas.

Carlier, I. V. E., Lamberts, R. D., & Gersons, B. P. R. (1997). Risk factors for posttraumatic stress symptomatology in police officers: A prospective analysis. *Journal of Nervous and Mental Disease, 185,* 498–506.

Conn, S. M., Amundson, N. E., Borgen, W. A., & Butterfield, L. D. (2015). From hero to zero. *The Canadian Journal of Career Development, 14(1),* 48–57.

Conn, S. M., & Butterfield, L. D. (2013). Coping with secondary traumatic stress by general duty police officers: practical implications. *Canadian Journal of Counselling and Psychotherapy, 47(2),* 272–298.

Coombs, A. (2008). A matter of the heart. *Nature Medicine, 14(3),* 231–233.

Crothers, D. (1995). Vicarious traumatization in the work with survivors of childhood trauma. *Journal of Psychosocial Nursing and Mental Health Services, 33(4),* 9–13.

Davey, J. D., Obst, P. L., & Sheehan, M. C. (2001). It goes with the job: Officers' insights into the impact of stress and culture on alcohol consumption within the policing occupation. *Drugs: Education, Prevention, and Policy, 8(2),* 141–149.

Digliani, J. A. (2016). *Police and sheriff peer support team manual reference and resource manual* (6.3 ed.).

Duxbury, L. (2007). *The RCMP yesterday, today and tomorrow: An independent report concerning workplace issues at the Royal Canadian Mounted Police.*

Duxbury, L., & Higgins, C. (2003). Work–life conflict in Canada in the new millennium—A status report. *The Sydney Papers, 15,* 79–97.

Dwyer, L. A. (2005). *An investigation of secondary trauma in police wives.* Unpublished doctoral dissertation, Hofstra University, Hempstead, New York.

Feder, A., Nestler, E., & Charney, D. S. (2009). Psychobiology and molecular genetics of resilience. *Nature Reviews Neuroscience, 10,* 446 457. doi: 10.1038/nrn2649.

Ferrari, P. F., & Rizzolatti, G. (2015). *New frontiers in mirror neurons research.* Oxford Scholarship Online. Retrieved on October 12, 2016, from www.oxfordscholarship.com/view/10.1093/acprof:oso/9780199686155.001.0001/acprof-9780199686155

Figley, C. R. (Ed.). (1995). *Compassion fatigue: Coping with secondary traumatic stress disorder in those who treat the traumatized.* Levittown, PA: Brunner/Mazel.

Frankl, V. E. (2006). *Man's search for meaning.* Boston, MA: Beacon Press.

Gershon, R. R. M., Barocas, B., Canton, A., Li, X., & Vlahov, D. (2009). Mental, physical, and behavioral outcomes associated with perceived work stress in police officers. *Criminal Justice and Behavior, 36(3),* 275–289.

Ginzburg, K., Ein-Dor, T., & Solomon, Z. (2009). Comorbidity of post-traumatic stress disorder in primary care: Prevalence and relationships with physical symptoms and medical utilization. *General Hospital Psychiatry, 27,* 392–399.

Hart, P. M., Wearing, A. J., & Headey, B. (1995). Police stress and well-being: Integrating personality, coping and daily work experiences. *Journal of Occupational and Organisational Psychology, 68,* 133–156.

He, N., Zhao, J., & Archbold, C. A. (2002). Gender and police stress. The convergent and divergent impact of work environment, work–family conflict, and stress coping mechanisms of female and male police officers. *Policing, 25(4),* 687–708.

Hirshfeld, A. (2005). *Secondary effects of traumatization among spouses and partners of newly recruited police officers.* Unpublished doctoral dissertation, The California School of Professional Psychology, San Francisco, CA (UMI No. 3191973).

Hochschild, A.R. (1983). The managed heart: The commercialization of human feeling. Berkeley, CA: University of California Press.

Honig, A. (2007). Facts refute long-standing myths about law enforcement officers. *National Psychologist, 16(5),* 23.

Howard, S., & Crandall, M. W. (2007). *Post traumatic stress disorder. What happens in the brain?* Washington Academy of Sciences. Retrieved November 22, 2016 from www.washacadsci.org/Journal/Journalarticles/V.93-3-Post%20Traumatic%20Stress%20Disorder.%20Sethanne%20Howard%20and%20Mark%20Crandalll.pdf.

Huddleston, L. M., Paton, D., & Stephens, C. (2006). Conceptualizing traumatic stress in police officers: Pre-employment, critical incident and organizational influences. *Traumatology, 12,* 120–177.

Kessler, R. C., Chiu, W. T., Demler, O., & Walters, E. E. (2005). Prevalence, severity, and co-morbidity of twelve-month DSM-IV disorders in the National Co-Morbidity Survey Replication (NCS-R). *Archives of General Psychiatry, 62(6),* 617–627.

Kessler, R. C., Sonnega, A., Bromet, E. Hughes, M., & Nelson, C. B. (1995). Posttraumatic stress disorder in the National Comorbidity Survey. *Archives of General Psychiatry, 52(12)*, 1048–1060.

Larson, R. W., & Almeida, D. M. (1999). Emotional transmission in the daily lives of families: A new paradigm for studying family process. *Journal of Marriage and the Family, 61(1)*, 5–20.

Marshall, E. K. (2003). *Occupational stress and trauma in law enforcement: A preliminary study in cumulative career traumatic stress.* Unpublished doctoral dissertation, Union Institute and University, Cincinnati, OH.

McCann, L., & Pearlman, L. A. (1990). Vicarious traumatization: A framework for understanding the psychological effects of working with victims. *Journal of Traumatic Stress, 3*, 131–149.

McCarty, W. P., & Skogan, W. G. (2012). Job-related burnout among civilian and sworn police personnel. *Police Quarterly, 16(1)*, 66–84.

McCaslin, S., Rogers, C., Metzler, T., Best, S., Weiss, D., Fagan, J., Liberman, A., & Marmar, C. (2006). The impact of personal threat on police officers' responses to critical incident stressors. *Journal of Nervous and Mental Disease, 194*, 591–597.

McCoy, S. P., & Aamodt, S. P. (2010). A comparison of law enforcement divorce rates with those of other occupations. *Journal of Police and Criminal Psychology, 25(1)*, 1–16.

Merikangas, K. R., Bromet, E. J., & Spiker, D. J. (1983). Assortative mating, social adjustment, and course of illness in primary affective disorder. *Archives of General Psychiatry, 40(7)*, 795–800. doi:10.1001/archpsyc.1983.01790060093012

Miller, L. (2007). Police families: Stresses, syndromes, and solutions. *The American Journal of Family Therapy, 35(1)*, 21–40.

Newman, M. A., Mastracci, S. H., & Guy, M. E. (2005). *Burnout versus making a difference: The hidden costs and benefits of emotion work.* Paper presented at the annual meeting of the American Political Science Association, Washington, DC.

Neylan, T. C., Brunet, A., Pole, N., Best, S. R., Metzler, T. J., Yehuda, R., & Marmar, C. R. (2005). PTSD symptoms predict waking salivary cortisol levels in police officers. *Psychoneuroendocrinology, 30*, 373–381.

Pearlman, L. A., & Saakvitne, K. W. (1995). Treating therapists with vicarious traumatisation and secondary traumatic stress disorders. In C. R. Figley (Ed.), *Compassion fatigue: Coping with secondary traumatic stress disorder* (pp. 150–177). Levittown, PA: Brunner/Mazel.

Pierce, H., & Lilly, M. M. (2012). Duty-related trauma exposure in 911 telecommunicators: Considering the risk for posttraumatic stress. *Journal of Traumatic Stress, 25(2)*, 211–215.

Roberts, N. A., & Levenson, R. W. (2001). The remains of the workday: Impact of job stress and exhaustion on marital interactions in police couples. *Journal of Marriage & the Family, 63(4)*, 1052–1067.

Shanahan, M. J., & Hofer, S. M. (2005). Social context in gene–environment interactions: Retrospect and prospect. *The Journals of Gerontology: Series B, 60(Special Issue 1)*, 65–76. Retrieved February 5, 2016 from https://doi-org.ezproxy.library.ubc.ca/10.1093/geronb/60.Special_Issue_1.65.

Sherlock, J. M., Verweij, K. J. H., Murphy, S. C., Heath, A. C., Martin, N. G., & Zietsch, B. P. (2016). The role of genes and environment in degrees of partner self-similarities. *Behavior Genetics, 47(1)*, 25–35.

Sippel, L. M., Pietrzak, R. H., Charney, D. S., Mayes, L. C., & South, S. M. (2015). How does social support enhance resilience in the trauma-exposed individual? *Ecology and Society, 20(4)*.

Smith, J., & Charles, G. (2010). The relevance of spirituality in policing: A dual analysis. *International Journal of Police Sciences and Management, 12(3)*, 320–338.

Smith, K. P., & Christakis, N. A. (2008). Social networks and health. *Annual Review of Sociology, 34*, 405–429.

Southwick, S. M., & Charney, D. S., (2012), *Resilience: The science of mastering life's challenges*. New York: Cambridge University Press.

Southwick, S. M., Vythilingam, M., & Charney, D. S. (2005). The psychobiology of depression and resilience to stress: Implications for prevention and treatment. *Annual Review of Clinical Psychology, 1(1)*, 255–291.

Stellman, J. M., Smith, R. P., Katz, C. L., Sharma, V., Charney, D. S., Herbert, R., . . . Southwick, S. (2008). Enduring mental health morbidity and social function impairment in World Trade Center rescue, recovery, and cleanup workers: The psychological dimension of an environmental health disaster. *Environmental Health Perspectives, 116(9)*, 1248–1253. Retrieved January 9, 2017 from http://doi.org/10.1289/ehp.11164.

U. S. Department of Veteran Affairs. (2016). *How common is PTSD*. Retrieved January 12, 2017, from www.ptsd.va.gov/public/PTSD-overview/basics/how-common-is-ptsd.asp.

van der Velden, P. G., Rademaker, A. R., Vermetten, E., Portengen, M.-A., Yzermans, J. C., & Grievink, L. (2012). Police officers: A high- risk group for the development of mental health disturbances? A cohort study. *BMJ Open, 3*, 1–10.

Violanti, J. M. (2003). Suicide and the police culture. In D. Hackett & J. M. Violanti (Eds.), *Police suicide: Tactics for prevention*. Springfield, IL: Charles C. Thomas.

Violanti, J. M., & Drylie, J. J. (2008). *Cop-i-cide: Concepts, cases, and controversies of suicide by cop*. Springfield, IL: Charles C. Thomas.

Vroom, V. H., & Jago, A. G. (2007). The role of the situation in leadership. *American Psychologist, 62(1)*, 17–24.

Chapter 2

Critical Police Incidents
Reactions and Recovery

> It is not the critic who counts; not the man who points out how
> the strong man stumbles, or where the doer of deeds could have
> done them better. The credit belongs to the man who is actually
> in the arena, whose face is marred by dust and sweat and blood;
> who strives valiantly; who errs, who comes short again and again,
> because there is no effort without error and shortcoming; but who
> does actually strive to do the deeds; who knows great enthusiasms,
> the great devotions; who spends himself in a worthy cause; who at
> the best knows in the end the triumph of high achievement, and
> who at the worst, if he fails, at least fails while daring greatly, so
> that his place shall never be with those cold and timid souls who
> neither know victory nor defeat.
>
> (Theodore Roosevelt, *The Man in the Arena*, April 23, 1910)

THE CALL

Police Officers

A tragic event is experienced on physical, emotional, and cognitive
levels. Which level you pay attention to at any given time depends on
factors such as the amount of time that has passed since the event, your
trauma history, personality differences, and the nature of the event.
I will discuss each of the categories of traumatic experiencing in turn.
My categorization of physical, emotional, and cognitive processes in
no way implies that they are unrelated. The physical experience of
trauma affects an individual's thoughts and feelings and vice versa.
I am discussing these separately in hopes of highlighting the complexity

of each of these processes apart from the added complexity when they're considered together.

Physical Experience of Trauma

When a person is exposed to a traumatic event that involves shock, horror, or fear, it sets into motion a series of neurological events. The critical, higher-order thinking part of the brain, the cortex, is hijacked by the part of the brain that processes and stores emotions such as fear, the amygdala. It's only after several seconds of deliberate effort to get the cortex back "online" that a person can have a sense of control over thoughts, behaviors, and reactions. In the meantime, the person, despite any training, personality traits, or amount of willpower, will be at the mercy of the evolutionary-based reactions directed by the amygdala. These reactions may be surprising, given your police training and personality, since they might involve behaviors such as physical or mental retreat, loss of control over bodily functions, and/or feelings of sickness. These natural reactions are normal reactions that are designed to keep you safe. How you respond to these reactions influences how you will adjust to the traumatic event in the long term. If you "should" on yourself—I *should've* done this, I *should not* have done that—you will make your adjustment much harder and longer, as you are asking yourself to have done the impossible. If, instead, you recognize that your reactions were involuntary in the situation, you can move on with acceptance of the realities of the traumatic response.

For the sake of simplicity, let's use the very common example of an officer-involved shooting to discuss the traumatic experience. When you're involved in a shooting, you will likely be intensely aware of the physical sensations of fear or horror at the time of the event, remembering details such as your heart was beating out of your chest, your vision narrowed to the weapon, your legs felt wobbly and weak, and your hands shook as you fumbled to pull your gun from the holster. Alternatively, there may be a moment of freezing, of feeling nauseous and paralyzed, of disbelieving or not registering what is happening. In the immediate aftermath, your body is bathing in stress hormones. You might pace to try to walk it off. Your mind is racing. You're thinking to call your loved ones to tell them you're okay. You start replaying the incident in your head. It doesn't feel real. It feels like your stomach is in your throat. You're wondering about what happens next. What will come of the investigation that follows? They're going to take your gun, and take your statement. The call is far from over. If you're lucky, you'll be removed from the scene fairly quickly, returning to the station to be interviewed. This is where you'll start to notice the effects that trauma has on your memory. Officers involved in traumatic events don't recall the entire event. They're surprised when they hear what others said happened or when they see it on video, when one exists.

> If you "should" on yourself—I should've done this, I should not have done that—you will make your adjustment much harder and longer, as you are asking yourself to have done the impossible.

Trauma and Memory

Trauma impacts the coding, storage, and retrieval of memories of the event. These processes involve different parts of the brain and depend on the kind of memory. For instance, explicit memories such as details of what happened are stored by the hippocampus into long-term memory. However, high levels of stress, combined with a rapidly unfolding event, result in memories of traumatic events that are usually fragmented. Secretion of stress hormones during the event increases the accessibility to the memory at a later time. It's the body's way of making sure emotionally charged material is not forgotten. Furthermore, the traumatic memory is state-dependent, meaning subsequent high states of arousal will stimulate the memory (van der Kolk, 1998). Decades of research demonstrate that traumatic memories are coded, stored, and retrieved differently than non-traumatic memories (LeDoux, 1992; McGaugh, 1992; Nilsson & Archer, 1992; Pitman, Orr, & Shalev, 1993). Unlike "normal" memories, traumatic memories tend to be detailed, accurate, and persistent (Yuille & Cutshall, 1989). Yet, it is the implicit, perceptual memories that are detailed, accurate, and persistent, not the narrative (explicit) memory. In a nutshell, this means that you are left with no cohesive story as to what happened. Instead, the traumatic memories are stored as behavioral re-enactments, sensory perceptions, and obsessional ruminations (Nemiah, 1995; van der Kolk & van der Hart, 1989, 1991). (I did this. I heard that. I'm stuck on this detail of the event.) In fact, neuroimaging of the brain shows that when symptoms are provoked in individuals with PTSD, there is a decrease in activation in Broca's area, which relates to speech (storytelling), and an increase in activation in the right hemisphere where emotions and images are processed (Rauch et al., 1996) (sensory perceptions such as sights and sounds). When the traumatic memory is personal, versus becoming aware of someone else's trauma, it's more likely to be remembered with such details, accuracy, and persistence for evolutionary purposes. In this way, we are better able to make decisions to keep us safe from harm.

During a critical incident, parts of the declarative memory may be missing due to narrowing of focus (Christianson, 1984; Safer, Christianson, Autry, & Österlund, 1998). You may narrow your focus to the flash coming out of the barrel of the gun, to the hand of the suspect, to the face of a victim and miss other details and events occurring around you. You're not recording the unfolding of events, as a story, as much as you are homing in on perceptual details. An officer relayed a story of being so focused on the suspect that he didn't notice a fellow officer drive right beside him, taking off the door of the police car. Similarly, the officer who took the police car door off didn't remember seeing the other officer firing his weapon from the passenger side door. Both officers had narrowed their focus to the suspect to the exclusion of each other.

Emotional Experience of Trauma

If you ask many police officers how they're doing after a pretty tough call, their response is likely to be "fine." In fact, this response is so common that those in the police psychology field have taken the word "fine" to represent Feelings on the Inside Not Expressed—F.I.N.E. Yet, there's no such thing as bravery without the feeling of fear. Think about that for a moment. It seems that some emotions are more acceptable than others (bravery, happiness, anger, etc.). The stigma of having so-called "negative" emotions (fear, sadness, overwhelm, etc.) is so strong that I don't even use the word "feeling" to ask police about their traumatic experience. I use the word "reaction," although I am tapping into the same thing, just giving it a name they're more likely to acknowledge. I learned this from a staff sergeant/police psychologist who is as much a cop as a cop doc.

Police are human beings and, as such, have the full range of emotions. This is a very good thing. This means you're not a sociopath or a robot. Dr Daniel Goleman (1995), author of several of books on emotional intelligence, states:

> All emotions are, in essence, impulses to act, the instant plans for handling life that evolution has instilled in us. The very root of the word emotion is *motere*, the Latin verb 'to move', plus the prefix 'e' to connote 'move away', suggesting that a tendency to act is implicit in every emotion.
>
> (p. 6)

So, emotions mobilize police, like others, to action. We don't want to do away with emotions. We need them. They tell us when something's wrong, pushing us to deal with it. They tell us when something's right, so that we can do more of that for more of the good stuff (happiness, etc.). We just need to listen to these emotions for the information they provide, instead of regarding them as nuisances to be avoided.

Cognitive Experience of Trauma

When it comes to negative experiences, especially traumatic ones, there is a tendency to think in a number of ways that contribute to worsened outcomes, robbing individuals of their capacity to be resilient. You may recognize these tendencies in everyday situations because they occur often. As you read through the list given in the box, pause after each one to see if you can recognize their presence in your daily life. You will also likely see these thinking styles in family and friends, demonstrating that these tend to occur automatically and are not reflective of a flawed intellect or personality style. The good news is that, since they occur automatically, once you draw attention to them, you can take steps to STOP relying on these thinking styles. The list offered here is not comprehensive but captures the problematic thinking styles that you will likely encounter in traumatic experiences.

- **Black or White (AKA all-or-nothing or dichotomous) Thinking:** As the name implies, the belief that someone is all good or bad, the action was right or wrong, etc. This extreme form of thinking tends to exclude the middle part; the "gray" in a situation or a person, which is usually more accurate.
- **Jumping to Conclusions:** This includes the mistaken assumption that you can 1) read other peoples' minds and 2) predict the future. "I know they think I'm broken after this event" or "Since I botched this call, I won't ever get that promotion I want."
- **Emotional Reasoning:** The fear that something might be true leads us to believe that it must be true. "I feel sorry about what happened. So, I must have done something wrong."
- **Labeling:** Assigning yourself or someone else a global label that may be difficult to dispute. "I must be *stupid* if I missed that call detail."
- **Personalization:** As the name implies, inappropriately making the situation about yourself. If others are laughing, they must be laughing about you. If a policy is changed, it must be in response to an error you made.
- **Catastrophizing:** Believing things are far worse than they actually are (AKA blowing things out of proportion). "If I don't get over this soon, my spouse will leave me. I'll lose my job. I'll lose my friends. My dog won't respect me so he'll run away from home. I'll be alone. Nobody will want me. I'll let myself go. Then nobody will ever want me. So, I'll die alone."
- **Discounting the Positives:** Thinking that a good act or quality does not count or that the praise of another was given for other reasons that make it disputable. "I may have helped 3 people on that call, but I failed to help that one" or "They're just saying that because they're trying to be nice. They know I really botched that call."
- **"Shoulds":** Thinking or saying to ourselves that we *should* have or *shouldn't* have done something. It is a form of shaming that is usually not based on evidence. It may also include "must," "ought," "have to," and other variations.
- **Mental Filter:** Only paying attention to certain information that usually supports an existing negative belief. For instance, when thinking about how you're doing following a series of traumatic calls, you only notice problems with your sleep but don't notice that you have been doing better with exercise and diet.

Did any of them sound familiar? We all tend to do these from time to time but especially when dealing with a negative situation. Police are notorious for black or white/dichotomous thinking because they tend to work with matters of law. They also draw clear lines between "innocent victims" and "bad guys" (unless, of course, they've become cynical. I'll talk about cynicism in the next chapter).

Chapter 2
Reactions and Recovery

What is Happening?!

When we encounter an event, good or bad (dichotomous thinking), we try to make sense of what is happening to us. This can happen in seconds when hit with a rapidly occurring event (which is oftentimes the case in policing) or can last minutes, hours, or days when the event is slowly unfolding. We try to determine the nature of the threat, what it means to us, how we anticipate it will affect us, and so forth. This is what is referred to as the *primary appraisal* of the situation (Lazarus & Folkman, 1984). Once we have wrapped our head around this, we jump to the next phase, *secondary appraisal*, where we ask, "How am I going to deal with this?" Can I deal with this?", and variations of this as we are sussing out our ability to cope with the situation, as appraised. We may then enter into the third phase, the *re-appraisal* phase, where we monitor the situation to make adjustments to primary and secondary appraisals. This is not a linear process and we may jump back and forth between appraising the situation and our ability to manage it. So, as you can see, how you appraise the situation and how you appraise your ability to manage it have strong implications for your ability to cope with the situation while it's happening and afterwards.

Part of the appraisal process involves looking to others to gain cognitive clarity about what happened (Festinger, 1954; Kulik & Mahler, 2000). We don't just look to anyone but, rather, to people we feel affiliate with. In short, police look to other police to determine how they "should" be responding to the situation. That's that "should" stuff. This is especially true when in a high threat or novel situation. In addition to looking at those with whom they affiliate with, they look to those who are deemed credible. I found this to be true when debriefing police involved in an officer-involved-shooting. Police without prior officer-involved-shooting experience looked to police with it to normalize their responses. They don't look to citizens or even to other first responders. They are looking for someone who can clear up their confusion about the situation—a trusted, knowledgeable source. Since we're social beings, everyone does this. Take an everyday example: When you're flying and encounter heavy turbulence, you scan the faces of flight attendants to determine if you should be worried. When they don't look worried, you tell yourself that the turbulence is nothing to worry about. Notice that you're not looking to fellow passengers for information. You want to go to a credible source for information, right?

Emotions are another part of the appraisal process. Two theories propose opposing sources of emotions. The first one states we feel physical arousal such as a racing heartbeat or a lump in our throat, we recognize these symptoms and *then* label the emotion, James-Lange Theory (James & Lang, 1922). The second one states we feel the emotion first and *then* our body responds accordingly, the Cannon-

Bard Theory (Cannon, 1927). Schachter and Singer (1962) added reasoning and cognitive labels to this process. According to them, part of the labeling process depends on the information that we get from others in our environment (Schachter & Singer, 1962). As social beings, we factor in others' reactions when we make sense of our own. Initial appraisals are likely to be modified if you notice that the visible emotional response of another is very different from your own (Schachter, 1959). Police are going to look at other police reactions to judge their own. This process contributes to emotional contagion. Schachter (1959) proposed "Misery doesn't just love any kind of company, it loves only miserable company" (p. 24). In other words, we look to those who are in the same boat as us to make sense of what is happening and what we are feeling. Ideally, we get feedback that matches our own feelings.

Some experts believe that emotions and appraisals come *after* and are due to our facial expressions. According to primitive contagion theory, we automatically mimic the facial expressions of those we come in contact with and then experience the emotion that accompanies that expression (Hatfield, Cacioppo, & Rapson, 1992, 1993, 1994). Paul Ekman, an expert on emotions, has found this in his work as well (Ekman, 2003). Ekman and colleague, Wally Friesen, found that simply making the face of the emotion produced the feelings. Ekman and Friesen were making recordings of facial expressions for Ekman's coding system for facial expressions of emotions. In making various emotional expressions, Ekman and Friesen noticed feeling flooded by the emotion they were attempting to demonstrate for the camera.

Whether the emotion comes from our appraisal of the situation or from mimicking the facial expression of others, it is an integral part of the experience of trauma. How you think and feel about these emotions has implications for your resilience. When you shun a natural emotional response because you feel like you have to put on a brave face for others, this can be at your own expense. Suppressed emotions can build up, causing physical damage to your immune system, and can create distance between you and your loved ones. One way that you can worsen your situation is to make sense of the tragedy at your own expense with inappropriate guilt, which is discussed next.

Trauma-Related Guilt

Part of determining what happened in police traumas involves identifying who is to blame for it happening in the first place. In this way, you (mistakenly) think that it can be avoided in the future. Edward Kubany, Tyler Ralston, and Susan Watson, experts in trauma, proposed that the magnitude of trauma-related guilt people struggle with is a combination of the amount of distress about a negative outcome accompanied by four mistaken beliefs about their role in the situation: wrongdoing, responsibility, justification, and hindsight bias (Kubany & Ralston, 2006; Kubany & Watson, 2003). When faced with a negative outcome in a critical incident, police may equate the "output" with their "input," reasoning that they must've done something wrong for it to have turned out this way. They might negate the fact that they didn't have any good options to choose from. Sometimes, you're stuck with choosing the best of the worst options because there are no good options available. Therefore, you can't be on the hook for an option that wasn't available to you. You might also interpret "wrongdoing" when you think about your instinctual physical response to a situation. For instance, you might grimace when you see the lacerations on the face of a victim and feel guilty that you reacted this way, regarding it as an affront to a person who has been through enough. You might also regard a small mistake as bigger than it was based on the outcome. Calling a suicidal person standing on a bridge by the wrong name is a small error. We tend to forget the names of people we just met all the time. Yet, in this circumstance, you might regard it as a major error which you (mistakenly) believe led to the person jumping. This belief discounts all the circumstances that led the person to be on the bridge in the first place.

Another "mind trick" I've seen police (and non-police) play when they are dealing with the aftermath of a tragedy is asking themselves "Why didn't I do this?", "If I had done that, this would have been avoided." They assumed that things would've turned out better. They never think that they may have turned out the same, or even worse. Sadly, the second guessing you do to yourself, disregarding how little time and information you had to make decisions, isn't terribly different than the hated Monday morning quarterbacking that others sometimes do after the fact. We would be quick to remind others of this but might internally be questioning ourselves. The problem with the tendency to think this way (and many of the others listed here) is that you can rarely fact-check your "what if" conclusions. Sometimes, this is doable when you can speak with other people who were there. This is oftentimes accomplished in critical incident debriefings. Oftentimes, though, this thinking takes a life of its own, making you feel guilt that isn't appropriate or healthy.

The last category of trauma-related guilt refers to one's sense that they are *responsible* in some way for the event. This is slightly different than the *wrongdoing* category in that it relates to the sense that one was supposed to do something but didn't. For police, it might be believing that it was your "job" to prevent something from happening. This is a tricky one to get rid of because we want to feel like we have some kind of influence in our work. I don't do therapy without thinking that, in doing my job, people will get better. Police also take ownership of their work and feel a sense of responsibility. The problem is that policing, like therapy work, isn't magic. We can't make all of the forces that cause a situation better, no matter how good we are at our job or how bad we want it to turn out well. You must remind yourself that there is a difference between being *responsible* and being *accountable*. "The main difference between responsibility and accountability is that responsibility can be shared and accountability cannot" (Diffen LLC, 2017). You would be wise to share responsibility for what happened with all the other people, systems, and events that have contributed to the outcome.

We can't forget old, reliable hindsight bias. We tend to use information we learn *after the fact* to assess the situation; how we should have acted, what we should have known, and so forth. Even though it doesn't make any sense, we still do it. The key is to notice this and the other errors in thinking that will interfere with your ability to be resilient. In Table 2.1, these errors that Kubany and Ralston (2006) created to assist in reducing inappropriate guilt in individuals struggling with the aftermath of a traumatic event is listed. I've shown this list to plenty of clients, police, and otherwise, who have found that many of these apply to them. It can be an eye-opening experience to know that you're not alone in thinking this way. It's a thing people do when they are trying to make sense of something that just doesn't make sense.

> The main difference between responsibility and accountability is that responsibility can be shared and accountability cannot
> Diffen LLC

A related thinking error that occurs in traumatic events is a skewed notion of what *caused* an event— an attribution error. One's belief about this is important, especially since it may be skewed and, therefore, difficult to manage in a healthy way. The *fundamental attribution error* is the tendency to overemphasize the personal characteristics and behaviors and underemphasize environmental factors to explain what happened. This is akin to Kubany and Ralston's (2006) Responsibility #2 (R2): Obliviousness to totality of forces that cause traumatic events. This, in turn, is worsened by the tendency for people to believe that everyone else agrees with them (false consensus effect). If you add all of these thinking errors up, you will have a terrible time moving past an event because your thinking is skewed and does not get checked against reality or at least the opinion of others. Problematic thinking tends to reinforce itself by interpreting information as agreeing with the underlying belief and discounting any evidence that contradicts it. For instance, if you believe you're a terrible person, your interpretation of things will be biased toward confirming this belief. It *must* be because of you. You tend to discount evidence that contradicts this notion—the fact that your spouse has struggled periodically with depressive episodes prior to even meeting you. You likely also discount evidence that supports that you are actually a pretty nice person—you do your best to make your spouse happy, you generally get along well with others, you don't mistreat people or abuse animals. After all, what makes a person worthy of the label "terrible" anyway? That's also part of the problem—assigning

TABLE 2.1
Thinking Errors that Lead to Faulty Conclusions and Trauma-Related Guilt

Thinking error that contributes to faulty conclusions about knowledge possessed before the outcome was known (regarding the *foreseeability and preventability* of negative outcomes)

HB   Hindsight-biased thinking

Thinking errors that contribute to faulty conclusions about *justification* or goodness of reasons for acting as one did

J1   Weighing the merits of actions taken against idealized actions that did not exist

J2   Weighing the merits of actions taken against options that only came to mind later

J3   Focusing only on "good" things that might have happened had an alternative action been taken

J4   Tendency to overlook "benefits" association with actions taken

J5   Failure to compare available options in terms of their perceived probabilities of success before outcomes were known

J6   Failure to realize that 1) acting on speculative hunches rarely pays off and 2) occurrence of a low-probability event is not evidence that one should have "bet" on this outcome before it occurred

J7   Failure to recognize that different decision-making "rules" apply when time is precious than in situations that allow extended contemplation of options

J8   Failure to recognize that in heightened states of negative arousal, one's ability to think clearly and make logical decisions is impaired

Thinking errors that contribute to faulty conclusions about degree of *responsibility* for causing negative outcomes

R1   Hindsight-biased thinking

R2   Obliviousness to totality of forces that cause traumatic events

R3   Equating a belief that one could have done something to prevent the traumatic event with a belief that one caused the event

R4   Confusion between responsibility as accountability (e.g., "my job") and responsibility as having the power to cause or control outcomes

R5   Existential beliefs about accountability and the need to accept the consequences of one's actions—which fail to take into account the causal power of situational forces

Thinking errors that contribute to faulty conclusions about *wrongdoing* or violation of values

W1   Tendency to conclude wrongdoing on the basis of outcome rather than on the basis of one's intentions before the outcome was known

W2   Failure to realize that strong emotional reactions are not under voluntary control (i.e., not a matter of choice of willpower)

W3   The tendency to "inflate" the seriousness of a minor moral violation—from "misdemeanor" to "felony" status—when the minor violation leads unforeseeably to a traumatic outcome

W4   Failure to recognize that when all available options have negative outcomes, the least bad option is a sound and moral choice

Thinking error that contributes to all of the faulty conclusions

ALL Belief that an emotional reaction to an idea provides evidence for the idea's validity—also called *emotional reasoning*

Source: Reprinted with permission of Guilford Press (Kubany & Ralston, 2006).

a label without considering what it even means. I have had many clients who claim that they are lots of things and when we break down the label and define it, they are able to conclude that they don't fit the description. The label is meant to punish themselves for a perceived wrongdoing— a mistaken wrongdoing at that!

Behavioral Responses to Trauma

Following a traumatic event, police officers might wish to isolate themselves from others until they feel they "have it all together." Many people have told me that they didn't want to burden someone else with their problems. Instead, they withdraw from their social support— family, fellow officers, and friends. They might even withdraw from situations that would remind them of the event. There are numerous problems with this way of coping. Running from your problems is a race you will not win. In fact, you will likely feel exhausted and be no further away from your difficulty. Social support is vital to getting through traumatic events. Family and friends oftentimes can sense that something is upsetting and will draw their own conclusions if they're not told about the officer's struggles. Withdrawal behavior might be misinterpreted as a lack of interest in the family. Friends might assume that the officer just doesn't care to hang out anymore. Everyone suffers when the officer withdraws from those who can provide emotional or practical support. Instead, officers would be advised to talk to trusted others about what is going on for them. They don't have to relay gory details or the details of a case they are not allowed to discuss to receive support and relief. In fact, they can just stick to talking about their reaction to the event and how they feel it is weighing on them now. In this way, others won't be drawing their own conclusions about the officer's behavior and then responding in a negative manner.

Police also find ways to check out to not have to think about the event. Drinking alcohol, using prescription drugs, mindless Internet surfing, and shopping offer an escape from the thoughts, feelings, and reminders of traumatic events. Numbing these out makes it easier to manage day-to-day life but has dire consequences in the long run. What is being avoided isn't being resolved. It's just being stored on the back shelf of the mind, so to speak. Eventually, it's going to have to be dealt with. Perhaps, it can be delayed until retirement (which is believed to be why so many have delayed-onset PTSD). What you resist, persists. Additionally, these numbing tactics create more problems such as alcoholism, addiction, financial difficulties, relationship strain, and health issues.

> Running from your problems is a race you will not win.

Spiritual Experience of Traumatic Event

When police are exposed to traumatic events, it can take a toll on their spiritual beliefs. Events such as the death of a child challenge police to make sense of how this could happen. "Why" questions can run rampant: "Why did God let this happen?", "Why is this happening to me?", and so forth. Individuals exposed to trauma are believed to make sense of the trauma through one of three processes: assimilation, accommodation, or over-accommodation (Falsetti, Resick, & Davis, 2003). When individuals assimilate the information, they adjust their interpretation of what is happening to fit their existing beliefs. For example, if a person believes that good things happen to good people and he's confronted with a situation where something bad happens to a seemingly "good" person, he will adjust his beliefs about the person's "goodness." This is how victim blaming happens (e.g., "He should have known better than to go there"). Lerner (1997) says that we "automatically reason backwards in time" in that we will try to make sense of what happened by looking for some moral or behavioral flaw in the person who was a victim of tragedy.

Some of police officers' reasoning in traumatic events can be explained by the *Just World Hypothesis*, which refers to the notion that people get what they deserve, for good or bad (Lerner & Miller, 1977). Having this belief helps individuals ward off anxiety that they, or those that they love, will also become victims. All they have to do is be good people and everything will be alright. Other times when something bad happens to a "good person," individuals believe that this will eventually be rectified; that the tragedy is only temporary (Lerner, 1997). This allows us to make sense of the tragedy using our existing belief system. We might think that justice will eventually be served and the wrongdoer will get his (or hers) and the victim will be better because of it. Anyone who has been doing police work for a while would know that this doesn't happen on a regular basis. Knowing this leads to cynicism. Police have identified their inability to help the victim as interfering with their ability to cope with their exposure to secondary traumatic stress (Conn & Butterfield, 2013). Acknowledging these human limits sometimes comes at a cost to officers' spiritual beliefs, sense of influence, and purpose, and can have lasting effects on their ability to be resilient.

When individuals accommodate, this means that they alter their beliefs based on the situation(s). For instance, they would change the belief "good things happen to good people and bad things happen to bad people" to "sometimes bad things happen to good people." This, as you can imagine, would be adaptive and healthy but might worsen anxiety, as it means that it could happen to them. This feeds hypervigilance. Lots of police have justified their hypervigilance, pointing to the countless innocent victims they have encountered on the job. This is especially true for police who work with children. This contributes to police "policing" their family members, managing their whereabouts and activities.

It becomes even more problematic when the individual over-accommodates and generalizes the new "rule" to all people and situations. The new rule might sound something like "All people are out to get you so you have to keep your guard up." Officers' faith in humanity has suffered and they and their families are paying the price for this damage. They fail to realize that they are actually only exposed to a small slice of the population, not the whole of it. Yes, people abuse children, rape, and steal from others. But most people don't do any of this. It's easy to forget this when the dominant picture of society comes from calls for service (or media, which will be discussed later).

Research on Spirituality and Trauma

Police officers report changes in their spiritual beliefs after entering the profession (Carlier, 1999; Marshall, 2003). In a study on cumulative career traumatic stress, 53 percent of police officers reported that their faith or religious beliefs had changed due to the job (Marshall). It is clear that the work impacts officers' spiritual health. What isn't clear from the research is the direction of change. For some, their beliefs may be *conserved*, strengthened to assist them in doing the work (Pargament, 1996). Some police with strong spiritual beliefs view the tragedy and suffering they are exposed to as a test of faith that they strive to pass. Others take the *transformative* coping approach and begin to question their spiritual convictions, formulating new notions about themselves, others, their god, and the connections between them all (Pargament). Judith Herman (1992), world-renowned expert on traumatic stress, writes:

> Traumatized people suffer damage to the basic structures of the self. They lose their trust in themselves, in other people, and in God. Their self-esteem is assaulted by experiences or humiliations, guilt, and helplessness. Their capacity for intimacy is compromised by intense and contradictory feelings of need and fear. The identity they have formed prior to the trauma is irrevocably destroyed.
>
> (p. 56)

Research by Falsetti et al. (2003) suggested that 30 percent of a sample of individuals with PTSD reported becoming less religious after their first traumatic event. This rate was five times higher than the sample without PTSD. Another 18 percent of individuals with PTSD became *more* religious after their first trauma event. Their research also showed that 56 percent of the sample reported that their religious beliefs were helpful in dealing with their traumatic event. It is difficult to determine if this research suggests that PTSD disrupts belief systems or if disrupted belief systems lead to PTSD. Since religious beliefs helped some but took a hit for those with PTSD, there must be other factors that are influencing individuals' PTSD and belief system. Lastly, having experienced multiple traumatic events was correlated with stronger religious beliefs about the meaning of events, but it's not clear as to why. Spiritual health helps many officers but becomes a casualty for others.

Summary of Immediate Impact of a Traumatic Event

Following a traumatic event, you might experience any number of physical, cognitive, emotional, behavioral, and spiritual symptoms. Most of the symptoms will subside with time, but, if they don't, it's a good idea to see someone to deal with them so that they don't get worse (not to mention, there's no need to suffer with them even if they stay the same). Some may not appear immediately, but will show up after days, weeks, or even months. Again, this is normal, given that you've experienced a traumatic event. Table 2.2 gives a list of various symptoms you might experience. The list isn't exhaustive but captures the most common experiences.

AFTER THE CALL

> From the initial event, where you may be fighting for your very survival, you must learn to transition to the ongoing fight for your well-being down the road.
>
> (Neily, 2016)

TABLE 2.2
Common Symptoms Immediately Following a Traumatic Event

Physical	Cognitive	Emotional	Behavioral	Spiritual
Sleep difficulties—falling asleep/staying asleep	Racing thoughts	Angry	Withdrawal from others	Questioning beliefs
Headaches	Confusion	Sad	Escape behaviors—drinking, shopping, Internet surfing	Anger at God
Body aches	Intrusive thoughts and images	Afraid	Increased risk-taking	Loss of meaning
Nervous energy—need to be moving	Nightmares	Irritable		
Heightened startle response	Forgetfulness	Lost		
Loss of appetite	Making careless errors at work	Numbness		
Elevated blood pressure	Difficulty making decisions	Shock/disbelief		
		Depression		
		Panic		
		Lack of interest in normal activities		

For police, the impact of a traumatic event is usually short-lived (a few days or weeks). Most of the time, the symptoms subside with time on their own. However, for a small percentage (roughly 7–9 percent), they linger. It's a balance of risk and protective factors in the situation and the individual that determines if one has ongoing issues from the trauma. This is why resilience is regarded as a process. Again, resilience doesn't mean the absence of symptoms. It's the active approach to and management of them.

One tendency in the first responder field following a traumatic event is to try to avoid the feelings about the event. Colin Wastell investigated the impact of emotional suppression on over 400 ambulance officers. He found that suppressing emotions was linked to physical and psychological stress reactions such as sleep disturbance, anxiety, nausea, high blood pressure, and backaches, and emotional and cognitive defense mechanisms such as numbing out or mentally manipulating the event so that it doesn't register as stressful (e.g., blaming the victim) (Wastell, 2002). He also found that those with higher levels of alexithymia, which refers to difficulty recognizing and naming emotions, also experienced higher levels of distress. In short, suppressing the emotions made it WORSE. Healing from traumatic experiences requires integrating the emotions that accompany intrusive memories with the unmanipulated content of the traumatic event (Horowitz, 1997). It's important not to lie to yourself about how you feel about the event and to be truthful with yourself about what happened. You can try to defend against these, but it will catch up with you. I've worked with plenty of people who have tried.

Even though emotional expression is vital to recover from traumatic events, it's oftentimes considered a weakness, so police keep their feelings to themselves. Consequently, everyone assumes that what they see on the outside reflects what the person feels on the inside. This error in thinking is called the Fallacy of Uniqueness in that the person who feels sadness about a call assumes he is the only one feeling it. This mistaken belief leads him to think all kinds of negative things about himself: "I'm not cut out for this work," "Something's wrong with me," and so forth. My colleague, a veteran police chaplain, calls this "stinkin' thinkin'." I spoke with two officers who responded to a horrific car accident where a family died. Both officers felt grief and sadness for the senseless loss of life at the hands of an impaired driver. Yet, each of them surveyed the responses of others on the scene and concluded that they were the only ones who felt that way so they kept it to themselves. It was only after leaving the call did one admit to the other in private that he thought it was a shitty call. The other then felt free to admit that she too was having a hard time with the call. I've learned that the word "shitty" is equivalent to my substitution of the word "reaction" for emotion. "Shitty" can be substituted for so-called "weaker" emotions like sadness.

Police suppress their emotions because of the sheer volume of tragedies that they see on a regular basis. They would be emotionally drained, suffering from compassion fatigue, if they were emotionally connected and expressive about their feelings every time they were exposed to suffering. Yet, if police get used to turning off their emotions at work, they may have difficulty turning them back on when they get home at the end of the shift. This is not a good thing for two key reasons: 1) it prevents them from healing because they need the emotional experience, combined with the cognitive, to heal from the event (Herman, 1997; Horowitz, 1997), and 2) it isolates police from their families (Herman, 1997; Rees & Smith, 2008). It's important for them to have strategies for transitioning to their home life, shedding their emotional "armor" and talking about how they feel about their work with their significant others.

As much as police attempt to suppress certain emotions, it doesn't actually work very well. In fact, the more one tries to suppress a feeling, the stronger they will actually feel it. This is referred to as the *rebound effect* (Clark, Ball, & Pape, 1991; Petrie, Booth, & Pennebaker, 1998; Wegner & Gold, 1995). When you suppress negative emotions, you actually increase activation of the sympathetic nervous system, which is responsible for stimulating the body's fight or flight system (Gross & Levenson, 1997). This activation increases the demands placed on the cardiovascular system, which could have serious health consequences. These physical reactions have been linked to compromised immune responses and poorer health outcomes.

Cognitive: This Can't Be Happening

The long-term psychological response to trauma is greatly influenced by how you interpret the event and your sense of control over uncontrollable circumstances. For instance, you may interpret the event as preventable if only you had responded differently (faster/slower; did this, not that, etc.). Making matters worse, believing you could have done something differently to prevent the event sometimes gets mixed up with the idea that you actually caused the event. A client once told me that because he could not think quickly enough to save his friend it was his fault that his friend died. It was heartbreaking to see him take ownership of what was not his to have. His pain was immense. Unfortunately, this kind of thinking is oftentimes compounded by police officers' mistaken belief that it was their job to prevent such an outcome. There are times when police officers are able to think and act quickly in a situation and things turn out well but many things are not in their control. These are the limits of all human beings, regardless of your training and experience.

Counterfactual thinking refers to the tendency to imagine alternative outcomes that did not happen. It's a way of denying the reality of what *is* by negotiating for what *could have been*. Needless to say, it's generally not a productive way of moving forward. It's one thing to do an operational debrief to learn from one's mistakes to *plan to act* differently in the future. It's quite a different thing to replay the past event and *wish* things were different. The first scenario is *constructive* while the second one is *destructive*. Police officers may find themselves wishing that the suspect had not reached for his waistband and imagining a neutral or positive outcome had that *one thing* not happened. They may wish that they had taken a different call for service and hadn't had to shoot someone that day. Their ability to move forward is hampered because they haven't accepted it so they could let it go. Making matters worse is the tendency to inflate the likelihood of an alternative outcome based upon the ease with which you can imagine this outcome. This is referred to as the availability heuristic. An example of this would be imagining that you cleared a call for service earlier and, as a result, you were able to respond sooner as an assist for your partner. You assume that this earlier arrival would have prevented your partner from being shot. Yet, there's no evidence that would be the case. In fact, it might have meant that you would have been shot as well.

Related to this line of thinking is officers' beliefs regarding their *locus of control* (Rotter, 1966). When individuals believe that they have the ability to influence their circumstances, they are said to have an *internal locus of control*. This isn't to say that they are delusional in that they falsely believe they are all-powerful and able to have the outcome they want. Instead, they believe that they have the power to control certain aspects of the situation, even if it means that they control their response to the situation. Therefore, it is key that you separate what you do/don't control. As you may have guessed, those with an *external locus of control* believe that they are at the whim of external forces. They are powerless to change the situation and become resigned to let themselves be acted upon. There is an overwhelming sense of defeat in a person with an external locus of control. Individuals with an external locus of control are more likely to develop PTSD (Norris, Friedman, Watson, Brne, Diaz, & Kaniasty, 2002; Zhang, Liu, Jiang, Wu, & Tian, 2014), while an internal locus of control seems to be a protective factor for both acute and chronic distress (Hoge, Austin, & Pollack, 2007). Additionally, individuals with a strong belief in an external locus of control may develop *learned helplessness*, which is discussed next.

I Give Up: Learned Helplessness

Sometimes you feel battered when, despite your best efforts, things just don't turn out as you had hoped. You might struggle to cope with an overwhelming difficulty and when it doesn't seem to be working, you can fall into a state of *learned helplessness*. Maybe when you're trying to cope with the aftermath of traumatic events, you come to the conclusion that you just can't manage, and give up. You lack the motivation to even try anymore because you think "Why bother?" You feel defeated because you've learned that you are helpless to change things.

The research on learned helplessness began as early as the 1970s. Tests with animals and eventually humans showed that when they felt that no matter what they did, they couldn't control their environment, they gave up (Abramson, Seligman, & Teasdale, 1978). What's worse is that they seemed to be locked into this mentality. When the situation changed and they *could* influence their environment, they didn't know or believe it so they didn't even bother to try. The determination that one was helpless depended on a variety of factors relating to the cause of the helplessness. Was the cause of the helplessness temporary or enduring? Was this helplessness global, in that it occurred across people, places, and situations, or was it specific to a person, place, or situation? Was the helplessness related to something internal, such as a lack of confidence in one's abilities or due to external circumstances? How people answered these questions influenced their sense of how chronic or acute their helplessness would be; where it would show up in their lives, and if feeling helpless reflected on them as people. In other words, if they were helpless, was it because they were weak or because the situation couldn't be helped by anyone? Police are not immune from developing learned helplessness. This might sound strange since police help the helpless. Yet, police have reported their inability to help victims or to have a sense of control over their work as hindering their own coping (Conn & Butterfield, 2013).

> The fact that this is a person that you really can't help. There's nothing you can do to make it better. I can't use any tools that I would normally use to kind of get myself out of here sooner. All of the things that we could have possibly done and not one of them happened and that's what makes it that much more sad.

A big contributor to individuals' learned helplessness is when others handle people with "kid gloves" following an incident. What I mean by this is that people are sometimes treated as if they were fragile, incapable of managing on their own. I truly believe people mean well when they do this but it perpetuates a "sick role," undermining the individual's self-confidence, and creating dependency on others. Capable people are treated like broken toys and convinced that they can't make their own choices about important life matters such as returning to work. Unfortunately, I see this too often in the mental

> Avoiding danger is no safer in the long run than outright exposure. The fearful are caught as often as the bold.
> (Keller, 1940, p. 11)

health field. I'm not referring to fitness for duty evaluations. They have their utility. What I'm referring to are those that assume that a person who has been exposed to a critical incident will be negatively affected by it and convey that belief. Police are NOT destined to be affected by a critical incident. That's why it is oftentimes called a potentially traumatic event, not simply a traumatic event. I've had officers in individual debriefings following an incident ask if something is wrong with them because they're eating, sleeping and feeling well. Don't worry. If you're not negatively affected by a call it doesn't mean you're a sociopath.

To be clear, learned helplessness should not be confused with freezing during a critical incident. When you "give up" during a critical incident it's an instinctual reaction. You're freezing because, from an evolutionary perspective, that's the best response for your survival. In the case of a critical incident, you might immediately shut down and no longer fight for your life or the lives of others. In policing, this might be mistakenly regarded as weakness. It couldn't be further from the truth. Just like fight or flight, the freeze response is an instinctual reaction. In other words, the most rigorous training and mental strength is not going to overcome this instinctual reaction. However, learned helplessness can contribute to having more crisis situations where you feel frozen. For instance, if you believe that you can't change anything anyway, you might compromise officer safety and end up in a critical incident that could have been avoided. For example, I've known officers to stop wearing their vests and to cancel their assist officers. It's as if they're saying "If it's my time, it's my time. There's nothing I can do about it."

EMOTIONAL AFTERMATH: ANGER

Another lingering impact from trauma is anger. Oftentimes people come to see me about "anger issues." They feel that they are on edge all the time and are mad at everyone they encounter. It doesn't take long before their "anger" begins to be explained by other more critical (vulnerable) feelings such as hurt, shock, and a sense of betrayal and resentment. They may feel betrayed by co-workers, supervisors, a situation, their God, their body, or all of mankind. The problem with anger is that it can sometimes spread from being aimed at one person and one situation to every other situation and person. Your anger may be justified. Systems fail, allowing people with mental health issues to further decompensate, leading police to handle mental health matters in the public. People sometimes do unthinkable things to children. Anger at these situations is healthy and appropriate.

However, holding onto anger allows resentment to build, eroding your resilience. You may come to resent the criminal justice and mental health systems and others involved in the call. Resentment is like drinking poison and hoping the other person dies. I've witnessed clients agonizing over how someone else needs to change (systems, a boss, co-workers, parents). I remind them that there is no point in this suffering because we can't change another person no matter how much we agonize over it. It seems as though they keep saying in their head "But she must change for me to be happy." If this is your logic, you'll likely never be happy. You will likely keep circling that thought, feeling powerless and defeated. So, you have to figure out how to let it go and not let your happiness depend on someone else's behavior.

Unacknowledged anger and resentment tend to wreak havoc in our lives. They affect our physical and emotional health, our relationships, our work and, consequently, our financial health. Physically, ongoing anger leads to headaches, stomach aches, muscle tension, poor focus, poor sleep, and diet. It can wear us down emotionally, causing depression and/or anxiety from ruminative thoughts. Our personal and professional relationships suffer because the pent-up anger is released while interacting with others. You might be passive aggressive, directly aggressive, and/or inattentive to the needs of others because you are so preoccupied with your own anger. You're probably not very fun to be around. Have you been around a person who is always angry? Every conversation you have somehow finds its way back to how they have been wronged. At the beginning, friends and family are empathetic to their feelings. After a while, it gets tiring for others and they tend to stop coming around.

EMOTIONAL AFTERMATH: IT'S OVER. WHY AM I STILL HAVING A REACTION?

When a negative experience is so bad, so tragically memorable, it only has to happen one time for your brain to decide "Hey, I need to remember some stuff that I just saw, smelled, felt and heard because I need to avoid them in the future." It's an involuntary decision the brain makes behind your back, so to speak. The brain associates certain sights, smells, and sounds with danger and sounds the alarms, triggering emotional and physical reactions when it registers something similar to the prior dangerous situation. It's for this reason that seemingly mundane objects, places, or people create a trigger response to fight, flight, or freeze. This involuntary response occurs when you perceive the triggering object, place, or person, because that sensory input goes straight to the emotional part of the brain, the amygdala, bypassing the frontal cortex, where rational thought occurs. Making matters worse, when the original experience is highly arousing, as most critical incidents are, the functions of the hippocampus, which is encoding and storing the memory, is also disrupted, resulting in a fragmented memory

> Resentment is like drinking poison and hoping the other person dies.

of the event. Since the memory was not stored properly, individuals can have strong, involuntary reactions to cues in the environment and lack a cohesive story to explain what is happening. This is terrifying and confusing. They never really get a chance to consider the objective threat because it isn't consciously recognized. In a millisecond, the information is fast-tracked to the part of the brain that is designed to arouse fear in us to keep us safe from harm. This has been referred to as the "low road" to the amygdala, while the "high road" refers to the information passing through the frontal cortex where it can be considered cognitively to determine if it is a threat (LeDoux, 1998). A simple example of this process is when we are on a hike and we encounter what appears to be a snake on the path in front of us. We will instinctively run away or freeze (unless we have something in our hand to kill it with) before we are able to recognize that what appeared to be a snake was actually a branch. In a mistake of this kind, we tend to be more forgiving of ourselves and others than when triggered by something that reminds us of a horrible call/case. There is a tendency to downplay our evolutionary response and demand that we be stronger, smarter, or more level-headed than to react with fear. This is an impossible demand. We can't stop instinctual behavior!

Oftentimes, environmental cues that were originally associated with the trauma extend to include many other things that simply *resemble* the cues. This is called stimulus generalization because there is a failure to discriminate between the original threat cue and non-threatening cues. For instance, some officers have told me of being startled when seeing a person in the grocery store that vaguely resembled a person from a traumatic event. Only upon further observation, do they realize it's just another bald man who doesn't actually resemble the person very much at all. Other times, they don't even make the connection between the man in the store and the traumatic event because they don't even remember seeing him. This occurs because, during a traumatic event, the brain establishes a connection between a group of cells in the brain, referred to as a *cell assembly* (Hebb, 1949; Johansen et al., 2014; Löwel & Singer, 1992). This cell assembly permanently records the triggering situation, in this case, the bald man and danger. However, the brain subconsciously recognized the stored emotional memory of the event and believes it must mobilize its human (you!) to action. The brain stimulates a bodily reaction like a racing heart, shallow breathing, sweating, but does so without your conscious awareness. This generalization can be crazy-making because you have a strong physical response but can't understand why it's happening. This is one of the many reasons why mindfulness approaches are helpful in alleviating traumatic responses—individuals increase their awareness of what is happening and orient themselves to be in the present moment, recognizing that they are safe and that the physical response was involuntary and nothing to be self-critical about. You can also weaken or even break up this cell assembly by deliberately exposing yourself to the triggering situation and preventing yourself from acting on the impulse to respond in a certain manner (e.g., immediately using force, fleeing when you feel afraid) (Ekman, 2003). For instance, if you typically avoid going to the store because you routinely see a bald employee who reminds you of a shooter on a call, then you would go there intentionally to see that nothing bad is going to happen while there.

Officers have also told me of being troubled and confused by the automatic negative reaction they had when they encountered a smell that was similar to a smell during a traumatic event. A prime example of this would be the smell of a car fire. Responding to a car fire where a family died can create a vivid olfactory memory that can be activated later when you respond to another car fire where no one dies. This can be confusing, given that it's just a car fire and everyone's okay. The reason this happens is that, unlike the other four senses, the sense of smell has a direct link to the emotional part of our brain and can be activated involuntarily and without your awareness of why (no story comes with it). So, in short, smell doesn't run through the normal channels for processing the sensory input. This means that the body responds immediately to the scent because the amygdala (emotion brain) mobilizes the body, to keep you safe. Implicit memories can be unintentionally retrieved without having any conscious recall of the event that gave rise to the implicit memory. This is because perceptual memories involving our five senses (implicit) are managed by a different part of the brain than the part that manages the storyline of the critical incident (explicit memory). This is why PTSD is so disturbing—you may experience perceptual memories, such as the smell of a burning body or the sound of gunfire, without consciously recognizing what is happening.

The problem is that you're responding to a faulty alarm system. This could activate an overlearned behavior, such as a takedown you've repeatedly practiced in training, increasing the likelihood of excessive force. You could also respond to the false alarm by removing yourself from the situation, which might make you feel better for the moment. This might sound like a good thing but it isn't. Removing yourself from the situation actually reinforces the faulty alarm. You come to learn that you weren't safe so you did what you needed to do and feel better for having done it. Imagine that you ran out of your house every time the alarm went off (and it goes off daily) instead of checking to see what was wrong with the alarm. You may go to great lengths to avoid people or places because you have come to regard them as dangerous. I've worked with first responders who avoid crowds, intersections, and certain people because they believe they are dangerous. This avoidance is regarded as a safety behavior and it undermines resilience. People don't learn that they're actually safe and that the alarm just needs some time (and maybe some assistance) to adjust. If they stayed put, they'd see that the alarm would sound for a bit and then it would stop. It won't go on forever. There's a brief period of time, what Ekman (2003) refers to as the *refractory period*, where we simply can't take in information that doesn't fit with the emotion we're feeling. We will likely have to be patient and let that period pass so we can make corrections to our interpretations. You can see proof of this if you've ever watched prank television shows. It oftentimes takes a while for the person being pranked to realize that they're safe; that it's just a prank. This happens even after hidden cameras are revealed and other people step forward to claim responsibility for the prank. These poor people are in the refractory period where they are struggling to accept that it's not a real threat. Eventually (and sometimes the camera doesn't run that long to catch it), you see that they realize they're okay and begin to laugh at the situation. Yet, people who have had old traumas activated don't tend to find it a laughing matter. It's horrifying and makes you feel like you're going crazy.

> We do not seek to challenge why we are feeling a particular emotion; instead, we seek to confirm it. We evaluated what is happening in a way that is consistent with the emotion we are feeling, thus justifying and maintaining the emotion.
>
> (Ekman, 2003, p. 39)

POLICE ADMINISTRATORS

The point of this book is to help police employees develop resilience so it wouldn't make sense to exclude the needs of police administrators from discussion. Sometimes, the suggestions for helping line officers be more resilient can be applied to police administrators but administrators have their own challenges to resilience. They are oftentimes crunched between the demands of the line officers and the mandates of the upper-level administrators or non-police government administrators. Oftentimes, administrators push help away from themselves, toward their officers. They think to themselves "I wasn't at that call. They were. I showed up when it was over so I don't need the help. They do!" Administrators may deny that it was difficult to see a gory crime scene or hear the stories of the responding officers, when comparing themselves to what the officers were dealing with. In fact, I regularly hear officers compare their experience to others that were suddenly worse off in an "I don't deserve help" kind of way. It's as if because their traumatic exposure was "less" than another's it doesn't count at all. Can you imagine if we had the same mentality with broken limbs? "My arm was only broken in one place, not two like hers was. I don't deserve medical treatment compared to her. Send all the treatment to her." A broken arm is broken. A gory scene and knowledge of what happened can be traumatizing, regardless of what your role was in looking at it. Besides, administrators were once line officers and have their own history of responding to horrific calls. Responding to manage the scene can be enough to activate the previous trauma memories, causing unexpected and involuntary reactions.

Some police feel that the worst part of the traumatic event isn't the event itself, but rather, is how the organization responds to their involvement in the event. Many officers have said that they feel alright about the choices they were forced to make in traumatic events such as shootings. What eats them up is not knowing what was going to happen next or feeling that they were being unjustly scrutinized.

Beyond the investigation following a critical police event, the response of administrators and co-workers also has a huge impact on how the police officer recovers. When people don't know how to respond to others during very difficult times they tend to just withdraw from them. This is the worst thing that could happen to a police officer who already feels isolated by his or her involvement in the event. A police sergeant called me to ask how to maintain team cohesiveness and support for two officers following a police shooting. He said some were afraid they would say the wrong thing or upset them, so they weren't saying anything. I advised him and his officers to say that they weren't sure what to say but that they were there to support the affected officers. Peter Neily (2016), an RCMP officer involved in a shooting suggested "Don't pretend nothing happened but don't wrap them in bubble wrap either." Instead, Neily recommends saying something as simple as "I'm glad you're okay."

Other times, co-workers use dark humor to respond to difficult situations. This may be helpful in many instances but it can be very isolating for an officer who is already struggling. Officers may crack jokes about use of force situations, calling the officer "Trigger" or joking that he isn't going to get the life-saving award this year since the car chase ended in the death of the suspect. Even if the use of force was justified and completely unavoidable, no one wants to take a life. The officer will still feel grief, anger, and guilt at having to make the difficult choice of using force. Jokes from co-workers dismiss these feelings. Dark humor is a defense mechanism though. Police use it because they feel it helps them to stay sane in insane circumstances. I get it. I've used it myself. However, it's not helpful to use it in lieu of supportive comments to a co-worker in a tragic situation.

Grief Leadership

The loss of a fellow police officer is one of the most, if not the most difficult, tragedies police officers face. Police officers lose their lives in the course of their work as well as at their own hand. When it's suicide, it might be even more difficult because it occurs at work or officers respond to the scene. When it's believed to be due to the impact of traumatic events experienced on the job, others can feel guilty for not having noticed or acted on it. The officer's death can impact those who did not even know the fallen officer because they can identify with his or her difficult experiences. Some might even fear that they might one day meet the same fate. So how do supervisors assist their troops in coping with the loss of a fellow officer? Supervisors and senior officers can assist others by demonstrating grief leadership. In short, grief leadership refers to leaders demonstrating their genuine humanness to those who are grieving a tragic event. Grief leadership entails the healthy expression of grief, facilitating communications, empowering others with information, and demonstrating adaptive coping.

True leaders openly express emotional reactions to tragic events. This healthy demonstration of emotions helps to de-stigmatize normal human reactions that have typically been labeled as signs of weakness. Traditional police culture calls for an artificially stoic reaction to ALL events, not just events where officers must suppress their fears and emotions to focus on getting the job done. During times of tragedies true leaders will offer a healthy demonstration of grief. Personally, I am not motivated by nor trusting of people who hide the way they feel or, worse yet, feel nothing when a tragedy strikes. By demonstrating their grief, leaders show that you don't have to stuff your emotions and pretend that everything is alright when it isn't. It takes a lot more courage to show emotions than it does to act like everything is fine. The leader's healthy demonstration of grief makes it more likely that others will express their grief too. Senior officers, whether or not they are supervisors, will be role models for more junior officers on how to react to a tragic event.

Leaders say what isn't being said by the troops but is felt by them. In doing so, leaders are increasing the likelihood that officers will talk to each other about how they are feeling and thinking about the event. When tragic events occur, there is a tendency to try to make meaning of the event, evaluating it to determine what could have been done or should have been done to prevent it. Sometimes, the meaning-making is vocalized in the form of people playing the "blame game" regarding how the event could have been avoided. The blame game tendency is exacerbated by the fact that police officers have training and experience detecting suicidality in others and taking measures to prevent, or at least delay, suicidal behavior with members of the public. For this reason, they may blame others for not preventing the officer's suicide—an uncaring supervisor, police administration, a work partner, or a spouse. They might even blame themselves if they knew the suicidal officer. Normalizing feelings of guilt as part of the grieving process would aid officers in realizing that just because they feel the guilt does not mean that it's appropriate or deserved. It would also help officers to learn that they are not alone in how they are thinking about the event. If others feel the same way, the reaction feels more normal than a personal failing or weakness.

Leaders provide as much information as possible. Clearly, there are circumstances where some of the information can't be disclosed but this does not preclude the disclosure of other information with an explanation as to what can't be disclosed and why. Some of the information provided would relate to the details of the event itself. This will hopefully stifle the rumor mill and officers' search for information, which might not be accurate. General information about suicide, grief, and coping would also be helpful for police officers trying to make sense of the tragedy. For instance, leaders would be well-advised to inform officers that most police suicides are a surprise because officers are skillful at hiding their pain. So, instead of blaming people for not noticing an officer's pain or for not doing something about it, officers could learn that they might be asking for something that was just not possible.

Lastly, leaders aim to lead by example in every aspect of healthy coping—taking care of their health with exercise, nutrition, and abstaining from substance abuse, making use of social and professional support, and maintaining work–life balance. Grief leadership isn't about telling others what they should be doing to cope with the impact of the event. It is about showing what is helpful. Grief leadership is walking the walk and inviting others to walk with you.

There's a long list of behaviors that leaders DON'T do. For one, leaders don't penalize officers for having reactions to traumatic events by reflecting it in their performance evaluations or allowing it to affect promotion opportunities. I'm not saying that you ignore signs that your police member isn't doing well. Instead of stigmatizing normal reactions when it comes time to evaluate, provide a referral to support services at the first sign that the police member is suffering. Even better, make sure they know about support services as soon as the event happens. I've had officers tell me that they didn't know where to even get help, if they wanted it. They vaguely remember something being mentioned in the academy and nothing since. They only ever hear of their co-workers *having* to see someone in order to get cleared to come back to work, which is not a glowing endorsement for getting help.

Leaders don't ever say "If I went through it, then you can," "That's what you signed up for," or any variation of these statements. These are cop-out statements that deny their own humanity and convey that the police member should do the same. Just because one went through a traumatic event without help doesn't mean that it was a good idea. In fact, the jadedness of the comment contradicts that. Leaders also don't talk about one member to anyone else without their permission. Admitting you're having a hard time is difficult enough without feeling like your business is being discussed with everybody else. When officers take leave following a traumatic event, others will notice their absence. So, something has to be said about it. Simply put, tell others in a "matter of fact" way that they're taking time off to better manage their reaction to the event, meaning that it isn't shameful or scandalous. There's no need to discuss symptoms or other private matters. Leaders maintain contact with the police member, as do members of the team, to keep the affected member from feeling isolated or shunned. Communications should be centered around support and keeping the member up to date on what is going on at work; excluding talks of how the officer's absence is affecting others' workload. This shaming would be the antithesis of support and could counter the benefit of the leave. The affected officer is likely very aware that his/her absence is felt in the workload of others and hearing about it isn't going to make things better.

CIVILIAN EMPLOYEES

The impact of traumatic calls on civilian employees is oftentimes overlooked. Since many of them are not responding to the scene, or are responding "after the fact," they're mistakenly assumed to be saved from the traumatic nature of the call. In fact, many civilian employees have even taken on this idea for themselves, denying their own traumatizations and "right" to be affected by calls. Yet we know that they ARE affected by calls. It can be horrifying to hear the things that happen on a 911 call and even non-emergency calls. Call takers are the first person to hear someone's cry for help. They have to maintain their cool with a person who is anything but cool to figure out what is happening on the other end of the line. Hearing parents wailing as they have discovered their child is not breathing can haunt call-takers long after the call. People tend to fill gaps to complete a story. If you can only hear the wails, you will picture their faces filled with agony. Sometimes the images you imagine are worse than reality and no less damaging than if you had seen it personally.

In addition to the calls, dispatchers can be traumatized by radio traffic. I remember feeling like my heart stopped when I was waiting to hear from an officer after they hit their radio emergency button or when I heard one was in distress. From the other end of the radio as an officer, I remember dispatchers telling me that they were worried about me when they hadn't heard from me during in-progress calls when the fight or foot chase was underway. In most departments, police officers and dispatchers have developed friendships and nobody wants to hear that their friend is in trouble but feel powerless to help them. In debriefing dispatchers, I learn that they oftentimes are forgotten as being involved immediately following the traumatic event. While officers from the scene gather to debrief on the scene, or offsite, the dispatcher is usually left on the radio for the remainder of the shift. This can be a very isolating experience. They may not get the details of what actually happened for quite some time, if at all. In the meantime, they have to tuck it away and plug along. Even worse, they may not even be included in the formal debriefing at a later time. I hope this changes since these men and women are the lifeline for both the public and officers.

POLICE FAMILY MEMBERS

Even though family members are not on the scene of traumatic events, they're still affected. Figley's (1995) trauma transmission model can explain the process by which family members are traumatized by the critical incidents police employees are involved in. According to Figley, significant others attempt to console their trauma-exposed loved one by empathetically listening to the details and reactions of a traumatic event. The "cost of caring" for family members is secondary traumatization, as family members bear witness to the disturbing details of the situation. Research suggests that it is less a matter of the disturbing details and more about the affective bond between the family member and the one exposed to the trauma (Albeck, 1994; Solomon et al., 1992). In listening to the stories of their loved ones, empathetic spouses seemed to take on the stories, including the disturbing images, as if they were their own.

Police who have experienced traumatic experiences expect that others see that they're not well because they know they're not well. They seem to forget that they have been hiding most of their reactions to the event because they believe it would make them appear weak. In relationships, people mistakenly hold the belief "If they love me, then they will know what I'm going through and what I need from them." I see this all the time in marital counseling. It's a dangerous assumption to believe that someone else knows what you're thinking, feeling, and needing. I can't count how many times spouses have been surprised to learn what's going on inside the heads and hearts of their spouses. Sometimes, they learn this after a considerable delay, when the relationship has deteriorated significantly. In the meantime, spouses draw their own conclusions about what is going on. Unfortunately, it sounds more like "She doesn't love me anymore" than "She is suffering and wants my support but doesn't know how to ask for it." People have a tendency to make sense of matters in a self-referent way since we know how it's making us feel. We start from that place to reason about what is happening. It's a good idea to ask yourself "What don't I know here?" and to ask your police spouse what they need. Be prepared for the answer though. They might ask for space, which can feel personal. It might be personal. In which case, you have some other stuff to work through, like a history of unresolved arguments and resentment. Avoiding that isn't advised. However, if it isn't about you, it would be important to look into what it IS. If your spouse doesn't want to talk about it, you shouldn't just give in and stop talking about it altogether. Instead, let him/her know what you've noticed in them, describing their behavior without assigning intent to it. This is a tricky one because we tend to include the intent part. "You've hardly spoken to anyone in the family the last few days" is better than "You've been giving us the silent treatment, acting like we don't matter." Both communicate the underlying concern but the first one is neutral and the second one is an attack, which will likely result in defensiveness. Your "job" as a supportive significant other is to be a mirror for your police member; reflect what you are seeing and go a step further to ask what is going on, what they need, and how you can help. How you go about doing this makes all the difference in the world. If you go at it in a manner where they feel like they are being attacked because you are hurting, they'll shut down and you both lose. If you reflect and ask in a caring manner, you just might get somewhere. Notice I said "might." Your significant other can still shut you down by refusing to talk. You might get an "I'm fine. Stop asking." You might be tempted to follow this instruction, even if you know your partner isn't fine. Don't do this. What you allow continues. It's not nagging, if it's done right. Reflect again. "I care about you and I can see a difference in your behavior." Then describe the behavior as objectively as possible. If you give up when you get some pushback, nothing changes. Your significant other gets to avoid how (s)he thinks, feels, and behaves and it becomes entrenched. This doesn't mean that you *have* to have the conversation right then, right there. Sometimes, it's not the best time to have the conversation. Somebody is getting ready for bed, trying to eat dinner, get some relief by watching their favorite television program. These are not great times for big conversations. The delivery and timing of difficult conversations are very important. They're just as important as the content itself.

Sometimes, support doesn't look like we think it should. At times, we have to be willing to say things that are hard to hear but vital to

> Your "job" as a supportive significant other is to be a mirror for your police member; reflect what you are seeing and go a step further to ask what is going on, what they need, and how you can help. What you allow continues.

talk about. "I'm concerned because I've noticed that you haven't been returning your family's calls" is far better than "You need to call your mom back" or saying nothing at all. It doesn't make you the bad guy or gal for reflecting what you're seeing, even if it upsets your loved one. This isn't a free pass to unload your frustrations. That would likely add to the burden your loved one already feels. However, it doesn't mean that your feelings don't count. It's a delicate dance to express your hurt and frustrations with your police loved one without it being interpreted as their "fault."

One of the key elements of being supportive, is to make your desire to support known. This might seem like a no-brainer, but it's worth saying it because it makes it easier for another to receive the help when it's outright versus having to ask for it. The other key element of support is that it is a matter of quality, not quantity. Tons of people can say "I'm here for you if you need me" and maybe they're just being polite. Only offer support if you mean it, following through with your time and attention. Nowadays, lots of people divide their attention between people and technology. Watching television or scanning social media while "supporting" a loved one doesn't cut it.

Furthermore, the officer has to value the support. This statement warrants explanation. What I mean by this is that you have to have some credibility in terms of providing supportive reassurance to someone about a decision they made on call. If you don't know much about the situation, it is hard to accept that your reassurance means that much. Try to understand by being a good listener. It helps to learn the jargon. The officer can easily discount that your support has any bearing, saying that you are just being nice because you're family. It's hard to not be offended by this, but you would do the same if someone was trying to reassure you of something for which they didn't fully understand.

When people think about support, they usually think of offering emotional support; talking someone through something or, at a minimum, being an ear for their woes. As a therapist, I think many people are surprised when I speak of the value of NOT talking about matters but, rather, being a source of non-verbal support. Going fishing or shopping with a person so that they feel that they are not alone is a very important form of support. It's not that you're avoiding talking about matters but, rather, you're helping someone to get their mind on something else for a while. There's nothing wrong with that. We don't want to be so consumed with the traumatic event that nothing else matters; that other parts of our lives are neglected. In my study on coping with traumatic stress, officers told me that it was very helpful just to spend time with family, to be reminded that they are more than their job, they have hobbies and other interests. One officer relayed:

I can be me and not police officer me. If I'm with my mom or my dad, for instance, I can almost be the kid again. It's like my dad will protect me.

Unhealthy Relationship Dynamics

Sometimes support can take on an unhealthy dynamic, especially when one person is mentally or physically compromised. The "Over-functioner–Underfunctioner" dynamic entails one partner assuming more responsibility for the relationship or family tasks based on their assumption that they're more capable than the other one. An example of this would be a police member who is dealing with a traumatic event is assumed by a well-meaning partner to be too fragile to deal with the demands of home so she (or he) assumes responsibility for all of the partner's responsibilities in the family. This kind and loving gesture might inadvertently create a dynamic where the overfunctioner carries too much of the load, eventually becoming resentful of the underfunctioner. Making matters worse, the underfunctioner comes to believe he/she isn't able to function because they haven't had to and might become resentful of the very person who seems to demonstrate capabilities they are lacking. The relationship that was once based on two people as equals has now become more like a parent–child or savior–victim relationship. A healthy relationship cannot exist with these unequal dynamics. I'm not saying you shouldn't help a wounded partner with additional needs while they're healing from their injury. It's ridiculous to think we have to have an equal share of responsibilities all the time. It's not good to rigidly keep score of who is doing what. I *am* saying to be mindful of the message you are sending by doing things for someone who *could* do them. You may feel your gestures say "I love you. Let me help you" when they're actually conveying "You can't do this for yourself because you have a problem."

Another unhealthy relationship dynamic following a trauma event is the *policed* family. Here the police member brings the work role home. Although some home problems can be addressed using work-role problem-solving, oftentimes they cannot. Significant others become resentful because they feel they are being treated like the victim, civilian, or even the suspect by the police member. Family members relinquish decision-making to the police member, who is trying to maintain control of situations as he would at work. This treatment might also include first responders' hypervigilance to threats and attempts to control the behaviors of significant others, believing this will prevent them from harm that the police member witnesses at work. Consider also the manner of speaking required of a 911 call taker/dispatcher. They have to maintain control of conversations to get needed information in the most efficient manner possible. This same manner would not bode well in speaking with a partner about their day or a teenager having relationship difficulties. One firefighter married to a 911 call taker told me of recognizing that he was being "worked" by his wife in conversation. He felt that she began talking *at* him about their marriage instead of *to* him. After 15 years of marriage, they divorced. The call taker may tighten up their control of the conversation even more after experiencing a traumatic event. The police member role can also spillover into the home in the form of emotional numbing. They may have been emotionally detaching from the victim(s) on a terrible call and continue this when they encounter their own family. Officers have spoken of how it was hard to see child victims at work and then look at their own kids a short time later without seeing the victim.

Media Scrutiny

Following a traumatic event, police family members tend to be consumers of media depictions of police events. When the event is ongoing, spouses may tune in to the television or social media to monitor what their loved one is dealing with. I know when my husband was working during a riot that lasted for hours, I alternated between television and Twitter to determine if any shots were being fired or officers hurt. The problem with this is that the media is a key source of MISinformation. It can be *more* unnerving because it tends to be filled with inflammatory stories, fueling fear to keep viewers tuned in. During the riots, friends were also watching the media and telling me what they heard and asking what I knew. This just made matters so much worse. I knew better than to tune in but I did anyway, since my husband wasn't available to fill me in. Nowadays, I imagine that this happens to police families on a regular basis. What is meant to be helpful in terms of becoming informed about critical incidents, seems to have the opposite effect. It adds stress having to sift through the information, wondering what you can count on being true, and what you have to try to ignore.

I think it's generally a bad idea to turn to unreliable sources of information when you're concerned about your loved one. Beyond the misinformation, the images and inflammatory descriptions seem to add to the trauma (and drama) of the event. I remember seeing the disturbing images of people jumping from the towers to their death in the media depictions of the 9–11 attacks. Those images are stuck in my mind and come up every time I think about the event. I'd rather they didn't. I'm not suggesting you stick your head in the sand, pretending that nothing is happening. I'm just saying limit your media viewing to avoid unnecessary traumatization.

Beyond the disturbing images you expose yourself to, some media portrayals of police events paint a portrait of police officers as being trigger happy and lacking in humanity. It's infuriating to see the biased portrayal of police officers and the selective inclusion of information relating to the exchanges between police and individuals such as those with mental illness, adolescents, and others. The media emphasizes the vulnerability of those who are harmed by police and completely ignores the vulnerability of the police due to the actions of the adolescent, mentally ill individual, or career criminal.

Public Scrutiny

Following a highly publicized police event, the public can also be a source of strain for police. You may be contacted by people you haven't heard from in a while who want the inside scoop on what they saw on the news. If you live in a small community, you may be recognized in public and can be met with a variety of responses such as questions, unsolicited opinions about the event, or outright harassment. If you encounter someone who is just being nosy, I would offer them "pocket statements." These are concise responses that you've already prepared and can sort of "pull out of your pocket to read," so to speak. For instance, when someone asks you, or your kid, "What happened on Main Street last night? I saw it on the news," you can say "Thanks for thinking to ask but I'm not able to talk about it. How are things with you?" If someone asks how your loved one is doing, again, "Thanks for caring enough to ask. We're taking care of ourselves. How are you doing?"

You may be tempted to answer questions you are asked or respond to emails, calls, or texts about the event. In my opinion, that's what the delete button is for. Unless this person is expressing a genuine interest in you, your police member, and family, there's no need to respond for THEIR sake. You likely don't have time to be concerned with what they need. You have to worry about your own needs and the needs of your family.

Your kids may also have to face scrutiny at school. Classmates and even teachers watched the event on the news and know that this is the child of a police member and have their own questions and opinions about the event. It's important to prepare children for questions and comments. Give them brief, age-appropriate information about the event and encourage them to ask you questions, if needed. Talk to them about how they can briefly respond to others. Help them develop their own pocket statements.

Beyond the busy-body people who may ask you about the event, there are those that are just outright anti-police. A large portion of the people police encounter are not exactly happy to see them. Police are called when bad things are happening and those doing the bad stuff don't exactly appreciate the attention they receive. Unfortunately, even some of the victims of crimes don't offer a warm welcome to responding officers. They may have a relationship with the offending person or have an opinion about how police work should be done based upon the most recent episode of C.S.I. They think that suspect profiles are generated from DNA pulled from a door handle, interrogations conducted, confessions received, and arrests made in under an hour (with commercial breaks). I can't count, nor do I want to, how many times I have heard people say that the police are not doing their jobs. This is very frustrating for the men and women who are doing their best to serve the public. You might encounter this group of people in social media or on television. Unfortunately, they are free to "troll" on social media and the media interviews those that will talk to them, give them an opinion. It doesn't have to be based on anything in reality to still make the news. Seeing this can add so much misery to an already stressful situation.

The problem is that the majority of the public don't understand police work. Why would they? I don't know anything about accounting because I've never been an accountant. Yet, plenty of people have opinions about police work even though they've never done the job. They base their information on media depictions, which is problematic. Little by little, police have to educate the public on the reality of their work, which requires patience and understanding. It's hard to remember that people don't know what they don't know. Because police can't "not know" what they've learned on the job, it's hard to identify with an unknowing public. You can become jaded about people in general. I can clearly remember my surprise the first time I received a "Thank you" for doing my job from a member of the public. I had been on the job for a couple of years at this point and had only ever been cursed at or worse by the public I served in a high crime area. Yet, this was a thin slice of the population. I had forgotten about the rest. That's easy to do when you're only ever exposed to the suffering of others. This brings us to the topic of the next chapter: secondary traumatic stress.

*

TOOLS FOR YOUR DUTY BAG

▮ Question "should" statements and feelings of guilt. Are they appropriate? Would you hold the same standard for someone else? Why or why not?

▮ Are your "what ifs?" balanced? Are you asking yourself these questions in a biased way? Is your reasoning backwards in time flawed? (using information you didn't have at the time, assuming you had time to consider all options, etc.).

▮ Question assumptions about how others are reacting to the traumatic event. You can't compare your insides to someone else's outsides.

▮ Don't assume responsibility for what's not yours. Consider all the factors contributing to a traumatic event (days, weeks, months, and years before the traumatic event day).

▮ Avoiding people, places, and things only helps in the short-term and reinforces anxiety, making it more intense over time and harder to face those people, places, and things.

▮ Suppressing feelings about events intensifies them and also has negative consequences for your health, particularly your cardiovascular and immune system.

▮ Focusing on what you control, and not what you don't, fends off learned helplessness, improving problem-solving and resilience.

▮ Shocking, terrifying traumatic events interfere with memory encoding, storage, and retrieval so you may have to work harder to overcome conscious and unconscious reminders to the event but it IS doable.

▮ Leaders are people too and should not simply push support to their troops, but accept support for themselves.

▮ Leaders are in a great position to demonstrate grief leadership, normalizing reactions to traumatic events.

▮ Emergency communicators can be traumatized by 911 calls and handling radio traffic for a traumatic event. They should be included in debriefings and other support services.

▮ Family members should speak up about what they are seeing in the police member, conveying concern, even if it is uncomfortable. Pay attention to timing and delivery.

▮ Support includes emotional support as well as being available for non-verbal forms of support such as spending time with someone to avoid isolation behaviors.

▮ Be mindful of relationship dynamics, avoiding savior–victim-like interactions.

▮ Media and public scrutiny can compound traumatic reactions. Limit contact with these sources of strain and develop plans to deal with questions and unsolicited advice.

▮ Assist children to adjust to the traumatic event and to respond to questions and comments directed at them.

REFERENCES

Abramson, L. Y., Seligman, M. E. P., & Teasdale, J. D. (1978). Learned helplessness in humans: Critique and reformulation. *Journal of Abnormal Psychology*, 87(1), 49–74.

Albeck, J. H. (1994). Intergenerational consequences of trauma: Reframing traps in treatment theory—A second generation perspective. In E. B.

Williams & J. F. Sommer (Eds.), *Handbook of post-traumatic therapy* (pp. 106–125).Westport, CT: Greenwood Press.

Cannon, W. B. (1927). The James-Lange theory of emotions: A critical examination and an alternative theory. *The American Journal of Psychology, 39,* 106–124.

Carlier, I. V. (1999). Finding meaning in police traumas. In J. M. Violanti & D. Paton (Eds.), *Police trauma: Psychological aftermath of civilian combat* (pp. 227–240). Springfield, IL: Charles C. Thomas.

Christianson, S. A. (1984). The relationship between induced emotional arousal and amnesia. *Scandinavian Journal of Psychology, 25,* 147–160.

Clark, D. M., Ball, S., & Pape, D. (1991). An experimental investigation of thought suppression. *Behavior Research and Therapy, 29,* 253–257.

Conn, S. M., & Butterfield, L. D. (2013). Coping with secondary traumatic stress by general duty police officers: practical implications. *Canadian Journal of Counselling and Psychotherapy, 47(2),* 272–298.

Diffen LLC. (2017). *Accountability vs. responsibility.* Retrieved July 26, 2017, from www.diffen.com/difference/Accountability_vs_Responsibility.

Ekman, P. (2003). *Emotions revealed: Recognizing faces and feelings to improve communication and emotional life.* New York: Henry Holt & Co.

Falsetti, S. A., Resick, P. A., & Davis, J. L. (2003). Changes in religious beliefs following trauma. *Journal of Traumatic Stress, 16(4),* 391–398.

Festinger, L. A. (1954). A theory of social comparison processes. *Human Relations, 7,* 117–140.

Figley, C. R. (1995). Compassion fatigue: Coping with secondary traumatic stress in those who treat the traumatized. New York: Brunner-Mazel.

Figley, C. R. (1998). Burnout in families: The systemic cost of caring. New York: CRC Press.

Goleman, D. (1995). *Emotional intelligence.* London: Bloomsbury.

Gross, J., & Levenson, R. W. (1997). Hiding feelings: The acute effects of inhibiting negative and positive emotion. *Journal of Abnormal Psychology, 106,* 95–103.

Hatfield, E., Cacioppo, J. T., & Rapson, R. L. (1992). Primitive emotional contagion. In M. S. Clark (Ed.), *Review of personality and social psychology* (pp. 151–177). Newbury Park, CA: Sage.

Hatfield, E., Cacioppo, J. T., & Rapson, R. L. (1993). Emotional contagion. *Current Directions in Psychological Science, 2,* 96–99.

Hatfield, E., Cacioppo, J. T., & Rapson, R. L. (1994). *Emotional contagion.* New York: Cambridge University Press.

Hebb, D., (1949). *The organization of behavior.* New York: John Wiley & Sons.

Herman, J. L. (1992). Trauma and recovery: The aftermath of violence- from domestic abuse to political terror. New York: Basic Books.

Herman, J. L. (1997). *Trauma and recovery: The aftermath of violence- from domestic abuse to political terror.* New York: Basic Books.

Hoge, E. A., Austin, E. D., & Pollack, M. H. (2007). Resilience: research evidence and conceptual considerations for posttraumatic stress disorder. *Depression and Anxiety, 24(2),* 139–152. Retrieved July 4, 2017 from http://dx.doi.org/10.1002/da.20175.

Horowitz, M. J. (1997). *Stress response syndrome* (2nd/3rd ed.). Northvale, NJ: Jason Aronson.

James, W., & Lange, C. G. (1922). *The emotions.* Baltimore, MD: Williams & Wilkins Co.

Johansen, J. P., Diaz-Mataix, L., Hamanaka, H., Ozawa, T., Ycu, E., Koivumaa, J. . . . LeDoux, J. E. (2014). Hebbian and neuromodulatory mechanisms interact to trigger associative memory formation. *Proceedings of the National Academy of Sciences of the United States of America, 111(51)*, E5584–E5592.

Keller, H. (1940). *Let us have faith.* New York: Doubleday, Doran, & Co., Inc.

Kubany, E. S., & Ralston, T. C. (2006). Treatment of trauma-related guilt and shame. In V. Follette & J. Ruzek (Eds.), *Cognitive behavioral therapies for trauma* (2nd ed., pp. 258–287). New York: Guilford.

Kubany, E. S., & Watson, S. B. (2003). Guilt: Elaboration of a multidimensional model. *The Psychological Record, 53*, 51–90.

Kulik, J. A., & Mahler, H. I. M. (2000). Social comparison, affiliation, and emotional contagion. In J. Suls & L. Wheeler (Eds.), *Handbook of social comparison* (pp. 295–320). New York: Springer.

Lazarus, R. S., & Folkman, S. (1984). *Stress, appraisal and coping.* New York: Springer Publishing.

LeDoux, J. E. (1992). Emotion as memory: Anatomical systems underlying indelible neural traces. In S. A. Christianson (Ed.), *Handbook of emotion and memory* (pp. 269–288). Hillsdale, NJ: Lawrence Erlbaum.

Lerner, M. J. (1997). What does the belief in a just world protect us from: The dread of death or the fear of understanding suffering? *Psychological Inquiry, 8(1)*, 29–32.

Lerner, M. J., & Miller, D. T. (1977). Just world research and the attribution process: Looking back and ahead. *Psychological Bulletin, 85*, 1030–1051.

Löwel, S., & Singer, W. (1992). Selection of intrinsic horizontal connections in the visual cortex by correlated neuronal activity. *Science, 255*, 209–212.

Marshall, E. K. (2003). *Occupational stress and trauma in law enforcement: A preliminary study in cumulative career traumatic stress.* Unpublished Doctoral Dissertation, Union Institute and University, Cincinnati, Ohio.

McGaugh, J. L. (1992). Affect, neuromodulatory systems, and memory storage. In S. A. Christianson (Ed.), *Handbook of emotion and memory* (pp. 245–268). Hillsdale, NJ: Lawrence Erlbaum.

Neily, P. (2016). Canadian Critical Incident Stress Foundation Annual Conference. April 19, 2016.

Nemiah, J. (1995). Early concepts of trauma, dissociation, and the unconscious: Their history and current implications. In D. Bremner & C. R. Marmar (Eds.), *Trauma, memory, and dissociation* (pp. 1–26). Washington, DC: American Psychiatric Press.

Nilsson, L. G., & Archer, T. (1992). Biological aspects of memory and emotion: Affect and cognition. In S. A. Christianson (Ed.), *Handbook of emotion and memory* (pp. 289–306). Hillsdale, NJ: Lawrence Erlbaum.

Norris, F. H., Friedman, M. J., Watson, P. J., Byrne, C. M., Diaz, E., & Kaniasty, K. (2002). 60,000 disaster victims speak. Part I. An empirical review of the empirical literature, 1981–2001. *Psychiatry, 65(3)*, 207–239.

Pargament, K. I. (1996). Religious methods of coping: Resources for the conservation and transformation of significance. In E. P. Shafranske (Ed.), *Religion and the clinical practice of psychology* (pp. 215–239). Washington, DC: American Psychological Association.

Petrie, K. J., Booth, R. J., & Pennebaker, J. W. (1998). The immunological effects of thought suppression. *Journal of Personality and Social Psychology, 75(5)*, 1264–1272.

Pitman, R., Orr, S., & Shalev, A. (1993). Once bitten twice shy: Beyond the conditioning model of PTSD. *Biological Psychiatry, 33*, 145–146.

Rauch, S., van der Kolk, B. A., Fisler, R. Alpert, N. M., Orr, S. P., Savage, C. R., . . . Pitman, R. K. (1996). A symptom provocation study using position emission tomography and script driven imagery. *Archives of General Psychiatry, 53*, 380–387.

Rees, B., & Smith, J. (2008). Breaking the silence: The traumatic circle of policing. *International Journal of Police Science and Management, 10(3)*, 267–279.

Rotter, J. B. (1966). Generalized expectancies for internal versus external control of reinforcement. *Psychological Monographs (General and Applied), 80(1)*, 1–28. http://dx.doi.org/10.1037/h0092976

Safer, M. A., Christianson, S.-Å., Autry, M. W., & Österlund, K. (1998). Tunnel memory for traumatic events. *Applied Cognitive Psychology, 12*, 99–117.

Schachter, S. (1959). *The psychology of affiliation*. Stanford, CA: Stanford University Press.

Schachter, S., & Singer, J. E. (1962). Cognitive, social, and physiological determinants of emotional state. *Psychological Review, 69*, 379–399.

Solomon, Z., Waysman, M., Levy, G., Fried, B., Mikulincer, M., Benbenishty, R. . . . Bliech, A. (1992). From front line to home front: A study of secondary traumatization. *Family Process, 31(3)*, 289–302.

van der Kolk, B. A. (1998). Trauma and memory. *Psychiatry and Clinical Neuroscience, 52(S1)*, S52–S64.

van der Kolk, B. A., & van der Hart, O. (1989). Pierre Janet and the breakdown of adaptation in psychological trauma. *American Journal of Psychiatry, 146*, 1530–1540.

van der Kolk, B. A., & van der Hart, O. (1991). The intrusive past: The flexibility of memory and the engraving of trauma. *American Imago, 48*, 425–454.

Wastell, C. A. (2002). Exposure to trauma: The long-term effects on suppressing emotional reactions. *The Journal of Nervous and Mental Disease, 190(12)*, 839–845.

Wegner, D. M., & Gold, D. B. (1995). Fanning old flames: Emotional and cognitive effects of suppressing thoughts of a past relationship. *Journal of Personality and Social Psychology, 68*, 782–792.

Yuille, J. C., & Cutshall, J. L. (1989). Analysis of the statements of victims, witnesses, and suspects. In J. C. Yuille (Ed.), *Credibility assessment*. Dordrecht, The Netherlands: Kluwer.

Zhang, W., Liu, H., Jiang, X., Wu, D., Tian, Y. (2014) A longitudinal study of posttraumatic stress disorder symptoms and its relationship with coping skill and locus of control in adolescents after an earthquake in China. *PLOS ONE, 9(2)*, 1–7.

Secondary Traumatic Stress
Uncomplicated Strategies for Complex Trauma

> You are not supposed to be happy all the time. Life hurts and it's hard. Not because you're doing it wrong, but because it hurts for everybody. Don't avoid the pain. You need it. It's meant for you. Be still with it, let it come, let it go, let it leave you with the fuel you'll burn to get your work done on this earth.
> (Glennon Doyle Melton, *Love Warrior: A Memoir*, 2016)

You have likely heard of post-traumatic stress disorder (PTSD) but, chances are, many of you haven't heard of secondary traumatic stress (STS). I would like to draw awareness to STS since police officers who repeatedly respond to trauma victims are at risk of developing STS, if not PTSD (Hafeez, 2003; Marshall, 2003; Salston & Figley, 2003). I also want to distinguish STS from burnout, because these conditions are oftentimes discussed as if they are the same condition. They come from different sources and call for different responses to deal with them.

PTSD and operational stress injuries are typically associated with what is referred to as a "primary" trauma, where the event involves a threat to the safety of the police member. This distinct event is easier to identify as the source of traumatic reactions. It's called a "Big T," in that it is considered a "Big Trauma." For example, on this day, the police responded to a shots-fired call. Officers were shot at and returned fire, killing the suspect. This is the material of Chapter 2. In addition to the explicit acknowledgment of the event, there is usually a formal provision of support such as a debriefing, contact with a peer support or critical incident stress management team member, or at least a verbal acknowledgment that it was a "helluva" call.

On the other hand, STS refers to a set of psychological symptoms that mimic PTSD but, unlike the singular critical incident that tends to accompany PTSD, STS occurs when a police officer is continuously exposed to the suffering and traumatization of others. These are referred to as "Small T's" or "Small Traumas," even though they certainly don't feel small, especially over time. The impact of this ongoing exposure to suffering is insidious. The officer cannot point to a single event as the culprit. Initially, this made it difficult to file claims with the workers' compensation board. Fortunately, a few compensation boards have recently recognized the cumulative effects of ongoing exposure to trauma (STS) on police officers. Some provinces in Canada now offer presumptive coverage, where the stress injury is assumed to be from the work and the burden of proof that it's NOT work-related is on the board. In my opinion, this is better than the police having to prove it's related to their work.

THE IMPACT OF CHRONIC EXPOSURE TO STRESS

So, what does STS look and feel like to the person that has it? As with PTSD, the effects of STS are psychological, physiological, behavioral, and spiritual. Psychological symptoms include depression, anxiety, distressing emotions, intrusive imagery, numbing or avoidance, and, sometimes, dissociation. It also affects your perception of situations. It may result in chronic suspicion of others, a heightened sense of vulnerability, feelings of powerlessness, and a lack of control. Physiological symptoms include headaches, gastrointestinal distress, heart palpitations, hypertension, heart disease, kidney diseases, hyperglycemia, hypoglycemia, fatigue, and premature aging. Behavioral symptoms include addictive or compulsive behaviors such as substance abuse, physiological arousal, relationship difficulties, absenteeism, excessive force, and sleep disturbances. Police work also changes the "soul" of police officers as they repeatedly face human suffering, deception, and violence.

In a study of cumulative career traumatic stress, an alternative name for STS, police officers reported high levels of disturbance from their exposure to trauma on the job (Marshall, 2003):

■ 74 percent of participants reported experiencing recurring memories of an incident;
■ 62 percent experienced recurring thoughts or images;
■ 54 percent avoided reminders of an incident;
■ 47 percent experienced flashbacks of an incident;
■ 96 percent of participants reported that their opinions of others had changed;

- 92 percent reported they no longer trusted others;
- 82 percent believed the world was an unsafe place;
- 88 percent experienced prejudices they did not hold prior to being on the job;
- 11 percent experienced suicidal ideation as a result of the occupation.

These statistics are alarming; especially the 11 percent of officers who had considered suicide due to their job. I can't help but wonder about underreporting in this category due to a fear of negative consequences.

In Chapter 2, we talked about critical incidents and their under-lying physiological processes and effects. So, it makes sense to look at what happens to the body when it's exposed to chronic stressors such as secondary traumatic stress. When you're first presented with a stressor, your body tries to adjust to meet the demands of the situation. These adjustments occur through secretion of hormones from the hypothalamo–pituitary–adrenal axis, catecholamines, and cyto-kines. It's your body's way of trying to meet the demands of life, to eventually maintain a state of equilibrium (McEwen, 2000, 2005). However, over time, the repeated occurrence of stressful life events or worrying about them results in imbalances, also known as an *allostatic state*, a state of adaptation to the stressors (McEwen, 2005). If not corrected, you will reach a tipping point where allostasis, which was originally adaptive, becomes *allostatic load* or *overload*.

> "Allostatic load" refers to the price the body pays for being forced to adapt to adverse psychosocial or physical situations, and it represents either the presence of too much stress or the inefficient operation of the stress hormone response system, which must be turned on and then turned off again after the stressful situation is over.
>
> (McEwen, 2000, p. 110)

The strain of allostatic load becomes unbearable on individuals, breaking down adaptive coping, further impairing their functioning. Allostatic load makes you more vulnerable to stress-related illnesses such as heart disease, cancer, ulcers, and migraine/headaches. When cortisol levels remain high over extended periods of time the brain becomes damaged. Literally the structure and function of the brain change. For instance, chronic elevation of cortisol is associated with major depression (Sheline, 2003). Stress-related illnesses also include psychological injuries such as PTSD, anxiety, and chronic difficulties with memory.

Research shows that prolonged stress affects the immune system which, in turn, contributes to chronic anxiety and cognitive difficulties (McKim, Niraula, Tarr, Wohleb, Sheridan, & Godbout, 2016; McKim, Patterson, et al., 2016). Inflammatory immune cells in the spleen send messages to the brain, contributing to individuals also having exaggerated behavioral responses to stress. Chronic stress also contributes to difficulties with short-term memory. Based on these findings, researchers believe that targeting the immune system may help treat mental health conditions (McKim, Niraula, et al., 2016; McKim, Patterson, et al., 2016).

Exposure to stress in police work has been referred to as "death by a thousand cuts" (Kirschman, Kamena, & Fay, 2014). It's a daily occurrence that goes unnoticed by others because they're doing their own thing. Even worse, if you attended these calls with others, which is usually the case, others may question how you developed a stress reaction to these calls while others didn't. You may even question this yourself. It becomes a blame game where people blame the person who admits to having a reaction to the call for being "weak," "off-duty mad," or accusing them of claiming work-related trauma for symptoms actually due to personal problems.

There are several problems with this rationale. The most glaring problem is that there is an assumption that others are not affected because they haven't said anything yet. The likelihood of them saying anything after hearing that another is being judged is greatly reduced, inadvertently reinforcing the false assumption that the person was the only one affected by the calls. Even if the first person isn't blamed by others, others who are affected by these calls may still not speak up for any number of reasons—fear of losing desirable assignments, promotion, pride, and so forth.

The second problem in blaming the person who reported being affected by the calls is that no two officers have attended the exact same calls in their career. Even if two officers attended the exact same calls in their career, which is highly unlikely, there are other factors that affect how traumatizing a call is. An accident scene may remind one officer of a previous one where he had prolonged exposure to a victim. Worse yet, the victim may have resembled a significant person in the officer's life, increasing the psychological strain of the call. Further complicating matters, if this officer is having problems in other areas of his life—family, health, financial—then he is more vulnerable to being affected by a difficult call. In short, the factors of the call (how long you're in contact with the victim, intensity of contact with the victim, relatability to the victim(s), history of calls of this nature) interact with the personal factors of the officer (personal and professional trauma history, health, presence/absence of personal issues and support) to determine the effect of the call on the officer. So, no two officers will have the same reaction to the same call.

Continuous exposure to the suffering of others, an integral part of policing, can slowly take a toll on your wellbeing. Like poison, small, continuous doses of others' suffering can make you sick. You won't know why you're sick and you may even feel that your symptoms are "normal" because they have appeared so gradually. Symptoms such as difficulty sleeping or sleeping too much, changes in your belief system relating to your self-concept, others, and the world in general, and a desire to "tune out" by drinking alcohol, shopping, staying busy, or remaining glued to the television, may start to appear. You may find yourself thinking about difficult calls, crime victims, and the horrors of accident scenes when you are "tuned in" to your mind. You might notice tension in your body when you pay attention to it. This is why many people find ways to tune out. The problem is you can't stay tuned out indefinitely. There are negative consequences to this. Small ailments become bigger, chronic conditions that are harder to resolve.

DELAYED-ONSET PTSD

There is considerable research to support delayed-onset PTSD (McEwen, 2003; Smid, Mooren, van der Mast, Gersons, & Kleber, 2009; Solomon & Mikulincer, 2006). Chronic exposure to trauma throughout a police career can certainly contribute to delayed-onset PTSD. Individuals who develop PTSD at a later time typically have "partial PTSD," also called "subsyndromal" or "prodromal PTSD," following the event(s). These individuals might experience many of the symptoms of PTSD but don't meet all of the criteria for a diagnosis. The avoidance symptoms of PTSD are typically the criteria that are missing for full diagnosis (Andrews, Slade, & Peters, 1999). In police work, you may not be able to avoid situations and places because of the demands of the job. Furthermore, you may not have functional impairment immediately following your exposure to traumatic events. Despite this, subsyndromal PTSD is similar to PTSD as far as disability is concerned (Gillock et al., 2005). Ongoing exposure to traumatic events or even difficult life events continuously increases your risk for full PTSD.

Delays in addressing the accumulation of trauma exposure for police may make matters worse, as studies have shown that the longer the delay in following up with military personnel exposed to trauma, the higher the incidence levels of delayed-onset PTSD. Additionally, soldiers had fewer exposures to military trauma but a greater proportion of delayed-onset PTSD (Smid et al., 2009). It's possible that, if there had been more incidences, full PTSD criteria would have been met sooner. I share this because there are several parallels between policing and the military and because several members of the military eventually go into policing. The key takeaway is that delaying getting help is not advised. Accumulated unresolved traumas don't simply evaporate. They may pop up after you have retired and are no longer busy with the demands of the job.

McFarlane (2012) suggests two mechanisms by which delayed-onset PTSD occurs: *kindling* and *sensitization*. With kindling, life events have the strongest impact when they first happen. Then this event is impacted by how you process the information that follows. In other words, the initial event starts the "fire." Then negative thoughts about the event act as kindling branches laid on top of this fire. They keep the fire going, spreading the fire until it becomes full-blown PTSD. The sensitization process relates more to continuous trauma exposures and your reactions to them. To continue with the fire metaphor, it's as if one keeps lighting fires next to each other. The fires will come together into one large conflagration and consume the forest of the police officer's mind. Sensitization is dose-dependent, in that the more exposures, the more symptoms experienced (Copeland, Keeler, Angold, & Costello, 2007).

Delayed-Onset PTSD and the Aging Process

The delay of PTSD may also be attributable to the aging process (Aarts & Op den Velde, 2007). Aging is hard enough without this added risk factor! Initially, researchers thought that the age-related onset of PTSD was due to cognitive and physical decline that broke down individuals' coping mechanisms. More recently, research has challenged this "deficiency model," suggesting instead that, after decades of adaptive coping, other triggering events in late adulthood put individuals at higher risk for PTSD.

For instance, as we get older, we experience more losses—loss of spouse, siblings, and friends through death—which may trigger old losses that have not been resolved (Aarts & Op den Velde, 2007). If you've not allowed yourself to grieve these losses, you've just pressed on, doing your job, it can catch up to you. These parts of your past fuel the angst of your current loss. Trauma and loss can have an exponential effect when not dealt with. As the losses pile up, they can remind you of your own vulnerability.

Also during old age, individuals begin to reminisce, contemplating their lives, considering their selves prior to and since the traumatic events, in an attempt to make meaning at the end of their lives. This reminiscing can lead individuals to unearth unresolved traumas, feelings of guilt, sadness, and questions relating to their identity (Aarts & Op den Velde, 2007). Events such as hospitalizations or exposure to mass media depictions of war or racism can also "retraumatize" individuals, sparking the onset of PTSD (Aarts & Op den Velde). According to this research, delayed-onset PTSD could occur after decades of being relatively symptom-free. This can be confusing for the person experiencing these symptoms as well as the clinician treating them. It might even lead to misdiagnosis of depression or dementia in older people, since being hospitalized or watching media depictions of war would be considered normal events. The activation of PTSD would be misunderstood since there's no obvious trauma in recent history to explain these symptoms.

Changes in life, such as retirement, were also believed to make it where individuals could no longer be distracted by work (Krystal, 1981). However, later research indicated that retirement was not as detrimental to individuals' health as once believed (Palmore, Fillenbaum, & George, 1984). On the other hand, *early* retirement was detrimental but it was likely the case that there were already problems in functioning that led to early retirement, not early retirement leading to problems (Aarts, Op den Velde, Falger, Hovens, De Groen, & Van Duijn, 1996). So, the longer you're on the job, the higher the likelihood that you can develop PTSD from the sheer volume of traumatic exposures, as well as the impact of other life factors such as loss of loved ones and retrospective reflections that re-activate distant unresolved concerns.

Delayed-Onset PTSD and the Police Organization

Providing organizational support for subsyndromal PTSD is complicated by the reactive nature of most organizational initiatives. Subsyndromal PTSD is also challenging for organizations that attempt to categorize their employees in a black or white manner: well/not well, fit/not fit for duty. The gray area created by subsyndromal PTSD can be confusing, leading to skepticism. The employer's skepticism may lead to misattributing the cause to poor work performance, marital problems, poor health, financial difficulties, or drinking problems. Simply put, the *effects* of delayed-onset PTSD over time are mistakenly viewed as the *cause* of it.

On the other hand, police organizations may mistakenly conclude that police are hardened individuals, resistant to harm (Adamou & Halem, 2003). McFarlane (2012) suggests it is important for employers to identify the accumulation of workplace traumatic exposures. This is the rationale behind annual check-ups or rotations for specific overly hazardous assignments. He also recommends that alternative duties be presented to the employee, but this may not always be an option for those in first responder work. Police may feel stigmatized by the assignment change and co-workers might be resentful, claiming special treatment for one leading to more work for them.

The kindling and sensitization process of PTSD also occurs with depression. Making matters worse, the depression can reach a level where it sustains itself without any outside influence (Patten, 2008).

You don't need to experience additional traumatic exposures or difficult life events to be trapped by negative thoughts and reactive to triggers. The pain and fatigue, which tend to accompany PTSD, are also maintained.

Police Suicide

The ongoing suffering from PTSD, depression, or anxiety, can be enough for police to think that taking their lives is the only viable option. Even the problem solver can feel trapped and unable to find a solution for what they're facing. As I was writing this section of the book, I received a call from a police lieutenant who was concerned about one of his officers. He told me that he directly asked the officer, a friend of his, if he was considering suicide. Even though he knew what answer to expect, it really scared him to have his suspicions confirmed. The officer said he was at the end of his rope. He felt that all he could do was let go. The lieutenant wisely, and honestly, empathized with his plight and urged him to climb back up the rope. He knew that he could do it, as the lieutenant had been there himself. He shared this, as this is the kind of guy he is; a straight shooter who wasn't afraid to show his human side.

There are several signs that people are considering suicide. Some well-known signs include saying goodbyes, getting one's business in order, withdrawing socially, talking about suicide either directly or indirectly such as expressing a lack of hope such as "What's the point?", "It never ends," "I can't wait until it's all over," or making comments about being helpless such as "I can't do anything right" and "I have no control over anything." Increased substance use, deteriorating hygiene, and emotional volatility also suggest possible suicide risk. Persons facing unsolvable problems or problems that at least appear to be unsolvable are also at heightened risk for suicide.

Some of the less-common signs for suicide are taking excessive risks at work in hopes of being accidentally killed or an abrupt improvement in mood. This improvement comes because the person is no longer struggling with the indecision about suicide. He or she has made the decision and is experiencing a brief sense of peace as he/she knows that the suffering is "almost over." This sign tends to shock family and friends after the completed suicide, as they will report that the person seemed to be doing better.

Dealing with Suicidal Thoughts

If you find yourself thinking suicide is the only option, you're not alone. Many people have moments when suicide seems to be the only source of relief for them. It is a desperate time, and when things get this bad, it seems like the pain will NEVER end. Yet, nothing, other than death, is permanent—not pain, not happiness, not sunshine, nor rain. You may think it's hopeless and that you are helpless to change your circumstances but neither is true. I encourage you to reach out and ask for the support you need and deserve. I have had people show up at my counseling office unannounced (not my clients at the time) as a last-ditch effort to get help before they made the irreversible decision to end their lives. I asked them what I am now asking of you—give therapy a try. Talk to *someone*. What do you have to lose? More importantly, what do you have to gain?

If you think someone you know is contemplating suicide, I encourage you to directly, kindly ask them if they are considering taking their life. Tell them they're not alone. Tell them you are concerned for them and that you would like to help in some way. Ask them what they need. You may not be able to give it to them but you can help them find it. Don't pretend that you fully understand. In fact, say that you don't understand but you want to. Ask them if it's okay if you check with them again later in the week and then follow through. Get support from someone else to help you help this person—a peer support team member, mental health professional, family member, trusted friend, and/or pastor. There are hotlines for police struggling with mental health and/or suicidal thoughts. There are several options listed in the resource section at the conclusion of Chapter 5.

Going Home

You may find yourself depleted at the end of your shift. Yet, you may not have the option to go home and simply go straight to bed. You may be met at the door with demands for your time and attention for personal life roles such as spouse and/or parent. You have to find ways to make the transition from work to home a little smoother. Perhaps the transition will require a mental shift of your roles, reorienting yourself to your personal life. Other times it might be a matter of energy. Let's talk about what you can do for each challenge.

Police work is emotionally and physically demanding. At the end of any given shift, you may have been exposed to a variety of tragedies, insults and abuses, and adrenaline-filled situations. You may be physically and emotionally depleted as you make your way home to their family. Yet, your family life will call for you to have physical and emotional energy to interact with them, and perform your partner and/or parent role when you get there. This mismatch in needs can be problematic for you and your family. You want peace and quiet. Your spouse wants to tell you about their day. Your kids want you to play with them. Your patience may have been depleted long ago, leading you to be irritable, maybe even outright angry. I've had officers tell me that they feel terrible about their behavior when they get home but they're at a loss as to what to do about it. Their spouses aren't happy either. They can't understand why their spouse isn't happy to see their family. The funny thing is that people are prone to treating total strangers with more respect and patience than their own family members. This is because many don't fear negative consequences from family members because they know they are emotionally attached to them. I'd say this line of thinking is quite backwards! It might help to ask for a small amount of time for you to get reoriented to your home life. You might need to take the long way home, listening to your favorite music, or maybe listening to the absence of noise in your car, in order to get your head cleared of the chaos that you've been in for the last 8–12 hours. One officer told me of deliberately asking his fiancé to give him 20 minutes to himself when he got home. He took this time to be intentional about exiting the police role and entering his home role. It's a small sacrifice of time to improve the quality of interactions that follow.

On the other hand, you might be hopped up on adrenaline after a busy shift and notice that your family is operating at a much slower pace. I've heard it described as trying to plug in a 220-volt appliance into a 110-volt outlet. Things just might blow up, leaving you in the dark as to what just happened. You may find that spending time with your family is boring, compared to the excitement at work. You might try to chase this excitement by returning to work, hanging out with co-workers and talking shop, or watching TV shows that relate to your work. Some might try to recapture the high with risk-taking behaviors like driving fast, gambling, using substances, shopping, or extramarital sexual affairs. Unless you hit a jackpot when gambling, not much good will come from these behaviors. In fact, these are the kinds of things that get police into trouble, under investigation, and divorced. It's a good idea to make plans for your transition. Go for a run, hit the gym, go for a bike ride, and then go home. If your shift doesn't allow for any of these (people would call in on you for running the neighborhood at 2 a.m.), you may find it helpful to take even 20 minutes to do something to take the voltage down before you walk through the door. Take a brisk walk around the block (five times, if needed). Maybe even take the dog with you to get Fido some exercise as well. Dogs can be very calming too, or, at least, comforting most days.

One odd but effective recommendation that I give clients is to look at their feet. If you're wearing your work boots, you're in work mode. If you're wearing running shoes, you're personal you, maybe it's athlete-you, maybe it's puttering-around-the-house-you. If you can't tell from the footwear, look an inch beyond at the floor. Where are you? If you're at home, you're not police. You're a spouse, parent, child, sibling, roommate, anything other than police. I know. I know. They say police is a 24/7 job and I get it. But, if you don't put in the time in the other roles when you're not at work, you won't have anything to go home to.

POLICE ADMINISTRATORS

Police administrators are certainly not immune from secondary traumatic stress. In fact, they may be more likely due to having more years of service. Not only do they have their own work history, filled with trauma exposure, but they can also be exposed to the suffering of their officers. Police administrators also have risk factors such as longer hours, sedentary work, and less camaraderie than line officers. In smaller agencies, administrators still respond to calls for service or, at a minimum, respond to the larger, more public (and more heinous) calls to oversee the handling of the call. Most police administrators will also be older and may have worked the streets at a time when talking about reactions to the calls would never have been acceptable and when education and training relating to STS would not have been available. Adding insult to injury, if they're much older, they may also be dealing with the stressors that are common to older adults such as health declines and loss.

In addition to having the added risk of STS, administrators are in the position to take actions to minimize officers' suffering from it. Police have repeatedly named their work environment as their biggest stressor (Abdollahi, 2001; Bell, Kulkarni, & Dalton, 2003; Burke & Paton, 2006; Hart, Wearing, & Headey, 1995; Liberman, Best, Metzler, Fagan, Weiss, & Marmar, 2002; Marshall, 2003). Police have repeatedly cited supervisory support, or the lack of, as a key factor for their ability to cope with STS. They make decisions about workers' compensation claims that affect officers' rights to treatment for work-related injuries. As, I said at the beginning of this chapter, oftentimes, there's no one call that the officer can point to as the reason for their occupational stress injury. It is the accumulation of traumatic calls that led to PTSD, anxiety, or depression.

Administrators, particularly field supervisors, make decisions about how long officers stay on the scene, exposed to the suffering of others. Continuous exposure to the traumatization of others can tax an officer's ability to cope with his/her exposure to trauma. Officers reported feeling physically and emotionally exhausted when they got stuck on a call involving trauma to another. Some officers, especially those that work in remote areas, are oftentimes stuck on calls by themselves for ungodly amounts of time. Chronic physiological arousal can result in the officer's inability to use his/her emotions as signals (van der Kolk, 1996). Emotions are supposed to provide us with information about events but it gets lost if you're emotionally exhausted from continuous exposure to STS. After being on the call for a while, your adrenaline levels will drop off, leaving you even more vulnerable to the effects of STS. Administrators should make every effort to get their officers relieved from their duties, even if just briefly. Relieve them yourself, if you can, so they can run to the station (even the gas station) to use the bathroom or change out of a wet or contaminated uniform. If that's not possible, bring them something to the scene that'll help them hang in there; coffee, a bottled water, a snack, etc. It's the little things that can make a big difference.

Another very important role administrators play in the mental health of their officers is that they're the holders of information: what's happening in the department, how complaint investigations are unfolding, and where and how to get mental health support. Some departments are better at making information about mental health resources available to officers than others by placing these resources on an employee-only website. This prevents employees having to ask around, broadcasting their need for support. Many officers I've spoken with reported that it was difficult to get the information they needed to access mental health services. Some even had to go through their supervisors to find out what was available to them. As you can imagine, this can certainly be a barrier for getting support due to the stigma of being weak by asking for help. Sadly, many of the officers I've talked with relayed that police managers "scoff at the idea" of seeing a psychologist or counselor.

In an ideal world, police agencies wouldn't have staffing shortages and financial constraints. Police could take time off, as needed, to bounce back from the barrage of calls. Officers who have been battered by one shitty call after another would benefit from having time off. We don't live in an ideal world though. So, administrators might have to be creative in rotating assignments to more evenly distribute the call load. Just make sure it's understood that the rotation isn't punitive, or because you feel that someone isn't managing their calls, district, or workload. In some police positions, usually outside of patrol, there might be an option to even let officers flex their hours for non-work activities. When it's an option, it has been shown to be very helpful in restoring or maintaining work–life balance and, consequently, job satisfaction. I know that I appreciated getting to change my hours when I was a detective. I was able to take Spanish classes at the university in the morning and work my cases in the afternoons and evenings. I felt like it was a win–win for me and the department, and I appreciated my sergeant's support in my goal to learn Spanish.

Even if none of these options are available, and many times they're not, honest verbal support of line officers and their work can go a long way. Officers have told me that they knew their work was appreciated by their sergeants and they were happy to do it. Those that felt their admin was pushing them without concern for their wellbeing or felt that their accolades were hollow, did not fare as well. They don't get much satisfaction pleasing an admin that doesn't care about them. Police can also detect bullshit when it's being given to them from citizens AND administrators. The *perception* of support has a stronger impact than the *actual* support given (Kaniasty, 2005).

CIVILIAN EMPLOYEES

Just like officers, civilian police employees can be affected by continuous exposure to traumatic events. As mentioned in Chapter 2 on critical incidents, dispatchers, call-takers, and other civilian employees tend to have additional risk factors for being affected by their work that are not usually accounted for. They don't receive the same amount of support as sworn police members do. They're at the bottom of the organizational hierarchy, they feel an added sense of responsibility for officers and the other first responders they dispatch for, and they usually lack proper training to do their jobs (Burke, 1991). Beyond this, although their work environment may shield them from the dangers of the street, it has its own dangers: confinement to a dark, noisy, hectic, and uncomfortable room. This environment contributes to additional stress (Burke, 2005).

Beyond the horror that might be heard on the phone line or radio, dispatchers and call-takers have the added stress of having to rely on other people to provide them the information they need to do their job. They make decisions based on partial and incorrect information from others, which can be intentionally or unintentionally withheld. They don't have the benefit of getting information from the caller/radio other than by what they hear. Unlike sworn members, there's no visual information for them to assess. Dispatch/call-taker work has been referred to as "a gunfight with blinders on" (Patterson, 2005, p. 21). So, until people start "Facetiming" 911, they only have what they're told and what they can hear in the background, to make sense of what is happening. This can leave them feeling quite powerless over and over again.

Adding insult to injury, sworn members may dump on dispatchers and call-takers for gaps in information because they felt ill-informed to safely or adequately respond to the call. Callers routinely don't know where they are, or fail to relay self-incriminating details relating to weapons on scene, and so forth. Having been a dispatcher before I was an officer, I tried to stay aware of the challenges call-takers faced in trying to extract information from panicked, intoxicated, and uncooperative callers. I hate to admit it, but there were times when I *still* got mad at them if I felt I was endangered based on a lack of good information. Officers may also be dismissive of the stress dispatchers and call-takers have, since they're not in physical danger in the field. The denial of their difficulty heaps more stress on them.

Dispatchers and call-takers are stretched thin throughout their shift. While officers divide the call load and take breaks (even if to write a report), many times dispatchers and call-takers don't really get any downtime. The sheer volume of calls and radio traffic subject dispatchers and call-takers to ridiculous amounts of trauma. Studies of dispatchers have shown chronic elevation of cortisol, the stress hormone, throughout lengthy shifts (Bedini, Braun, Weibel, Aussedat, Pereira, & Dutheil, 2017; Weibel, Gabrion, Aussedat, & Kreutz, 2003). Because they're forced to be sedentary while doing their job, they aren't able to burn off any stress, as police in the field are sometimes able to do. Being sedentary also contributes to health issues, which, in turn, worsen the chances of recovering from STS.

POLICE FAMILY MEMBERS

Research indicates that if a police officer is suffering from STS, his or her partner is also at risk for STS (Dwyer, 2005). The partner is exposed to the trauma when the officer retells the events of the day. Even if details are left out, the partner may fill in the details and create a disturbing mental image to accompany the story. Family members also wrestle with the same questions about these events that police members do (Figley, 1998). Family member symptoms will mimic the symptoms of the police member, which can be very confusing. The more details are shared with them, the more symptoms they will experience.

Making matters worse, sometimes, in their efforts to support their loved ones, police and family members ruminate together about their fears and worries. This makes symptoms of anxiety and depression worse, not better. This is referred to as the "pressure cooker" effect, as the angst rises with the mounting pressure of these talks (Hobfoll & London, 1986). The more loved ones offer support, listening to their crisis, the worse things can get. I would add that this happens in the home, as well as in the workplace. Everybody gets riled up when you're all ruminating. Worrying excessively with your loved one can have the opposite effect of what you're hoping for. It's better to talk about worries and reactions but to not dwell on them, with them dominating all of your conversations.

Other times, it can be very tiring managing your family when the police member is struggling with STS. You might find your patience wearing thin. You may even come to believe that your police member is using their job as an excuse to explain bad behavior. Maybe they are. Sometimes, police, like everybody else, do things that make their situation worse. You may be tempted to take out your frustrations on your police member. No good can come from this. You'll just be batting your frustrations back and forth at each other, in a downward spiral. Instead, talk with them about it. Hear them out. If they say their job is making them drink (spend, yell, sleep all the time), try to mentally separate the frustrating consequences of their bad behavior from their underlying intentions; which is usually to shield him-/herself from the stress or pain. Every day I hear stories of wounded people trying to do their best in the world, but still making poor decisions to get by. I'm not suggesting that you be okay with the bad behavior. But if you villainize the doer for the deed, it will likely only add to their own beliefs that they're a bad person that's ruining their life and the lives of their family. Instead, appeal to the person you know and love, who is buried under a blanket of pain. You might find that it *does* relate to their work or that it relates to any number of other demons they're struggling with. You're not likely trained to be their therapist (nor would that be a good idea to be the treating clinician, if you were), but you can help them to feel understood and gain some insight into the destructive consequences of their behavior. This might open the door to them getting professional help or, at a minimum, motivate them to make change on their own.

Family members experiencing STS from supporting their police member can feel very isolated from others (Galovski & Lyons, 2004). Others may not understand their symptoms, or know what to say or do; leaving police family members to feel even more isolated. Family members don't get the same levels of support their police members do. If police members work for responsive supervisors, they're likely to get a referral for support. Most wouldn't think to include support services for family members who are also affected. Some of the information for family members might be geared more toward how to support the police member, not for the family, per se. You're not alone though. I have listed several organizations in the Suggested Resources section at the end of this book.

PREVENTING STS FROM BECOMING STSD

When asked about what hindered his ability to cope, one officer relayed an incident where an infant had been sexually abused, stating

> I mean you often hear that line, you know, 'I've seen it all'. I didn't see that one coming. It's just, wow, I can't believe there are people who actually do that, so it . . . it's hard to process something that you don't understand.

Instead, acknowledge that you are having a normal reaction to traumatic events and that your body is telling you that you need to deal with it. Talking with a professional can help. You can unload the burden you have been carrying and find ways to manage your reactions to previous and ongoing experiences of trauma. Secondary traumatic stress does not have to evolve to the status of "disorder" before you get support. You wouldn't wait until you got a cavity to brush your teeth. Your mental health warrants the same level of preventative care.

What can you do to insulate yourself from the effects of STS? My study on how police cope with their exposure to secondary traumatic stress resulted in 14 key factors that influenced their coping:

1. self-care—taking care of physical, emotional, and spiritual health;
2. support from family and significant others;
3. talking to co-workers—informally debriefing and supporting each other;
4. emotionally disengaging from emotionally draining calls;
5. having a supportive work environment;
6. access to mental health resources;
7. personality—being positive, not taking self too seriously, etc.;
8. ability to help the victim (might mean adjustment of your definition of this);
9. relatability to the victim (hindered when this happened, so emotional detachment helped);
10. scene reminders (made it harder when having to return to scene/area often);
11. continuous exposure to call or mentally dwelling on it;
12. exposure to human nature (hindered when only exposed to the negative/dark side);
13. vulnerability of the victim (especially children);
14. presence of additional stressors—health, financial, relationship.

Officers felt they had control of some of these issues (self-care, emotional disengagement, and connecting with supportive others) but some situations relied on organizational or situational factors to make it easier or harder on them (nature of the work environment, continuous exposure, scene reminders, ability to relate to the victim). Whether or not you control things influences what is most adaptive for you to do in the situation. When you can control it, it's best to act on it, approach the issue. When you don't control it, it's best to avoid trying to change it and, instead, change your response to it.

> Man is capable of changing the world for the better if possible, and of changing himself for the better if necessary.
>
> (Frankl, 2006, p. 131)

According to Anshel (2000), avoidance coping, the cognitive and behavioral process of creating distance from a stressful situation, is recommended for circumstances where you don't have the ability to change the circumstances. Some officers use avoidance coping by making a point not to learn personal details about victims or using dark humor to lighten the intensity of the situation. I know I did this when going to a tough call. I made it a point to NOT look at the pictures on the fireplace mantle when I went to someone's house to do a death notification. It didn't help me in that moment to see that this was once a (seemingly) happy family. What is particularly difficult is when the person who worked the death scene, is the same one doing the death notification. Ideally, these would be different people. Dark humor can also go a long way in lightening up something that you have no control over. I've heard (and made) sick jokes about going to lunch during an autopsy. It sounds like you're deranged to talk in such a way, but the reality is that you can't bring back the dead. You're not causing harm to the person's family if you are discrete about it and kind when interacting with them. It doesn't mean that you don't care; that you're calloused.

Avoidance strategies should be healthy ones like exercise or focusing on the aspects of the job that you do control. Maladaptive avoidance coping includes using alcohol or drugs or overeating and these mechanisms have a well-documented history in policing (Cross & Ashley, 2004; Gershon, 2000; Kohan & O'Connor, 2002).

There are many ways you can take care of yourself—exercise, participating in hobbies outside of work, maintaining supportive relationships, talking with co-workers, and talking with a professional. Officers have reported that it helped them to periodically unload their troubles on a person not involved in their personal life, such as a mental health professional. It's a good place to let it all out without fear of judgment or traumatizing the listener. Officers cited talking to co-workers as a helping factor even before being asked what helped them cope with STS. In the course of describing what it was like being a police officer, several spoke of camaraderie and teamwork as key reasons for enjoying their work. For some, talking with co-workers took place mostly at work following critical incidents. For others, it extended to off-duty activities such as playing sports and just "hanging out." Speaking a common language of police jargon makes it easier to feel supported and understood by co-workers. Talking about other things besides "shop talk" with co-workers can also be helpful. Oddly, officers are reluctant to talk about their reaction to traumatic events even though they recognize that they feel better after they do (Evans, Pistrang, & Billings, 2013). Research has found that a cohesive social network reduces the effects of traumatic stress (Ozbay, Johnson, Dimoulas, Morgan, Charney, & Southwick, 2007). Palm, Polusny, and Follette (2004) suggested that those who cannot talk to their co-workers may experience more isolation, creating difficulty for managing their exposure to STS.

CONFRONTING UNFIXABLE SUFFERING

Police who go from call to call, problem to problem, may find their worldview changing for the worst. Entering policing, you may have believed that the world was a benevolent, predictable place. After some time on the job, these beliefs can be shattered and replaced with beliefs that people, including you and your family, are vulnerable to harm. This change in worldviews is believed to result in anxiety, depression, or PTSD, as you become acutely aware of your mortality (Janoff-Bullman, 1992).

If you find yourself struggling with feeling that you are facing unfixable suffering, you may also wish to change your view of how you define success in your work. You will never eliminate crime. You must look for the smaller victories—the small changes that you can make in the lives of others. You may not be able to prevent the burglary, or even get their stuff back, but you can give people suggestions for making their home more secure. One officer relayed:

> This person had his house broken into and had a bunch of jewelry stolen. One of the pieces of jewelry was a ring that his deceased father had given him and his brother. It had some sort of inscription on it that was important to this particular person. He didn't care what happened to everything else. He just wanted that ring back and he was visibly distraught. He and his father had a very close relationship. So, you can't imagine what that person is going through, now that that one connection has been taken. I told him just call the pawn shops, let them know and if this particular jewelry shows up, have them call us. Well sure enough the next day two guys are in a pawn shop trying to sell it with a bunch of other jewelry. We end up getting the guys. I called him up and I said "Sir, thank you very much for your call" and he was like "Really? So, what did you get?" I'm like, "Well, I told you I'd get your ring back" and when I gave it to him, his face just lit up and he was just absolutely happy. That's why I do my job! It's never these big dramatic things.

For this officer, he had to adjust his definition of what success looked like in his work. Earlier in his career, he had a bigger picture idea of what his job was. It had been about preventing or reducing crime, which just isn't realistic.

You can define success as being able to comfort accident victims during one of their most difficult times. Working with crime and accident victims, I oftentimes hear of the difference it made to have an empathetic police presence. In fact, some police officers got into policing because they had a positive interaction with police during their darkest hour. They decided they wanted to be that source of comfort and protection for others.

When I switched from short-term response support as a police officer to a longer-term support as a therapist, I got to hear these stories. I learned that most people heal from traumatic events. I'm not saying they're unscathed. I'm just saying that life goes on and people can heal from even the most horrific of circumstances. However, police don't usually get to hear how the story ends, so to speak. They just see the person at their darkest hour and then go on to see the next person at their darkest hour, and so on. When I studied how officers coped with secondary traumatic stress, officers told me that it bothered them that they never really knew how it all turned out for the crime victim. They rarely got to see that the victim moves on and goes back to their daily lives. Their "victimhood" is the first and last impression of them. Occasionally, you might get some kind of closure. It's more likely with firefighters and paramedics who save peoples' lives in medical emergencies. The victims (patients) drop by the fire hall or write a letter to thank them for their help. This happens in policing too, but to a lesser extent. Without the ability to follow up with crime victims, you're stuck with having to fill in the blanks for yourself as to how they're doing. It helps to recognize that tragedy is as much a part of life as success is. It isn't the exception. It's always been that way. Throughout history, people have faced and moved past tragedies. They will continue to do so after you leave the call. You have to learn to live with believing in this without witnessing it. One officer told me of her prior experience of trauma as giving her this wisdom as she faced the tragedies of others in police work.

> I feel like I understand the grief that the people are going to go through. So, I don't take on as much of it. I know that I got through this. Now I know that these people will be able to. It was turning that dread of realizing that I know what the near future might be like and then thinking they're going to get through it the same as I did.

It's also important to recognize and accept your limitations as a human. You cannot fix problems that took months or years to develop. As I said in Chapter 2, there is a difference between responsibility and accountability. You share the responsibility with multiple others, including large systems, to address the problems that police are called to handle. You have to focus on the small part for which you could be held accountable. This means taking measures to keep others and yourself safe, taking good notes from victims and witnesses, doing your best in interrogating suspects, writing good reports, and leave the rest of the situation to all the other people you share responsibility with: the victims, witnesses, assisting officers, crime scene technicians, district attorney, and jury, to name a few.

LET GO OF THE OUTCOME

I remember my first week in field training as a mixture of excitement, pride, and nervousness about my ability to be a police officer. I was dispatched to meet a domestic abuse victim who had managed to escape her home to call for help. As I took her statement, I noticed the scars on her face and body, likely the remnants of previous beatings. I remember the fear and desperation in her voice as she pleaded for help with her situation. When we arrested the abuser that night I remember thinking that this is what it was all about –righting the wrongs, protecting the vulnerable, and bringing a sense of order to the world. A week later my idealistic views were dashed when I learned that the abuse victim had been beaten to death. I immediately began reviewing what I had done, not done, could've done, and should've done that might have created a different outcome.

Unfortunately, this was not an isolated event. There were many like it where my desire to make the world a better place just wasn't happening. Was I a bad cop? Should I have chocked it up to my inexperience as an officer? Or was there more to it? This was happening to every cop, regardless of their level of experience. So, clearly, it wasn't a matter of being a "good" or "bad" cop. I learned that it was the limited influence that cops actually have in the circumstances they face every day. So how do you do a job where you feel that your influence is limited in the big picture? You have to change your view of what success means.

If I had determined in week one that I was not effective in my work, there are countless instances that I would not have been able to prevent crimes, console victims, and catch bad guys and gals. You have to look at those instances when you evaluate your effectiveness. Unfortunately, human nature directs you to pay more attention to what went wrong than what went right. In this way, you (mistakenly) feel that you can have more control the next time you're facing a similar situation. This is not to say that you can't learn from experiences and get better at handling events in the future. It is to say that there is a limit to how much you control circumstances despite your best preparation, training, and wisdom. You are human beings, after all, faced with so many variables outside of your control. Even if you do make a "mistake" in a situation, the outcome is usually greatly influenced by so many other factors than your mistake. Take my personal example—I can reason that if I had not arrested him, he would not have been so mad as to beat her to death. This is tricky because you can't prove it either way, which makes this logic torturous. But *I* didn't beat her to death. I never even touched her. *I* didn't put them together as a couple and *I* didn't teach him that he should demonstrate his dominance by beating others to submission. In fact, what I did was what was expected of me as a police officer. What if I hadn't arrested him and he killed her that night? Am I responsible for that too? It can feel like a no-win situation when all of the options could have negative consequences. The problem is that we assume a better outcome if a different course of action were taken. We also discount how many times taking a certain course of action *did* turn out well. I arrested lots of abusers after that without this outcome. Sometimes we also learn other information *after* the event has concluded and hold ourselves to a standard as if we knew it at the time of the event. It is important to separate what we knew at the time from what we later learned to avoid punishing ourselves for crimes we did not commit. These are some of the trauma-related guilt-thinking errors I talked about in Chapter 2.

What I am trying to convey here through my personal story is that we can sometimes be our own worst enemy when it comes to evaluating our decisions and performance. Attaching the outcome of an event to your input is dangerous and based upon faulty logic that rarely gets questioned. You need to question this logic—Did your singular input create the outcome? Did you have all the information you needed at the time? Could it have turned out poorly if you had taken a different course of action? Could a different action have made the situation even worse than it turned out? Have you taken this action before without these outcomes, maybe even positive ones? These are important questions that can not only save you a lot of grief, but can help you see the big picture.

When chronically exposed to the suffering of others, it also helps to bear in mind that you are only exposed to a small slice of the population. Think about it. Nobody calls the police to come observe that little Johnny is doing well in school. You are only called upon when something bad happens. This is why it is so critical for you to maintain relationships outside of policing and participate in non-police activities—to expose you to the rest of the population, to keep a balanced view of humanity. I know this is hard to do with shiftwork but it's doable, with effort.

I have presented some pretty scary symptoms and staggering statistics regarding the effects of STS. I hope what you takeaway from this is that you have the power to take a proactive approach to counter these effects. If you are already experiencing these effects, I hope you find comfort in knowing you are not alone and that help is available. The effects of this can be worsened by many of the organizational stressors that come with police work. These are discussed in the next chapter.

TOOLS FOR YOUR DUTY BAG

▮ STS mimics symptoms of PTSD but comes from chronic exposure to the suffering of others.

▮ No two officers will have the same reaction to the same call because they haven't had the same accumulation of calls.

▮ The longer on the job, the higher the accumulation of traumas, and the higher the risk of PTSD from STS.

▮ Accumulation of STS can lead to thoughts of suicide. Suicide is a permanent solution to a temporary issue.

▮ Coming home following exposure to STS can either deplete you or key you up. Take measures to transition to your home environment: exercise, listen to music, read, make time for quiet (even if only 10–20 minutes).

▮ Supervisor support is one of the strongest protective factors against STS. Perceived support is more important than received support.

▮ Emergency communicators also have a higher risk for STS than expected due to sedentary work, confinement to an uncomfortable work environment, and a lack of support combined with having an added sense of responsibility.

▮ Family members demonstrate PTSD symptoms from exposure to police members. Family should take care of themselves and mentally separate the doer from the deed when the police member is coping in destructive ways.

▮ Take action early to counter STS: exercise, get support from family, talk to co-workers.

▮ Adjust your definition of success. Remember, you didn't create these situations and you can't "fix" them either.

REFERENCES

Aarts, P. G. H., & Op den Velde, W. (2007). Prior traumatization and the process of aging. In B. A. van der Kolk, A. C. McFarlane, & L. Weisaeth (Eds.), *Traumatic stress: The effects of overwhelming experience on mind, body, and society* (pp. 359–377). New York: Guilford Press.

Aarts, P. G. H., Op den Velde, W., Falger, P. R. J., Hovens, J. E., De Groen, J. H. M., & Van Duijin, H. (1996). Late onset posttraumatic stress disorder in aging resistance veterans in the Netherlands. In P. E. Ruskin & J. A. Talbott (Eds.), *Aging and posttraumatic stress disorder* (pp. 53–78). Washington, DC: American Psychiatric Press.

Abdollahi, M. K. (2001). *The effects of organizational stress on line staff law enforcement officers.* Doctoral dissertation. Retrieved from ProQuest Dissertations and Theses database (UMI No. 3103552).

Adamou, M. C., & Halem, A. S. (2003). PTSD and the law of psychiatric injury in England and Wales: Finally coming closer? *Journal of the American Academy of Psychiatry and the Law, 31(3),* 327–332.

Andrews, G., Slade, T., & Peters, L. (1999). Classification in psychiatry: ICD-10 versus DSM-IV. *British Journal of Psychiatry, 174,* 3–5.

Anshel, M. H. (2000). A conceptual model and implications for coping with stressful events in police work. *Criminal Justice and Behavior, 27(3),* 375–400.

Bedini, S., Braun, F., Weibel, L., Aussedat, M., Pereira, B., & Dutheil, F. (2017). Stress and salivary cortisol in emergency medical dispatchers: A randomized shifts control trial. *PLoS ONE, 12(5),* e0177094. Retrieved September 25, 2017 from https://doi.org/10.1371/journal. pone.0177094.

Bell, H., Kulkarni, S., & Dalton, L. (2003). Organizational prevention of vicarious trauma. *Families in Society, 84(4),* 463–470.

Burke, T. W. (1991). The relationship between dispatcher stress and social support, job satisfaction, and locus-of-control (Volumes I and II). Unpublished doctoral dissertation, City University of New York, New York.

Burke, T. W. (2005). Dispatch. In L. E. Sullivan & M. Simonetti (Eds.), *Encyclopedia of law enforcement, 1* (pp. 137–139). Thousand Oaks, CA: Sage.

Burke, K. J., & Paton, D. (2006). Predicting police officer job satisfaction: Traditional versus contemporary models of trauma in occupational experience. *Traumatology, 12,* 189–197.

Copeland, W. E., Keeler, G., Angold, A., & Costello, E. J. (2007). Traumatic events and posttraumatic stress in childhood. *Archives of General Psychiatry, 64(5),* 577–584.

Cross, C. L., & Ashley, L. (2004). Police trauma and addiction: Coping with the dangers on the job. *FBI Law Enforcement Bulletin, 73(10),* 24–32.

Dwyer, L. A. (2005). *An investigation of secondary trauma in police wives.* Doctoral dissertation. Retrieved from ProQuest Dissertations and Theses database (UMI No. 3177108).

Evans, R., Pistrang, N., & Billings, J. (2013). Police officers' experiences of supportive and unsupportive social interactions following traumatic incidents. *European Journal of Psychotraumatology, 4(1),* 1–10.

Figley, C. (1998). *Burnout in families: The systematic costs of caring.* New York: CRC Press.

Galovski, T., & Lyons, J. A. (2004). Psychological sequelae of combat violence: A review of the impact of PTSD on the veteran's family and possible interventions. *Aggression and Violent Behavior, 9,* 477–501.

Gershon, R. (2000). *National Institute of Justice final report "Project Shields"* (Document No. 185892). Retrieved February 19, 2010 from www.ncjrs. gov/pdffiles1/ nij/grants/185892.pdf.

Gillock, K. L., Zayfert, C., Hegel, M. T., & Ferguson, R. J. (2005). Posttraumatic stress disorder in primary care: prevalence and relationships with physical symptoms and medical utilization. *General Hospital Psychiatry, 27,* 392–399.

Hafeez, S. (2003). *The relationship of violence related trauma and length of trauma exposure to post-traumatic stress disorder in emergency medical services personnel.* Doctoral dissertation. Retrieved July 23, 2017 from ProQuest Dissertations and Theses database (UMI No. 3072174).

Hart, P. M., Wearing, A. J., & Headey, B. (1995). Police stress and well-being: Integrating personality, coping and daily work experiences. *Journal of Occupational and Organizational Psychology, 68,* 133–156.

Hobfoll, S. E., & London, P. (1986). The relationship of self-concept and social support to emotional distress among women during war. *Journal of Social and Clinical Psychology, 4,* 189–203.

Janoff-Bullman, R. (1992). *Shattered assumptions: Towards a new psychology of trauma.* New York: The Free Press.

Kaniasty, K. (2005). Social support and traumatic stress. *PTSD Research Quarterly, 16(2)*, 1–8.

Kirschman, E., Kamena, M., & Fay, J. (2014). *Counseling cops: What clinicians need to know*. New York: Guilford Press.

Kohan, A., & O'Connor, B. P. (2002). Police officer job satisfaction in relation to mood, well-being, and alcohol consumption. *The Journal of Psychology, 136(3)*, 307–318.

Krystal, H. (1981). *Massive psychic trauma*. Boston, MA: Little Brown.

Liberman, A. M., Best, S. R., Metzler, T. J., Fagan, J. A., Weiss, D. S., & Marmar, C. R. (2002). Routine occupational stress and psychological distress in police. *Policing, 25(2)*, 421–439.

Marshall, E. K. (2003). *Occupational stress and trauma in law enforcement: A preliminary study in cumulative career traumatic stress*. Doctoral dissertation. Retrieved February 19, 2010 from ProQuest Dissertations and Theses database (UMI No. 3098255).

McEwen, B. S. (2000). Allostasis and allostatic load: Implications for neuropsychopharmacology. *Neuropsychopharmacology, 22(2)*, 108–124.

McEwen, B. S. (2003). Mood disorder and allostatic load. *Biological Psychiatry, 54(3)*, 200–207.

McEwen, B. S., (2005). Glucocorticoids, depression, and mood disorders: Structural remodeling in the brain. *Metabolism, 54*, 20–23.

McFarlane, A. C. (2012). The occupational implication of the prolonged effects of repeated exposure to traumatic stress. In R. Hughes, A. Kinder, & C. L. Cooper (Eds.), *International handbook of workplace trauma support* (pp. 121–138). Hoboken, NJ: John Wiley & Sons.

McKim, D. B., Niraula, A., Tarr, A. J., Wohleb, E. S., Sheridan, J. F., & Godbout, J. P. (2016). Neuroinflammatory dynamics underlie memory impairments after repeated social defeat. *Journal of Neuroscience, 36(9)*, 2590–2604.

McKim, D. B., Patterson, J. M., Wohleb, E. S., Jarret, B. L., Reader, B. F., Godbout, J. P., & Sheridan, J. F. Sympathetic release of splenic monocytes promotes recurring anxiety following repeated social defeat. *Biological Psychiatry, 79(10)*, 803–813.

Ozbay, F., Johnson, D. C., Dimoulas, E., Morgan, C. A., Charney, D., & Southwick, S. (2007). Social support and resilience to stress: from neurobiology to clinical practice. *Psychiatry, 4(5)*, 35–40.

Palm, K. M., Polusny, M. A., & Follette, V. M. (2004). Vicarious traumatization: Potential hazards and interventions for disaster and trauma workers. *Prehospital and Disaster Medicine, 19(1)*, 73–78.

Palmore, E. B., Fillenbaum, G. G., & George, L. K. (1984). Consequences of retirement. *Journal of Gerontology, 39(1)*, 109–116.

Patten, S. B. (2008). Sensitization: The sine qua non of the depressive disorders? *Medical Hypotheses, 71(6)*, 872–875.

Patterson, B. (2005). Safety: A protocol priority. *National Journal of Emergency Dispatch, 7(1)*, 21–23.

Salston, M. D., & Figley, C. R. (2003). Secondary traumatic stress effects of working with survivors of criminal victimization. *Journal of Traumatic Stress, 16(2)*, 167–174.

Sheline, Y. I. (2003). Neuroimaging studies of mood disorder effects on the brain. *Biological Psychiatry, 54*, 338–352.

Smid, G. E., Mooren, T. T., van der Mast, R. C., Gersons, B. P., & Kleber, R. J. (2009). Delayed posttraumatic stress disorder: Systematic review, meta-analysis, and meta-regression analysis of prospective studies. *Journal of Clinical Psychiatry, 70(11)*, 1572–1582.

Solomon, Z., & Mikulincer, M. (2006). Trajectories of PTSD: A 20-year longitudinal study. *American Journal of Psychiatry, 163(4)*, 659–666.

Van der Kolk, B. A. (1996). The body keeps the score. In B. A. Van der Kolk, A. C. McFarlane, & L. Weisaeth (Eds.), *Traumatic stress: The effects of overwhelming experience on mind, body, and society* (pp. 214–241). New York: Guilford Press.

Weibel, L., Gabrion, I., Aussedat, M., & Kreutz, G. (2003). Work-related stress in an emergency medical dispatch center. *Annals of Emergency Medicine, 41(4)*, 500–506.

Chapter 3
Strategies for
Complex Trauma

Non-Operational Stressors

Catching the Sneaky Resilience Thief

You're in pretty good shape for the shape you're in.

(Dr. Seuss, 1986, p. 7)

I use the term *non-operational stressors* instead of organizational hassles because the latter doesn't include many of the stressors that are independent of the police organization such as media and public scrutiny. Even as I talk about organizational stressors, I want to be clear that I am not villainizing police organizations and the "brass" and "white shirts" that manage the organization. After all, police administrators have demands placed on them from above, below, and the outside. Non-operational stressors include shiftwork, overtime, call-outs, and policies and procedures relating to promotions, work assignments, discipline, and even retirement.

SHIFTWORK, OVERTIME, AND CALL-OUTS

Given the 24/7 nature of police work, you likely have, or have had, some difficulties with your schedule. Unless you've got seniority in your department, you have bad days off, swing shifts, and might even have your days off eaten up by court appearances and mandatory overtime. It makes it very difficult to make and keep plans with family and friends. Continuously breaking plans can take a toll on relationships. Loved ones may give you grief for cancelled plans because they're disappointed that you can't be there (AGAIN). Unfortunately, their expression of frustration might not be delivered in the most supportive manner, heaping guilt onto your own frustration. This, in turn, leads to friction with the very ones you wanted to spend time with. Over time, this friction can build up, causing relationship difficulties, isolation, and resentment *unless* you are proactive in managing these events.

The Hours

Many police agencies struggle to maintain adequate staffing levels. This means that officers end up being "voluntold" they are going to work over or, worse yet, on their days off. It can be a short-term scenario but, oftentimes, it's a chronic issue. In recent years, many police agencies have developed mental wellness programs that encourage work–life balance. Unfortunately, the messages from these programs are met with suspicion, if not outright disbelief, because police officers are aware of the competing message that says, "If you want to get ahead, you will take an extra shift and respond to work demands outside of work hours." So, combining the balance message with mandatory overtime can really kill morale. Police, like most bright people, believe what they see more than what they're told. Linda Duxbury (2012), an expert in work–life balance conducted a series of studies with the Royal Canadian Mounted Police in Canada which demonstrated close to half of the officers (40 percent) reported high levels of total role overload. Total role overload meant "collective demands are so great that time and energy resources are insufficient to adequately fulfill the requirements of the various roles to the satisfaction of self or others" (p. 56). I don't know about you, but I get tired just reading that definition.

Officers in small departments, detectives, SWAT officers, and negotiators in any size department are accustomed to receiving call-outs at the worst times: while sleeping, when sitting down for dinner, or at the beginning of the movie you've been waiting to see. Even if your pager/phone doesn't go off at these times, you still *feel* like it could, which puts you on edge. I was on-call when I was a detective and, although my loved ones understood that I had to go most times I was paged/called outside of work, they didn't particularly like it. It's irritating when criminals do stupid stuff when you're trying to spend time with your family. I remember instantly getting a "bump" of adrenaline: a racing heart, faster breathing, when I was being called in. Just because you get called in doesn't mean that you're exempt from your shift the following day. I can remember working all day, getting called in 5–6 hours after work, staying on a call-out for another 3–4 hours, sleeping for 4–5 hours, and then coming back in. Cases have to be filed during business hours. Other responsibilities don't just melt away because you didn't get a good night's sleep. Your sleep schedule is already wrecked but you have to be alert for your safety, the safety of other officers, and for the quality of the call you're working or the case you are building. Drinking coffee to wake up to do all this means you may have trouble sleeping a few hours later with the caffeine in your system. Making matters worse, you also have to contend with the adrenaline from the call.

You're not going to be able to do away with shiftwork, overtime, and call-outs. It might get better, if you promote, or if you get a specialized assignment in a non-operational section. However, most likely, you're going to have to get creative to work with these issues. It means coordinating with your loved ones for alternate times for dinner, for holiday celebrations, and for date night. For instance, date night might have to be breakfast in the morning, when you get off your shift. When my husband and I were both on overnights, we played roller hockey in the morning before going to bed. Just like folks on dayshift, you don't want to go to bed right after work. It would be weird for a person that works 9-5 to go to bed at 6 p.m., right? Make plans for events that are interrupted by a call-out to be reconvened at the next opportunity. As much as possible, keep your loved one informed on your delayed arrival when you get stuck at work. With technology, there's hardly any excuse to not send a quick text that updates them on your timeline. When possible, even let them know you're thinking of them. I don't mean that you have to be perpetually connected via technology. That would be annoying, not to mention distracting, since you need to have your mind on your job so you can be safe and get back home at a reasonable time. What I am suggesting is that you may have to find ways to let your loved one know that they matter; that they don't cease to exist in your mind when you walk out the door for work. A quick "thinking of you, wishing I was there" message can make a big difference.

Sometimes, overtime and call-outs are optional. I've known fellow officers who ate up all the call-outs, overtime, and off-duty jobs. It was like they were barely making ends meet or were competing to see who could work the most. If this is you, you need to ask yourself why you're doing this. I know the money is good, and good money is tempting, but at what cost? I can see doing it in the short term, because you're saving for a vacation or a special purchase. But doing it continuously is going to cost you in ways that are difficult to recoup—in your health and relationships. Loved ones are more likely to be tolerant and accepting if you're not able to decline overtime. I think it's a whole other story if they knew that you were consistently choosing the overtime over family time. The demands on your time from police work, whether voluntary or involuntary, can make you feel like you have no time for yourself. This feeling is called "time sickness" and is discussed next.

Time Sickness

If you're like me, you have a busy life filled with deadlines and demands. We live in a fast-paced world that shows no signs of slowing down. All this hurrying around is having serious consequences on our health, relationships and, oddly, our productivity. Not a day goes by that I don't hear someone (sometimes myself) say "I don't have time for that" or "I'm too busy to deal with that." Saying this is almost a badge of glory in a "who's the busiest" competition. Unfortunately, we live in a time where doing everything as fast as possible is a (twisted) sign of strength. Think of the many television programs based upon people doing tasks against a ticking clock. These programs seem to justify us rushing through life, constantly multitasking and trying to do more with less time.

Shiftwork, overtime, court appearances, and training days make you feel the crunch of time sickness. You might be tempted to fall back on the demanding police schedule to excuse yourself from participating in other aspects of your life. I did when I was a gang detective. It felt good to know that I was doing meaningful and exciting work. Yet, it can become addictive and consume your free time, even if it is just mentally consuming. Even thinking about a call or a case takes you out of your personal life, making you feel like all you do is work, all you ARE is work. I noticed (mostly because others pointed it out) that I was spending less time doing the things outside of work that were once important. I talked about work, which was easy to do since my husband was a police officer too. I was losing parts of myself in favor of being a police officer.

One of the most obvious costs I have observed as a psychologist is that eventually people meet their limits. They become physically ill with chronic headaches, muscle aches, insomnia, exhaustion, and digestive issues. Mentally, they are foggy, unable to focus, anxious, and riddled with worry. Relationships suffer because others are pushed away, ignored, and possibly even villainized because they try to slow us down. We justify our need to be busy like our life depends on it, dismissing advice to slow down and rest by saying the person doesn't understand our circumstances or has selfish or ulterior motives for wanting us to be less productive. Doesn't she get that I'm trying to get ahead?!?!?

Instead of feeling stronger and more capable, overly busy people feel they are not good enough because their bodies, minds, and relationships are falling apart. Their productivity actually declines because they haven't been taking care of themselves. Some will take stress leave from work but then recreate the busyness frenzy in their recovery time. They want their healing to happen at the same speed that got them there in the first place. I've had clients try to rush their progress while on stress leave. They try to give themselves a timeline for recovery, asking "How many sessions before I am good to go?" They don't get it. As the old saying goes "If you do what you have always done, you'll get what you've always gotten." I think this wisdom clearly applies here. Let's talk about another way of thinking about our daily lives.

Over the years, I've taught time management courses in organizational settings. Attendees were surprised when I advised them to eliminate things from their to-do lists rather than teach them time-saving techniques so they could do more. I'll let you in on a little secret. Time management is *life management*. Nobody is "too busy." It's all about priorities. When we don't take the time to reflect on how we spend our time, we tend to fill it with things that don't truly contribute to our lives in a meaningful way. Take a moment now and think about what is important to you. I imagine you'd name things like your relationship and health. These are important aspects of our lives that tend to be ignored because there are no immediate consequences to neglecting them. However, over time, there will be dire consequences. Some would argue that you can't tell your boss you're not doing what they asked you to do because it's not on the list of what is important to you. Fair enough. However, you *can* decide if you're going to help your neighbor with home repairs or if you're going to pick up that voluntary call out/overtime shift.

In short, the medicine for time sickness is changing your mindset about busyness. Reset the tempo of your life. Slow down by eliminating things not connected to your big picture life goals. Maybe this means saying "no" to favors for others and reducing time-wasting activities such as television programs, especially those perpetuating the "rush" theme, or mindlessly checking social media, when you're exhausted from constant busyness. Eliminating or at least limiting these activities will leave you more time and energy for what matters most. I'll return to this concept in Chapter 5 when discussing how having a moral compass contributes to resilience.

> If you do what you've always done, you'll get what you've always gotten.
>
> Anon

> Nobody is "too busy." It's all about priorities.

POLICE IDENTITY

Some jobs, such as policing, promote the embodiment of the position. You ARE the job. It's easy to be consumed with your work. After all, we spend roughly one-third of our time at work, preparing for work, or coming home from work. Police work is especially likely to consume your life because you're taught that being a police officer isn't what you *do*, but rather, who you *are*. Role models provide an identity that recruits can "try on" provisionally, to see how it fits them (Ibarra, 1999). The models that are available in the formative period of the police identity are examples of what a good cop is and what a bad cop is. Cautionary tales are offered in hopes of teaching recruits the difference. This officer is dedicated to his work and knows his beat very well. This keeps him safe and makes him a good officer. That officer takes a sick day for a hangnail. He can't hack it and it's going to catch up to him one day. That's why he didn't get promoted.

The Making of the Police Officer Personality

Socialization processes during the academy and training programs do a good job of fusing personal and professional identities. Right from the beginning, police recruits are socialized to assume the prized identity role of police officer. Conti (2009) studied the socialization process of police recruits and found that their civilian lives were degraded while their status of police officer was idealized. Deviations from the idealized police role rituals were considered shameful and reflected moral or characterological weakness. Becoming a police officer is regarded as a rise in status from their formerly lesser civilian self. I remember some of these messages from my own academy days. We were regularly reminded that there were sheep and there were sheepdogs. The public, to include ourselves if we couldn't hack it, were sheep who were oblivious to the dangers of the world. They needed to be herded and protected because they were too weak to manage themselves. There were signs in the academy hallways that reminded us that we had to earn our right to wear the uniform. It's no wonder that police give up their life, interests, and supports outside of policing! Who wants to be a sheep and be among other sheep when it's portrayed like that?

Police recruits and police officers are reminded that they are police officers 24/7, overshadowing other life roles such as husband, wife, parent, daughter, friend, and community member. I remember the speech given to my academy class moments before our graduation. The chief warned us that we would always be on duty and might have to act to keep others safe from harm. He urged us to always have our weapon on us, which I was accustomed to since my dad always carried his. Right out of the gate, the expectations were outlined from the top officer in the department. Who were we to question such a directive? We *were* the job. This was just the beginning of the change process.

Personality Changes

Police work changes people and it doesn't take long before the changes begin. A study of new police officers shows that personality changes begin at the recruitment phase, are more pronounced after 2 years on the job, and substantially more pronounced at the 4-year mark (Beutler, Nussbaum, & Meredith, 1988). The results suggested that the officers had higher risks for stress-related physical complaints and substance abuse after a mere 4 years of service. Police also become more suspicious and socially isolated (Cottle & Ford, 2000). This is likely due to both socialization processes as well as exposure to mostly the dark side of human nature. You can't unsee what you've seen so you look at the world a little differently.

Do you remember what you were like when you became a police officer? Maybe it was last year; maybe it was 30 years ago. How does this person compare to who you are today? I have included an annual check-in tool at the end of this chapter for you to answer this question. Chances are, if it was just last year that you joined, you are not a drastically different person but I would bet you *are* different. It doesn't stop there. It changes the people around you too—your family, your friends, sometimes it even changes your neighbors. I first took note of this when I joined. I may have even noticed it when I was a kid because my family wasn't like non-police families. For some reason, unbeknownst to me at the time, my dad needed to know my friends' last names and their parents' names and where they lived. But I digress. Your family is now a police family. They come to see the world a little differently, have to adjust their schedule around yours, and now have to consider who they spend their time with. Even your neighbors and non-police friends do things a little differently when you're around.

Changes that begin in the academy continue throughout your police career. You may not even notice some of the changes because they are occurring so slowly. Most people compare themselves to others in their environment to make sense of themselves anyway. This means that you would compare yourself to other police to get a sense of how you're progressing in your career. The flaw inherent in this comparison is that conformity is prized in police agencies. So, comparing yourself to police co-workers isn't going to be much help in terms of recognizing your individual changes and how these compare to the rest of the non-police world. At times, you might be challenged to make comparisons of your current self with your former self because others comment on how you've changed. Significant others have noticed the change in you over time. Lots of police spouses I've worked with have spoken of wanting the person they married back. A once fun-loving jokester has become a tired and grumpy couch potato. A spouse that once loved to spend time with his family hasn't put forth the effort in quite some time. This leads to marital and family trouble.

One of the most troubling changes is the tendency for police officers to begin narrowing how they define themselves. On entering policing, officers typically possess multiple identity roles—they are not just a police officer but they also identify as parents, partners, friends, community members, members of sporting teams, etc. As they spend more time in policing, these other roles tend to fade behind the ever-strengthening police role. The trend of police work not being "what you do," but who you are, is troubling for a number of reasons. First, when you narrow how you come to identify yourself, you also narrow your problem-solving skills. For instance, when an officer encounters a personal dispute with someone, perhaps a spouse or partner, he or she will likely call upon the police role to resolve the conflict. Most spouses/partners would not be particularly receptive to this kind of interaction. In fact, a colleague of mine conducted a study of police partners who complained of feeling that the family was being "policed" at times.

Narrowing one's identity to the singular police role can be even more troubling when the police officer loses his or her status as a police officer. This could very easily happen through retirement, injury, illness, or involuntary resignation. If all you are is a police officer and that is taken away, what is left? Cops have relayed to me that they couldn't bear to leave policing because they didn't really have a self outside of their police identity. Some who have left policing are still struggling to figure out who they are. A firefighter I interviewed summed up his feelings about leaving the first responder profession pretty well, saying he didn't want to go from "hero to zero." No one wants to feel like a zero. This is one of the reasons behind the heightened suicide risk and rapidly declining health for officers who have recently retired.

Over time, the person who began policing with a wide array of friends, hobbies, and interests, slowly lets them fade away. It happens little by little—declining a movie invitation by a friend, blaming shiftwork for being too tired to make it. Next, its giving up playing organized sports because it's too hard to make practice and the games. While letting go of friends, hobbies, and interests outside of policing, police-related friends and activities tend to increase. This creates a shift in the master identity of the police officer, as it is now largely made up of the work role of police officer. I have spoken with several first responders who have looked back on their careers with dismay as to what happened over the years. They recall having friends outside of policing that they lost touch with. Most of the time it isn't deliberate and, because it's insidious, it can be confusing as to what happened. Other times, it may be intentional since the police life often mandates that you be more selective about who you spend your time with. In discussing his friendships outside of policing, one officer relayed:

> The one thing that I always thought is how can I be friends with people that don't know the job I do. We always see the dirt bags and the less than desirable. It's always been that thought in my mind like 'How can I just be friends with just regular Joe Blows' But now that I do these other roles, I see that hey not everybody is like the people that we deal with,

not everybody is a dirt bag. I can't just paint that brush on everybody.

Not everybody is a dirt bag. That's hard to believe without proof and it's hard to get proof when you only ever do anything but work.

Strangely, there appears to a love–hate relationship between veteran police officers who, on the one hand, believe that incoming, younger police officers have figured it out when they see them take their vacation time. I have listened to officers speak of their regrets at not having taken a more balanced approach to their work, citing that their commitment to the job over the years has not provided them with the happiness they thought it would. They envied this new generation of officers who were willing to take time off when they needed it. Yet they also resent them because they're believed to lack the same level of commitment to the work. There is an expectation of paying one's dues. Paying one's dues demonstrates commitment to the job by agreeing to work extra shifts and staying late.

Having your identity limited to the police role is also problematic because you have pretty limited control over your work. When work is stressful and you lack the control to eliminate the stressors, you can easily find it overwhelming to manage. Nobody will ever have complete control over a situation but police work can oftentimes be the epitome of uncontrollable circumstances. As such, if the majority of your life, your waking hours, is spent performing this role, you may find yourself feeling quite powerless. On its face, this seems contradictory to the notion of the authoritative police role. Yet, if you've spent any time doing it, you know that there is so little you actually *do* control. For instance, you can't control how the public will perceive your job. You can't control what the courts will do with the bad guys and gals you arrest. You can't control the policies administration will pass down. When this reality sets in, your sense of control and self-efficacy take a hit. It's during this period that it's most vital that you have other life roles to provide you with a sense that you *do* control aspects of your life such as how you will parent your child, treat your partner, and spend your time doing what interests you. One officer I spoke to relayed her story of how she came to the realization that she needed to have more than her work in her world:

> I think I actually had the seven-year itch. I was in a house and it was a bit of a crack house and I was there with my partner and we were talking to these two people and, even though I'd never seen them before, it was like the same people that I dealt with before over, and over, and over again. I went 'You know what? You're fine' and I went out to my car and he came out and said, 'What's up?' I'm like

'I don't deserve this. I don't need to see this all the time; I'm just done with it.' So, once I realized that, I just realized that I really didn't have enough in my life to sort of take that taste out of my mouth. And so, I started investing a lot more time in everything else.

For her, it was an endless line of people making poor life choices, contributing to her continuous frustration. Instead of resigning or ignoring it, she developed her own interests.

Having the police role as a master identity makes it hard to shed identity role behaviors when you go home. Police officers come home and police their families, interrogating their children about their whereabouts the night before. Call-takers strictly manage conversations with loved ones to get the pertinent details and none of the extras. If you don't believe me, ask your family how you have changed since you began policing. It's also hard to shed this identity because others sometimes won't let you. You go to a party and people ask you questions about your work; how to get out of a ticket, what happened the other day when they saw the police road block, what your scariest call was, etc. Officers who are trying to play the parenting role at a PTA meeting are asked to offer security for the school. Officers trying to play a team sport, just be a softball player, are asked about their work or treated differently because others have varying opinions on police (usually based on half-truths and misinformation from media/others). Even if you make efforts to get away from it, others will pull you back in. One officer explained it this way:

> Everybody I know labels me as a police officer primarily and I feel like that impacts all of my other roles as well and how I perform. For example, I used to be part of a rugby team where the guys would have beer on the field after practice or after a game and of course that's not something I can participate in and they would just joke around on the field with me about "Oh you can't do this" and "Are you gonna show up and give us tickets?"

Develop Multiple Identities to Avoid Disorder

So, what do we do with this information? Are all officers doomed to feel like zeros? Absolutely not! Awareness precedes change. One of the best ways to be resilient is to maintain an identity independent of your work. I encourage you to take stock of the various roles you currently play in your daily life. Compare this information to when you first became a police officer. Do you notice that you have stopped doing certain hobbies you enjoyed or have withdrawn from other non-police activities or people? If so, make the commitment to return to these non-police activities. It might be that you join a baseball league or running club. It might mean reconnecting with an old friend or returning to the relationship rituals you shared with your partner that have fallen to the wayside. Sometimes it helps to ask those close to you, your non-police family and friends, how you have changed since becoming a police officer. Ask them if there is anything they miss about the "old" you, or the way the relationship was when you first started as a police officer. Armed with this information, you can reconnect with all the other parts of who you are. I encourage you to be vigilant in maintaining all of the roles you play by routinely taking stock of how you spend your time. Having a well-rounded life, filled with multiple roles, will promote your resilience and overall quality of life.

When most people talk about playing multiple roles in their life, they're complaining about how stretched and stressed they are. So, having multiple roles gets a bad rap. However, the benefit of having multiple identity roles is well documented. According to Identity Accumulation Theory, having multiple identity roles offers you purpose, meaning, and behavioral guidance (Thoits, 1983, 1986, 2003). Thoits' theory fits the *revisionist* perspective which holds that having multiple roles can have a positive influence on mental health instead of a negative one. Having multiple roles is especially beneficial when the roles are voluntary such as friend, neighbor, and soccer coach (Pavalko & Woodbury, 2000; Thoits, 1991). This is believed to be because voluntary roles don't usually demand as much of your time, energy, and commitment and because you chose these roles because they give you a very specific benefit (Thoits, 2003). Most people don't participate in friendships that add nothing to their life or volunteer to coach a sport if they don't enjoy it. Having voluntary identity roles increases self-esteem and provides a greater sense of control over your life (Thoits, 2003). Greater self-esteem and sense of control are personal resources that you can carry over into other parts of your life such as your work. In short, it can make you a better officer, spouse, and parent.

> Awareness precedes change.

Consider the number of identities in the same way you would think of stress. With too little stress, you become bored. You're not challenged or motivated to do anything. You might be complacent. With too much stress you become overwhelmed. You can't function. You're overextended. But with the *just right* amount of stress, you're in an ideal situation. You will work optimally with the right amount of stress. It's a "Goldilocks and the three bears' porridge" kind of scenario. The same holds true with identities. There's a happy medium, which will vary based upon life demands. Some identity roles complement each other. For instance, you can easily combine social role activities by exercising or doing hobbies with friends or family. Parental roles can be combined with friendship roles by taking your kids bowling with your friend and their kids. When time is limited, you have to be creative. Necessity breeds invention.

Having multiple identities isn't something that is simply forced on you by life. That line of thinking is outdated but sometimes still mistakenly believed. The accumulation of identity roles isn't merely what *happens* to you in your social environments but is also the product of your choices (Thoits, 2003). You choose your roles, based upon your preferences and life goals.

I've learned a lot from first responders, most of which were police officers, about maintaining a life outside of policing. A lot of the research out there would have you believe that police officers are at the mercy of the demands of their agency and public and lack control over their circumstances. It's suggested that police officers just deal with this reality, barely wringing out an existence outside of their work. Many of the officers I have spoken with in my research over the years tell a different story. They tell a story of determination to maintain their life roles outside of their jobs. They are committed to being partners, parents, friends, fisherman, and community members. They had obstacles like shiftwork and overtime to overcome but they refused to succumb to the obstacles. Many of them spoke of how, initially, they let go of their life outside of their work. They reported noticing that they became cynical, tired, and unhappy. Some even reported a decline in health as their wakeup call. Others referred to relationship problems and spoke of the confrontations from their family members, pleading with them to spend time with them outside of work. They knew that they had to change directions and reclaim their lives.

Others spoke of noticing the cynicism of others and took that to be a warning of what was to come if they were not vigilant in maintaining their life outside of work. One officer told me a story about attending a funeral of a fellow officer where he encountered the son of another officer who had also passed away. The son said to the officer "There were times when I think you were closer to my dad than I ever was. He was always at work." The officer said to me:

> It struck a chord that it's wrong, not wrong, just a different generation; a different mindset. But that pressure is still there that your obligation should be to the job, to the job, to the job.

Given the enormous response I received from officers who had found a way to have a life outside of policing, I'm convinced that it's possible. Not only did several officers self-identify as striking a balance in their lives, but they provided very detailed accounts of how they were doing it. Other times, these officers were identified by others as being the epitomes of having full, but balanced, lives. So, I don't think I was hearing stories of wishful thinking or exceptional circumstances such as officers without the demands of parenting or that were financially well off. These were the stories of everyday police officers, of varying ranks and assignments, who had found their way to have a life outside of their work.

PROMOTIONS, ASSIGNMENTS, POLICIES, AND PROCEDURES

Procedures for promotions and specialized assignments are significant sources of organizational stress. In fact, these stressors are harder to manage because they weren't anticipated stressors and there aren't any courses in the academy training on how to deal with it. In my department, we had standardized promotion processes. You took a test relating to your knowledge of laws, criminal procedure, and leadership skills. You advanced based upon your demonstrated mastery of this information, not who you knew. Yet, this system is also flawed in that anyone can memorize this information to advance and still not be good at applying it, and lack common sense and people skills. Good test-takers don't necessarily make good supervisors or leaders. I've met these folks on the job. This can be infuriating for those who might not be good test-takers but have the skills, dedication, and people skills to do well in the desired position. Ideally, promotional processes would involve testing that includes a written portion, a panel interview, and a practical demonstration of skills. Hopefully, this would offset some of the biases that might occur with a single measure such as a test or an interview.

Another aspect of promotional and specialized assignment processes that challenges police resilience is the expectation that employees will demonstrate their commitment to the job with long hours, many of which are unpaid. Police culture calls for "face time," where hours worked are more important than output (Duxbury & Higgins, 2003). You have to put in the time, go full-bore, trying to outdo your fellow officers, so that you will be chosen for the desired position. Even if you put in all this time, you can still not get the promotion. With limited opportunities and multiple people applying, there's not a spot for everyone. This can be outright infuriating when you feel like people are chosen based on who they know and who is liked by those making the decision. This happens all the time.

THE LAST ORGANIZATIONAL STRESSOR: RETIREMENT

It might sound odd to think of retiring as an organizational stressor but the retirement process doesn't begin the day you turn in your notice.

It occurs YEARS earlier, not just the financial planning, but the mental planning as well. Officers complain that departments do a poor job of preparing them for this eventuality. They focus on the financial aspects, to the exclusion of the lifestyle change that comes from leaving the job. To be fair, most employers don't usually include this kind of preparation. But, in policing, it is critical that you get your head wrapped around what comes next since it is such a change from shiftwork and the adrenaline of going call to call to call.

What comes up for you as you think about retiring from police work? Excitement? Apprehension? Ambivalence? Do you know how you will spend your days? You can't wait until you are near retirement to prepare psychologically for leaving police work anymore than you can wait to prepare financially. There are three key areas to be considered: lifestyle, identity, and mental health.

Lifestyle

When you retire, how will you spend your time? Who will you spend your time with? Do you have non-police friends and activities? Ongoing research indicates that some choose not to retire because they don't have anything else to do and fear boredom and isolation. They regret not mapping out a plan sooner. Having a plan for how you will spend your free time, whether it involves spending time with friends, travel, or hobbies just makes sense. You plan your professional life so why not make plans for your personal life? Keeping a schedule of activities can help officers transition to retired life. It's kind of odd to think to maintain a schedule in retirement, but the reality is that when decades of your life are dominated by work, and a work schedule, you may feel lost after a few weeks of not having any kind of schedule. At first, you might welcome the change. It feels like you're on vacation. But what happens when the vacation doesn't end and you've caught up on rest and some of the things on your to-do list? You may not know what to put on the schedule because you don't know much about what you are interested in or good at. Even people who are still working struggle to know what they are interested in doing outside of their work. Making a decision of what to do can seem daunting when you've spent the whole day making decisions (sometimes for others). As crazy as it seems, a lot of people are so dedicated to work that they don't know what to do in their free time except the usual house and family tasks. It's such a problem that therapists provide lists of pleasurable activities like the one on the next page. Pick a few that match your interests, or could be potential interests, and give them a try. Not all of the suggestions on the list will make sense for you. Notice that they do NOT include online activity. I think we do enough of that without even thinking about it. Hours pass and we don't know what we've even been doing. It's sedentary and indoors and neither one is ideal.

Identity

For some, turning in their gun and badge symbolizes giving up a part of who they are. When you retire from policing, you are a "retiree." There isn't much that separates you from the retired dentist next door. This can be a very painful aspect of retiring from policing. Having a broad sense of identity, including recognizing the various roles you play in your personal life, can help you to manage losing your police officer identity. Part of the identity work for retiring officers involves looking at other retirees to determine what retirement is supposed to look like.

LIST OF PLEASURABLE ACTIVITIES

Try a new recipe	Watch old home videos
Do a puzzle	Gardening/planting
Go to a movie	Take the dog to the park
Go for a drive	Go to the gym
Take a woodworking class	Call a friend/family member
Go to a museum	Go for a hike (walk in nature)
Go to a hobby store	Listen to music
Take a cooking class	Ride your bike
Research travel destinations	Go hit baseballs, golf balls, etc.
Volunteer (animal shelter, etc.)	Take a painting class
Photography (nature, street, people)	Watch a little league game
Go to the aquarium and /or zoo	Attend a comedy show
Play an instrument	Go watch live music
Refinish furniture	Work on a car
Draw or paint	Stitch, sew, quilt
Read a book	Learn to do home repairs
Coach a team	Join a (book, motorcycle, etc.) club
Go fishing or hunting	Play a game (card, video, board)
Play ball/Frisbee with dog, kids	Organize photos, collections, etc.
Get involved in a cause (PTSD, cancer)	Go camping (even if just for the day)

Unfortunately, in police work, there are more bad examples than good ones. The ones who fully engage in their personal life are less visible than the ones that return to the agency for a part-time position. Sometimes returning to the agency part-time might be because they don't have other plans for their time, friends outside of policing, or may not have the financial freedom to not work. When I interviewed first responders about their decision not to retire, the financial aspect of it was only a small part of the equation. One seasoned officer relayed his observations about retired officers:

> When I saw them, I saw them go from being over confident, over the top, out there, life of the party to when they retired. Within six weeks you're basically forgotten. Within six months they've replaced you, and within a year no one knows who you are. And to see them live through that where they went from being you know a cop for 35–40 years to instantly overnight you're retired and then within a year people change, move, transfer, you're not even recognized in the office, and to see how that impacted them on an emotional level, and right into their physical level, because that was their golfing group, and their pick-up hockey league, and once they were disconnected from the police, they lost all that. I saw it impact their physical well-being and emotional well-being, their mental well-being and it was almost sad like to see them trying to hang on to it. When they died, they were you know trying to hang on to that. It reminded me a lot of that where they had poured their heart and soul into policing for 35–40 years and, in the process, their kids grew up and had their own families. When they realized the policing community was gone and they tried to reach out to their family, their family had their own lives to live.

Mental Health

For some officers, 25–30 years of police service comes with a cost to their mental health. Twenty-five years of being exposed to the traumatization of others exacts a heavy toll on the psyche of a police officer. Many veteran officers have shared stories with me of witnessing terrible tragedies early in their careers, at a time when debriefing meant having a drink after the call and cracking jokes with fellow officers about what they had seen. They were then forced to move on to the next call, the next shift, and so on without ever really talking about what they witnessed. They can still vividly recall the details of the event like it happened yesterday. It begs the question: What happens when you don't have another call to go to? Retirement opens the space for the mind to wander toward unresolved events because you no longer have the benefit of the distractions of work or the support system that accompanies it. This may result in vulnerability to traumatic stress disorders and depression (Patton, Violanti, Burke, & Gehrke,

2009). Dr Kevin Gilmartin (2002) warns of the "biological rollercoaster" of police work, where the high of police work cannot be sustained outside of work and results in a dip in mood which can lead to depression, relationship problems, and addictive behaviors.

The presence of these issues is complicated by the lapse in benefit coverage that typically occurs within three months of retirement. Veteran Affairs Canada has extended benefits to military members and their families beyond retirement with operational stress injury clinics because they recognize that soldiers experience problems after retirement. In addition to the loss of benefit coverage, police officers typically lose other forms of organized support when they retire, such as support from peer support programs. If you feel like you might have some skeletons in your mental closet that will have to be dealt with, go see someone. It's never too late to benefit from therapy. I've had clients in their 80s. I've worked with police who had their concerns about retirement. I offer advice on picking culturally competent therapists in the Chapter 5. If this doesn't float your boat, at least engage with peer support.

Staying Engaged Through Peer Support

When officers retire, a wealth of knowledge goes with them. Sure, they pass on their wisdom to junior officers but why does it have to stop at retirement? Peer support programs such as critical incident stress management teams would greatly benefit from having a retired officer section (and a family section, for that matter) operated by retired officers. Retired officers can offer peer support to other retired officers and continue to contribute to non-retiring officers by sharing their wisdom to those still working. Who would be better positioned to talk about the experience of retiring from police work than the ones who have? They can provide an invaluable service to officers nearing retirement while maintaining their social connections and contributions to the workplace. It's a win–win situation. Retirees can decide how much time they wish to devote to their involvement in the peer support team.

If your agency does not offer retiree support services, I encourage you to form your own informal support system. Ideally, this system would include people from work and from outside of work. Those that are still working will be harder to maintain contact with because they still have the demands of shiftwork and overtime. Even those outside of policing might be difficult to stay in contact with since first responders tend to retire at an earlier age than other professions. You might find that you're the only one in your age group that is retired. For this reason, it would be a good idea to have a variety of individual and shared activities on the agenda for your daily life. There is no doubt that retiring from policing may conjure up mixed feelings of happiness and sadness but it should not be an isolating experience. Once you are a brother/sister in blue, you will always be a part of the family in blue.

Physical Wear and Tear

Police work is hard on the body. Even if you don't get injured on the job during your career, you may still have work-related physical deterioration from sitting in a patrol car with heavy gear, or bathing in stress hormones for 20+ years. Extensive studies, including a project called Buffalo Cardio-Metabolic Occupational Police Stress, have highlighted the physical and psychological effects of police work (Violanti et al., 2006). Studies show that police, especially female police officers, have high levels of cortisol in the morning that don't drop during the day, as they're supposed to (University at Buffalo, 2008). This is believed to be due to the lack of elasticity in the arteries, a marker for cardiovascular disease. Police also tend to have higher levels of cardiovascular disease, due to higher levels of hypertension and obesity than the general population (Ramey, Downing, & Knoblauch, 2008). They have higher rates of various kinds of cancer, lymphomas, and melanomas (Forastiere et al., 1994). These elevations are also believed to be related to shiftwork, which is not only correlated with multiple forms of cancers, but is correlated with hypertension, higher cholesterol levels, cardiovascular disease, and occupational accidents and injuries (Chen, Lin, & Hsiao, 2010; Conlon, Lightfoot, & Kreiger, 2007). Working night shift also disrupts the circadian rhythm, which makes restful sleep difficult. Sleep deprivation, in turn, comes with its own health complications such as increasing allostatic load, placing extra strain on the body, contributing to immune, endocrine, and autonomic dysfunction (Navara & Nelson, 2007).

I don't share this research with you to help you build a worker's compensation case once you have developed a condition related to shiftwork or chronic stress. I realize this research can be very depressing, if you don't take the information with an eye towards what you can do about it. Forewarned is forearmed. You won't likely be able to make a case for only doing dayshift in an organization that has to offer around-the-clock coverage. But, individually, you can take other actions to counter some of these risk factors. The organization can also take steps to reduce the impact on their employees.

Individual Actions for Better Health

One of the easiest actions you can take is to monitor your health with regular check-ups with your doctor. At least once a year, even if you feel fine, check in with your doctor for a blood panel to determine if you're maintaining healthy levels of blood sugar, cholesterol, cortisol, blood pressure, and so forth. If you're not, you can make a course correction before it goes off the rails too far. Oddly, lots of people won't go to the doctor because they fear learning that they're not healthy. They feel shame about how they haven't followed advice from previous appointments about maintaining a healthy lifestyle. Some have told me that they don't want the lecture from their doctor, telling them to lose weight, stop smoking, or make other lifestyle changes. It's a stick-your-head-in-the-sand-and-pretend-it's-not-happening kind of situation. If you're not healthy, ignoring it doesn't make it go away. Your awareness of not feeling good or guilt for what you're doing to your body will just gnaw away at you in the background, day after day, after day. And the result is the same. Your quality of life is diminished, and your lifespan is shortened. Instead, go see your doctor and YOU lead with "I haven't been taking care of my health so I'm here to see what I've done" and go from there. Ask for help on *how* to make the changes, and *make them stick*. That would go a lot further than simply being told to lose weight. Your doctor might be able to refer you to someone that can help you build motivation for change. That's usually the hardest part. You likely know *what* to do. You just lack the motivation to do it.

Nutrition is also a very important part of physical health. Note, I use the word nutrition, not diet (diet is a loaded word!). Eating healthy will help to maintain a healthy weight. Obesity can contribute to a laundry list of health problems. Beyond being aware of *what* you eat, it's also important to pay attention to *when* you eat. Your body needs calories and nutrients at different times for different reasons. Some foods are better before going to bed, such as carbohydrates and foods with magnesium in them (see Chapter 5 for additional information). Some are better earlier in the day, even if your day starts at 9 p.m., because your body needs fuel that will sustain you through your shift. John Violanti, a 23-year New York State Trooper and one of the key investigators in the studies above, suggests having a high-protein meal just prior to shift because it energizes hormonal systems. For the same reason, he suggests that you exercise prior to the start of your shift. This makes sense anyway, in that you aren't trying to squeeze exercise in at the end of your day, right before going to sleep. Regular exercise will help you counter some of the risks of overtime, call-outs, and shiftwork. Lastly, getting good sleep is important for your health. This is discussed at length in Chapter 5, as sleep is a cornerstone for being resilient. If you find yourself overly tired and your shift is fast approaching, take a 20-minute catnap. This has been found to improve performance, mood, and even creativity (Vila, 2009).

Organizational Actions for Better Employee Health

Organizations can't take police off overnights just because they're not good for their health. However, they can improve officers' quality of life by scheduling them on 10-hour fixed shifts (National Institute of Justice, 2012). An investigation of shiftwork and health found that there were no differences in performance and work–life balance between 8, 10, and 12-hour shifts. However, officers on 10-hour shifts got more sleep than those on 8- or 12-hour shifts. The longer 12-hour shift also seems to increase the likelihood of accidents. Officers reported better quality of life at work when they work 10-hour shifts, compared to 8- or 12-hour shifts. Studies also show that those working 8-hour shifts worked a significant amount of overtime; five times more than those on 10-hour shifts, and three times more than 12-hour shifts. This makes the 10-hour shift more cost-effective, which is appealing to most cash-strapped agencies. Additionally, accident rates increase significantly after officers have been on shift for 9 or more hours. At 10 hours, the risk increases by a whopping 90 percent. At 12 hours, it increases by 110 percent (Folkard & Lombardi, 2006). This is a huge health risk factor for officers since they are more likely to be injured on the job from accidents than from assault (Vila, 2008).

Agencies should also limit the amount of overtime allowed per week, support annual sleep screenings so that officers can stay on top of their sleep quality, provide information to officers on how to get good sleep, and manage fatigue, as well as equip supervisors with information on how to recognize signs that their officers are fatigued (Vila, 2009).

Burnout

One of the consequences of non-operational stressors is burnout. Unlike, STS, which relates to a set of psychological symptoms that mimic post-traumatic stress disorder, burnout is "prolonged exposure to chronic emotional and interpersonal stressors on the job, and is defined by the three dimensions of exhaustion, cynicism, and inefficacy" (Maslach, Schaufeli, & Leiter, 2001, p. 397). Police and civilian police employees have similar levels of burnout. However, female officers are more prone to burnout than males (McCarty & Skogan, 2012). This is believed to be due to the additional demands still placed on women from home and family. It's also likely due to the hesitancy that women have to ask for support from others. Many female officers have told me of feeling like "double failures" if they can't handle family and work, as well as "mother guilt" for devoting themselves to work. It's tricky. There are also consequences for male officers who take off time for family. They might be seen as less dedicated to work, resulting in being passed over for promotions or desired assignments.

Burnout impacts officers on many fronts; oftentimes leading them to leave the profession mentally, if not physically. Research shows burnout can lead to harmful effects on officers' health, including physical symptoms such as exhaustion, headaches, and hypertension (Salston & Figley, 2003). It's regarded as a two-part process: 1) high demands from work leading to exhaustion and 2) lack of resources to meeting these demands worsening the exhaustion and contributing to cynicism and a sense of being ineffective, ultimately leading to withdrawal from work (Demerouti, Bakker, Nachreiner, & Schaufeli, 2001). Burnout begins with what is referred to as "burn in," where you remain at work despite having health issues that should keep you at home such as the flu, cough, gastro-intestinal issues, etc. (Josse, 2008). It's regarded as "presenteeism," in that you are there physically, but not mentally. You then transition from "burn in" to "burnout," which reduces your commitment to work and damages your relationships with others.

BURNOUT SYMPTOMS

Physical   Chronic fatigue, headaches, backaches, heart palpitations.
Emotional   Loss of interest in work, aggressiveness, cynicism.
Mental   Feelings of worthlessness, incompetence, and self-blame, slower thinking, cognitive "fog."

In a nutshell, emotional exhaustion might be thought of as being "all out of fucks to give." You may think you've got a shipment on back order but it seems like it's not going to get here any time soon. You can hardly muster up the energy to do your job, much less care about it. Emotional labor is needed to care about a situation and even to avoid losing your cool when the situation frustrates you. When you're depleted emotionally, you won't likely have anything to offer here. Emotional exhaustion is the key ingredient in burnout that leads to depersonalization, cynicism, and feeling ineffective in your work.

Depersonalization refers to when you treat people as if they were not people, but objects. Sometimes, police intentionally emotionally detach from victims to avoid being traumatized. I am not referring to this tactic here. Rather, I am referring to the chronic depersonalization of *all* people, not simply to get through a tough call. This is an ongoing numbness that occurs because you feel like you need to distance yourself from the public because you feel overloaded and exhausted. It's an avoidance technique. You become indifferent, or even cynical, about people, your work, even yourself and your family.

Cynicism is quite common in policing. I've met very few police officers who didn't speak sarcasm as a first language. When you enter the policing profession, it's like admission into a family. When this family fails to protect or support as expected, burnout can occur. Feeling that you are treated unfairly, whether it be relating to getting rewarded for the good work you do, or getting punished for the mistakes you made, unfair treatment contributes to cynicism and burnout. Punishments were so unfairly distributed in my department, that I was mandated to a discipline consistency panel. I didn't think that was fair, but I quickly learned they didn't really care what I felt. As you can probably guess, the discipline doled out in my department wasn't very equitable and it was causing quite a bit of resentment and cynicism. Some officers who needed training or equipment were getting days off without pay, while others who were doing worse were getting verbal or written reprimands. These disparities contribute to officers feeling like they don't have any control over their circumstances; that they're at the mercy of whoever happens to be deciding things that day and what kind of mood that person is in. Which leads me to the next burnout component, lack of self-efficacy.

The loss of self-efficacy can lead to learned helplessness, which is the antithesis of resilience. If you don't believe you're able to change anything in your environment, you certainly aren't going to put forth the effort. Sometimes, this is because you feel like you don't have the resources you need to do your job. For instance, you might need equipment, or you're using outdated equipment, lacking in supervisory support, departmental support, or even community support, to do your job. High levels of burnout and stress combine with low levels of commitment to the job and the prioritization of home life and life satisfaction, resulting in "retirement on the job" (Duxbury, 2007, p. 113). Once committed officers feel betrayed by their employer they stop doing more than the bare minimum to keep their job. It's good that they are committing more to their home life and satisfaction, but it's not good for the department, fellow officers, or the community that they don't feel compelled to do more than required. The officer also suffers because he or she is spending a third of their time doing a job they've grown to resent.

I've spent my whole life in a police organization because my dad was married to the job throughout my childhood and then I went into policing myself. So, I have had a fair amount of experience listening to people talk about their jobs as police officers. I will say that those that complain like a broken record about how things *should* be as opposed to how they *are* not the easiest people to be around. They get tuned out by others; regarded as grumpy, crusty complainers. This is not to deny that things should change or to imply that certain practices or policies are acceptable. This is not to deny the difficulty of shiftwork or the 24/7 nature of police work but, rather, to figure out how you work within that reality. Progress is desirable and I don't mean to silence anyone's voice in speaking out against what needs improvement. This kind of conversation is different because it's in hopes of creating change and/or removing the barriers to progress. The other kind of conversation is circular complaints without any purpose other than to vent. Yet this kind of venting actually makes people feel *worse*, not better. Have you noticed that? Complaining with co-workers has the benefit of feeling that you're not alone in the suffering. It's a "misery loves company" kind of situation. Yet, when it is repeating the script of defeat and helplessness, it makes you *more* miserable. Admittedly, I've done this. I've been the leader and the follower in these "bitch sessions." You start off feeling righteous and you end up feeling anything but right.

Deputy "Meh"

I met with an officer relating to a suicide call. Although she felt like she was doing well with this event, she was bothered by the numbness she felt about her life in general. It wasn't an attempt to cope in the aftermath of the incident, but, rather, this indifference had been slowly building over time. She felt "meh," which, in my opinion, says "I can't even muster up the energy to make a full word, and I wouldn't even know what the word would be anyway because I don't really feel anything." It wasn't the only time I ever heard someone use "meh" to describe their blunted emotions. Unfortunately, it won't be the time last either. The problem is that it doesn't just change the way you do your job. It transfers to your home life, where you don't have the mental or emotional energy to care about your family, your health, even your future. You don't have to be a Deputy Meh.

Countering Burnout

Countering burnout is difficult because it requires effort, which you likely are too exhausted to put forth. But remaining burned out is not a good plan and it's not going to get better on its own. In large part, it's a matter of addressing the two sources of burnout: 1) demands placed on you and 2) resources available to help you meet the demands. You can't control all of the demands placed on you, as the agency may be mandating overtime, your good police work might result in routine court appearances, and so forth. However, you can reduce the demands you place on yourself by not voluntarily picking up extra work and reducing self-imposed exceedingly high expectations. In fact, it's the most committed officers, with the highest standards, that are most prone to burnout (Netotea, 2012). Trying to convince people to lower their standards is an uphill battle. After all, people are usually rewarded for having high standards, it's tied to entrenched values such as

"If you're going to do something, do it right." However, there's wisdom in recognizing that you are a human being with limits. When you pour yourself heavily into your work, you won't likely have much more than a drop or two left for everything else. It's not that you *can't* take that voluntary overtime shift. It's that you choose not to because you've decided something else (yourself) is more important.

Building resources to meet demands means acting on what you can control in your life. It also includes accepting what you can't change, letting those things go, and challenging overly simplistic negative thinking. I'll talk about each of these, in kind.

In recruiting for my work–life research, I received a flood of responses from police about how their organizations don't let them have a life outside of work. Between the shiftwork, the uncaring attitude of supervisors and the organization as a whole, court on days off, etc., they report that there is no chance of a personal life. Feeling like your life is dictated by your work is a lousy way to live. You feel powerless to navigate your own way through life. Feeling powerless can lead you to being angry, anxious, sad, and resentful. Despite all of these "less than positive" responses, I received several emails from police officers who identified as having work–life balance and other emails telling me about someone they knew who did. In speaking with the officers in this research, I learned that they felt a sense of choice, personal responsibility, and ability to influence their circumstances.

I asked one officer, who had been policing for 30 years, how he made sense of this. He gave me permission to share his words here. He told me of a story of a very unhappy co-worker that he felt had lost sight of why he chose the policing profession in the first place. This unhappy officer no longer felt the sense of purpose and enjoyment in his work. The officer I interviewed offered his wisdom to the unhappy co-worker and others like him. His advice to them, which I am sharing with you now is this:

> Challenge yourself to consider and make choices in order to be the cop and the person you want to be. You will not ever have control over police work or the organization, but you can decide how you will spend your personal time. You can spend it in a way that makes you happy or you can spend it in a way that makes you miserable. It's roughly the same amount of work. You can spend your free time ruminating on the ways you are powerless and how police work sucks the life out of you or you can catch yourself engaging in this downward spiral of negativity and change directions.

This was a powerful message from a person who was and likely still is practicing what he is preaching.

Countering burnout means determining what you can't change. Don't fight with it with the limited amount of energy you have. It's like banging your head into a wall repeatedly, hoping it'll move out of your way because your head hurts. This is not to say that we should just accept abuse from others. There are situations where we should act and the "this/they must change" idea is the motivator behind you advocating for that change. We just have to look at the situation and the way we are thinking about it to know whether to let it go or push for change. If we don't, then we must move on and stop thinking about it. Reflect on the serenity prayer—"God, grant me the serenity to accept the things I cannot change, the courage to change the things I can, and wisdom to know the difference." It might feel like defeat to accept the situation or the person, but it really is like drinking poison if you don't. It doesn't mean that you condone or approve of it. It just means you're wise enough to know that you need to put your energy somewhere else in your life.

The next trick is letting go. So how do you let it go? First, watch how you think about letting go. The quote "Winners never quit and quitters never win" can inspire you to hang in for the sake of hanging in, neglecting the benefit of knowing when it's wise to stop fighting for something. Instead, you might ask "Is this the hill you want to die on?" Do you want to hold your position at all costs? If it's worth fighting for, do it. If it's not the hill you are willing to die on, stop fighting. Some people feel like they're losing and the other person is winning if they let it go. They dig their heels in, taking their position of righteousness. Yet, they don't feel like they're winning at all. You're not winning if you're suffering. Remind yourself that you can't change another person or situation. I'm in the change business but I can't change anyone that doesn't want to change. It's helpful to recognize that if another person (supervisor, co-worker, etc.) is a jerk then they're probably just as miserable on the inside as they are to others on the outside. They're not winning either. Say to yourself "I can't change this. I can't waste my life and my happiness thinking that I can. What can I focus on to be happier?" Then focus on that. Remember, nothing besides death is permanent (and that hasn't been confirmed either). If you move on to other things you can control you might be surprised to find that down the road you get that promotion or assignment. You may also determine that you're glad you didn't get it after all. I know that has happened to me. How many times have you thought to yourself "I'm glad that didn't turn out as I had hoped. This is so much better." A quote from Helen Keller captures my message: "When one door of happiness closes, another opens; but often we look so long at the closed door that we do not see the one which has been opened for us." I urge you to look toward the open door.

Is this the hill you want to die on? Do you want to hold your position at all costs?

Lastly, the antidote to cynicism is to challenge the negative thoughts about yourself, people, and the world because they are over-simplifications of reality. Not *all* people treat each other horribly. In fact, if you look for it, many people are often kind and generous. You may have to look for examples outside of your work to improve your chances of finding it, but it's worth the effort. This may be especially difficult because once a person is struggling with burnout, there is a tendency to withdraw from others. Knowing this tendency can help you challenge yourself to broaden your worldview by spending time in your personal life looking for the good in people. Find your purpose outside of your work and with it you will find a way to feel you are making a difference and more examples that the world is not going down the drain.

Anger

Chronic cynicism can lead to anger. You might be angry at the public, your co-workers, administrators, your family, or the world in general. Anger is just as valid as any other emotion. It oftentimes gets a bad rap because it's strongly associated with bad behavior. Yet, feelings and behavior are two different things. Your anger about a situation might be completely justified. If someone says something rude to you, being angry about it makes sense. I would find it odd if you were indifferent about it.

Like any emotion, anger can be unhealthy and maladaptive in three key ways: 1) your interpretation of the situation was skewed, 2) your response was destructive, or 3) you stew in the anger instead of addressing the situation. If your interpretation was off kilter, then it's a matter of being open enough to make this discovery through communication with others. It's important to ask: "What information am I missing here?", "How is that person making sense of it?", "Could I be wrong here?" It takes quite a bit of nerve to eat some humble pie and ask these questions. It's far better to do it at the time you get mad than let it go on building up, only to let the anger multiply, widening the gap between you and others. I've worked with client couples who have suffered immensely from misunderstandings that never get resolved. Every time they become angry at each other (or a situation they are both dealing with), they argue but never make any progress. They're so certain that they have all the information, they're not listening to the other person. "Certainty locks us out of their story, curiosity lets us in" (Stone, Patton, & Heen, 2010, p. 37). So, they give up. Retreat. They thicken stories of how the other person is a villain. Ever notice you're never the villain in your version of the story? This leads to the next part; villainous behavior.

Some people take the right to be angry to extend to their right to behave in destructive ways to express their anger. I've never met anyone who became convinced of another person's point because they yelled it at them. I've been called a few names in my lifetime and never have I thought to myself "Wow! That person has a point." Slamming doors, throwing things, and sulking also shut down any hopes of resolution. You're never going to get your point across if you throw it at them like a bladed weapon. Instead, the situation escalates and someone storms off or shuts down. You're even further away from a solution to the problem.

Lastly, stewing in your anger isn't going to be very helpful. It's masochistic and doesn't change anything. In fact, the anger just intensifies. Anger can be very addictive. We can hold onto it; being self-righteous in our anger; repeating our self-righteous slogan: "I've been wronged and I am justified in my anger." Oddly, it gives us some sense of power over the situation because we feel that we are better than those who have wronged us. We can become smug, and condescending. Our throne is a comfy place from which to cast down rocks to those who have wronged us. Yet, this kind of behavior alienates us from many unintended others. The rocks we're throwing hit others; we don't treat family and friends as well as we should because we are not ourselves. We're defensive and on high alert for any perceived slight.

Managing anger requires noticing the first sign of it. In this way, you can think about why you're mad and cope with it before it gets carried away. Constructive problem solving is usually only possible when you're not overwhelmed and physically agitated. If possible, you might have to temporarily distract yourself or remove yourself from what's making you mad. Then you can get some clarity about what you think you can or would like to do about it. For instance, when you learn you've been bypassed for a promotion that you feel you deserved, you may be pretty ticked about it. Instead of blasting those that delivered the bad news, wait. Redirect your focus to something else for a few minutes to allow yourself to cool off. It'll be hard to do because you're going to want to mull over what just happened, but it's important to try. When you feel that your heart rate has lowered and your eyes don't feel like they're bulging out of your face, begin to think about the news. Check your assumptions about what happened and why. If you determine your anger is completely justified: someone gets a promotion they don't deserve because of who they know, you have to consider what you want to do with that information. Remember, emotions are there to tell us to get into *motion* (the Latin origin means move). It might literally mean move into a new assignment, a different department, or, if these aren't feasible, then to move your mental state about your work. You may have to redirect your focus to the parts of

> Certainty locks us out of their story, curiosity lets us in.
> (Stone, Patton, & Heen 2010, p. 37)

Chapter 4
Catching the Sneaky
Resilience Thief

your work that you do control. Talking to those that made the biased promotion decision wouldn't likely be helpful, if you intend to continue working there. It might feel good for a moment but would ultimately make you feel worse, and would likely have negative consequences.

On the other hand, when you ask yourself questions like "What information am I missing here?", "How is that person making sense of it?" and "Could I be wrong here?", you may determine that there are plausible explanations for someone else getting the promotion you wanted. The anger isn't justified but disappointment certainly is. It might be easier to feel anger than disappointment, much less sadness. Again, anger can sometimes make us feel more powerful in the moment but it isn't the real deal, emotionally.

If you're angry about something that you've been ignoring for a while, you might need another strategy. Chances are you're mad at yourself for ignoring the matter as well as being mad at the offending party. Oddly, even police can be conflict avoidant, allowing anger and resentment to build over time. The tendency is to go from ignoring (passive stance) straight to aggressive behavior (verbal and/or physical), bypassing the middle ground—assertive communications. Shoot for the assertive stance, saying in a kind, direct manner how someone's behavior is affecting you and what you'd prefer. This doesn't mean that they'll give it to you, but you can use that information to make whatever decision you need to make. For example, if I tell a friend that I haven't appreciated all the times she cancelled plans with me at the last minute and she doesn't see it as a problem, I can decide if I'm willing to still deal with it or if I need to let the friendship go.

Other Life Stressors

Sometimes the non-operational stressor that challenges you is one of life's many changes. Even positive changes bring stress, which is confusing for many. Getting a promotion is a good thing but probably means your days off and hours will change. You'll also have to learn new responsibilities, tasks (paperwork!), and so forth. Some of the biggest positive changes, getting married and starting a family, also create stress. You probably don't feel right complaining about these things, but even these life events can affect your stress levels, chipping away at your resilience, if you're not careful.

POLICE ADMINISTRATORS

Police administrators have their own non-operational stressors; namely long hours, political pressures inside and outside of the agency, and family stressors. Research on the Royal Canadian Mounted Police conducted by Linda Duxbury and Christopher Higgins consistently showed that police administrators have *very* stressful jobs that demand long hours (Duxbury & Higgins, 2003, 2012). My own research with police administrators reflects high levels of non-operational stress in the upper echelon of the police organization, mostly due to the number of hours dedicated to the job. Administrators may not be subjected to the traditional strain of shiftwork, but oftentimes work from home. Technology makes working from home by staying in contact with subordinates easy to do. Text messages, emails, and laptops means others can easily reach you, if needed. This comes at the expense of your down time. Administrators volunteer their time, as they have supervisory and administrative duties that just can't be done during work hours. Administrators in the mid-manager level have been shown to have the poorest mental health due to increasing levels of stress and burnout (Duxbury, 2007). Their physical health is declining, as well. My dad worked from home often. This was the reason behind my research on work–life balance and police identity.

Administrators are oftentimes stretched between loyalty to their officers and accountability to the public. Each group has its own list of priorities, demands, and needs. The public push for reductions in crime are at odds with officers' exhaustion from overwork. The public demands more officers in school zones while officers know that there's a drug ring in the same neighborhood that needs their attention. As an administrator, you have to navigate these waters, trying to maintain the faith of both sides. Yet, you can't make everybody happy. If you lose public support, you may suffer the consequences in terms of funding or even keeping your position. If you lose officer support, you've possibly crossed the thin blue line at the expense of your career and police identity.

Highly publicized use of force events places administrators in the unenviable position of balancing support for their officers without looking like they're defending or even covering up bad behavior. Let's face it. Occasionally, there's a bad apple in the bunch that makes the whole tree look rotten. If the administrator leans too far in favor of the officers, the public isn't happy. If he leans too far in favor of the public, officers would question his loyalty to his brothers and sisters in blue. It's a no-win situation, which heaps stress onto the administrator while also isolating them. That's a bad combination. When officers are justified in their use of force, which is oftentimes the case, administrators have to endure the hardship of trying to inform and appease a disgruntled public. Nowadays, there are a lot of disgruntled members of the public who don't have much, if any, understanding of police work. I've encountered it several times in a one-on-one conversation and it wasn't an easy go. I can't imagine trying to communicate to a crowd of people who are riled up, at least in the diplomatic manner expected of a police administrator. This is the epitome of an organizational stressor that can wreak havoc on the physical and mental health, eroding resilience over time.

Administrators were once line officers doing shiftwork, requiring accommodations by family members. This usually ends up with family routines that don't include the officer. One sergeant who never took time off from work decided he'd take the evening off, thinking this was a good thing for him and his wife. Much to his surprise, even though he was in a healthy, strong marriage, his wife was thrown by his presence at home and asked him in a loving but sarcastic tone "What the fuck are you doing here?" She had plans to curl up in her chair and read her book, as she had been most nights he wasn't there. This isn't an isolated story. Many officers have talked about their exclusion from their family activities after years of shiftwork. They struggled to make their way back into the fold of the family when they moved out of an operational position. They were an outsider inside their own home. If this is you, then you will need to be direct about your desire to be more involved now. Once you've made this declaration, follow through. This doesn't mean that you then work from home while your family is in another room watching a movie.

As a police administrator, you will have to lean heavily into your family and non-police support for many of these non-operational stressors. Due to your position, you may not be able to count on the support of your peers or subordinates. Like line officers, you will have to pick your battles, keep your voluntary overtime to a minimum, and carve out a life outside of your work. You may need to work harder to stay healthy, give that your position is probably more sedentary than working in the field. If you are a publicly visible administrator, you may also need to a develop a plan with your family for how to deal with an unsupportive public or media when you are out of the home. As a kid, my dad had given us explicit instructions on what he wanted us to do if he was approached by someone who wasn't happy.

CIVILIAN EMPLOYEES

Civilian employees have many of the same hassles as sworn members: shiftwork, overtime, lack of equipment, and unfair policies and procedures. Unlike sworn members, you aren't subjected to the added stress of being in physical danger and you rarely have to attend court. However, you also lack resources and may reach the promotional ceiling in your work much sooner than sworn members do. You also tend to have less control over your work environment. Even though you're in the controlled environment of a communication center, you have very little control over what people on the phone do and what officers on the other end of the radio do. Adding to this, the vast majority of dispatchers (allegedly 90 percent) have "Type A" personalities, which means that they tend to more easily feel overloaded and are more preoccupied with time (of which they don't have much to speak of) (Reddin, Van Hasselt, Baker, Larned, & Southgate, n.d.).

Non-sworn members are also sometimes regarded as "second class citizens" in the police world (Reddin et al., n.d.). I remember my days in dispatch when officers berated a fellow dispatcher (and occasionally me) during or after a call. Dispatchers don't get credit for much, even though they have to think like an officer, act like a mediator, speak like a radio announcer, and operate the console equipment as if they were an octopus with eight arms. Just like police officers, non-sworn members, such as crime scene technicians and victim service workers, are also subjected to non-operational hassles such as call-outs, shiftwork, and court appearances.

Although civilian members have many of the same organizational hassles that officers do, they usually have a lot less support from the organization and from each other. They don't seem to have the same level of camaraderie that officers do. Instead, there seems to be more back-biting. I've offered team building training for dispatcher/call-takers and have been surprised by the amount of conflict that occurs in this group. If there are personality differences between two dispatcher/call-takers, others are dragged into the drama because everyone ends up being aware of everyone else's business. It's difficult, if not impossible, to get away from it when everyone is crowded into a communication center. I'm sure there are several reasons for the interpersonal conflict, such as their overall diminished status in the organization, working in tight quarters with each other (sometimes even having to speak over one another), and the inability to burn off stress from a cruddy call or series of cruddy calls. I can't imagine having a room full of Type A personalities helps matters much.

Civilian police members will fare better with these organizational stressors by taking deliberate steps to build group harmony, pride in their work, and healthy lifestyles. Developing group harmony requires strong leadership. It's great if that leader is also the manager but leadership might also come from the bottom of the hierarchy. Harmony within and between shifts can be developed by creating opportunities for employees to socialize. For instance, you can organize a meeting, a luncheon, or a special way to start or end a shift or a crazy, busy summer. You want to communicate that they should be serious about the business of their work but still have fun in doing the job. Some suggestions for incorporating fun into the workplace include creating a bulletin board for jokes, birthday lists, personal newsletters, and events. Harmony also means managing conflicts that arise. It's beyond the scope of this book to teach conflict management, but a recommended resource, *Getting to Yes: Negotiating Agreement Without*

Giving In, offers the following key strategies (Fisher, Ury, & Patton, 2011):

- separating the people from the problems;
- focusing on shared interests of all parties;
- recognizing both sides have legitimate concerns and differences. Determining how can each side get what it wants;
- evaluating the options using objective criteria;
- developing fair standards and procedures for resolving the conflict.

Conflict also occurs when role expectations are unclear. Clarifying who does what can go a long way in preventing conflict. Cross-training and shadowing other roles promotes mutual understanding, improving group harmony. When people get what you're doing and why, they're more apt to be understanding of the choices you make. When missing this information, they might reason backwards from the negative impact it had on them.

As a civilian police employee, it's important to take pride in the work you do. Not everyone could do it. Sworn members may not fully understand how important your job is and why you do what you do. Don't let their lack of information taint your perspective about your work. If you *didn't* do your job, they'd probably be the first to be impacted by it. This speaks volumes to the critical nature of what you do. This applies to dispatchers, call-takers, crime-scene technicians, victim service workers, record clerks, and beyond. It's nice to be recognized by others for what you do, which would certainly add to your pride, but don't let it be necessary for you to recognize your own contribution to the police organization and public.

Beyond the advice I gave to sworn members for maintaining their health, I would add that some of the non-sworn positions call for even more activity, due to the sedentary nature of the work. Don't take your break at your console or in a break room. Go outside and go for a walk. Better yet, go for a walk with a co-worker. Also try to stand up and stretch at your console/desk at least every hour. I've been in dispatch centers that have treadmills and stand-up desks. Great idea! Nutrition is also important, which means bringing foods that will sustain you, keeping your blood sugar and energy levels stable. You can even take turns trying healthy recipes and bringing in these foods to share with co-workers, promoting both health and harmony!

POLICE FAMILY MEMBERS

Police family members also have to deal with non-operational stressors. They have to accommodate shiftwork, long hours, call-outs, and working holidays. Unless they're connected with other police families, they usually have to figure out how to make these adjustments along the way, on their own. At least police officers and non-sworn members have each other to compare notes to. For instance, one wife of a police dispatcher told me she had no idea how she would have a family, given her husband's variable shiftwork and her work schedule. She realized she was on her own with this one when she considered who in her work and social circle she might ask. If you or your spouse don't work shiftwork, especially shiftwork that is variable, you can't usually understand how complex this is to navigate. Her husband had been asking his co-workers for advice on how they did it. He was sharing what he learned with her, but she was still at a loss as to how it would happen. This was a monumental decision they were facing and one that many police families are forced to contend with.

One common consequence of non-operational hassles on police families is the lack of connection in intimate relationships. This can occur for a number of reasons but mostly happens when other demands on time or energy put the relationship with one's partner dead last. For instance, we can become consumed with work, responding to work emails and calls outside of work hours, taking call out when it's not mandatory or out of financial necessity (often referred to as "golden handcuffs").

Another common occurrence is the prioritization of parenting over the marriage. Although kids, especially young ones, are more reliant on their parents for their needs, it does not justify the neglect of the marital relationship. In fact, maintaining the health of the marital relationship contributes greatly to children. The children see a model for a healthy relationship. They see the fondness and affection displayed between parents and it becomes the example for their future relationships. Conversely, seeing their mother ignoring their father (and herself) to attend to them indicates that, when they are older, they should ignore their own needs in service of others. It's unlikely that this is the message intended by parents who focus on their children to the detriment of their marriage. Similarly, parents who are over-committed to work model this behavior to their kids, which is not going to be helpful when they are older and trying to navigate the balance between their work and relationships.

Bonds between co-workers can also create rifts between police and their significant others. The rifts may be due to actual infidelity or the non-sexual, emotional bond that occurs when spending so much time with a co-worker in such a stressful environment. Significant others may also have concerns about the attention given to their police member, as some uniforms may attract admirers. Over time, emotional affairs can easily become sexual affairs. People who are in unhappy marriages will find ways to get their needs met. If you had access to a time machine, I'd say to go back and start investing in your relationship at the first sign that things are not going well. Given the impossibility of that, you've got to take immediate action to recapture what you once had. What you allow continues. Couple's counseling can help you get this back, if you're both committed to doing it. If this isn't doable, or you or your loved one object to this, you can at least take action as a couple. Discover and get active in mutual interests (preferably, something not revolving around your kids). If you've both always wanted to do a marathon, train together. In addition to creating new points of connections, rekindle old ones. Pull up old photos or memories and reminisce about old times; your early days together. Snippy comments about their co-worker will only drive them away (and possibly toward the co-worker). You catch more flies with honey than you do with vinegar.

> What you allow
> continues.

It is difficult but vital to manage these difficulties. It requires deliberate efforts to revitalize the connection between partners by scheduling "adult time" to relate as a couple. This doesn't mean that the couple goes out to dinner and discusses parental matters. It means going out to dinner to talk about their interests as adults and as a couple. Not only does one have to attend to the quality of interactions as a couple but also the frequency of adult time. It can't be something that occurs just once a month, time permitting. It needs to be a daily commitment, including even the smallest efforts such as having a cup of coffee together when the kids are in bed. Having a healthy relationship as a police employee might seem like a pipe dream but it is possible. Think of relationship health as you would officer safety: It requires daily commitment as if your relationship depends on it.

As a police family member, I recommend that you pull your oxygen mask over your face before you assist the "passenger" beside you. This means that you have to maintain your health by getting the exercise and nutrition that you need to manage daily stress. You will need to maintain some semblance of a schedule around your loved one's crazy schedule. You will need to put forth intentional effort to maintain balance in your life. You will also have to communicate early and often to avoid the buildup of resentment or misunderstandings. Make the implicit explicit. What do you need? What don't you need? Consider these questions for yourself and communicate them to your loved one. It doesn't mean that they will be the only provider for these needs. You may have to get some of your needs met by other family, friends, and support systems. It's important that you talk about your needs (and your loved one's) instead of assuming that the other should automatically know but is deliberately ignoring. Do you need help with the house? The kids? Alone time? Couple time? No one can read your mind. There's nothing wrong with asking for what you need, even from your police spouse who has their own demands to contend with. You two can hopefully have a problem-solving conversation where you can come up with some options for both of you getting what you need. You can't achieve this without at least talking about it.

TOOLS FOR YOUR DUTY BAG

- Keep in touch with loved ones when overtime or call-out keep you away. Update them and let them know you are thinking of them.
- Unless financially required, keep voluntary overtime to a minimum. You'll pay the price in other ways (family, health, etc.).
- Maintain a life and identity outside of policing to increase purpose, sense of control, variety of skill set, and various sources of support.
- Take stock in how you spend your time and with whom, asking loved ones how you've changed since you went into police work.
- Mentally plan for your retirement early, building interests, activities, and a network outside of work.
- Annual health check-ups with your doctor can detect issues early so you can counter the effects of shiftwork and stress.
- Exercise and high protein meals before a shift will energize you. A 20-minute catnap can improve performance and mood.
- 10-hour shifts are recommended for less fatigue, fatigue-related accidents, and overtime.
- Limit "bitch sessions" about work. What starts off feeling helpful leaves you feeling helpless and defeated.

ANNUAL CHECK-IN

How Have You Changed Since Beginning Policing

- Have these changes been positive? Or negative? Take inventory by considering the following questions.
- How have your relationships changed? Your family life? Friendships?
- Are you satisfied with your intimate relationship? What is something that you two used to do that brought you joy that you do not do now or do less often? Make a plan to reincorporate these activities into your life. Life will always be busy. There is always a limited amount of time. Instead of prioritizing your schedule, try scheduling your priorities. What are your priorities in life? How do relationships fare in this equation? As artificial and silly as it might sound, plan your recreation with the same amount of commitment that you would schedule work tasks and household chores.
- Do you find that your outlook has changed? Have you become cynical?

- Police work has been found to change the way police see the world and the people in it. Think about it. You only see a thin slice of the population on a regular basis. It would be easy to assume that all people are the same or similar to the people you see every day. Seeing is believing. It takes vigilance to remind yourself that police interact with a small segment of the population and that society, as a whole, is largely law-abiding and non-violent. Test your outlook by filling in the blanks to the following statements:
- I am _____. People are _____. The world is _____.

- Is there evidence of mistrust, cynicism, vulnerability, or some related concept? The challenge is to look for evidence to the contrary of imbalanced, cynical views based upon a thin slice of the population. If your outlook is that people are greedy, look for evidence that they are, in fact, generous. We tend to find what we are looking for so why not look for something positive?
- How about your health? Do you often feel stressed? How well do you feel you are coping with stress and strains from the job and from your personal life?
- Do you know what your physical signs of stress are? What do you do when you notice you are becoming overstressed? How do you alleviate stress? If you don't know the answers to these questions, chances are you are at the mercy of stress, responding in a haphazard fashion. Research indicates that there are a number of factors that buffer stress. Some of these factors impact at the point where one is coping in the aftermath of stress. Examples include seeking support from family and friends, physical activities such as exercise and meditation, distraction activities such as hobbies, and seeking professional support. Some of the factors that impact how we manage stress take place BEFORE the stressor even occurs. This includes proactive measures such as taking care of ourselves, having a spiritual practice, building positive emotions, preparing ourselves for potential stressors by building our confidence to manage tasks with preparation, and living a balanced life.

REFERENCES

Beutler, L. E., Nussbaum, P. D., & Meredith, K. E. (1988). Changing personality patterns of police officers. *Professional Psychology: Research and Practice, 19(5)*, 503–507.

Chen, J.-D., Lin, Y.-C., & Hsiao, S.-T. (2010). Obesity and high blood pressure of 12-hour night shift female clean-room workers. *Chronobiology International, 27*, 334–344.

Conlon, M., Lightfoot, N., & Kreiger, N. (2007). Rotating shift work and risk of prostate cancer. *Epidemiology, 18*, 182–183.

Conti, N. (2009). A Visigoth system: Shame, honor, and police socialization. *Journal of Contemporary Ethnography, 38(3)*, 409–432.

Cottle, H. G., & Ford, G. G. (2000). The effects of tenure on police officer personality functioning. *Journal of Police and Criminal Psychology, 15(1),* 1–9.

Demerouti, E., Bakker, A. B., Nachreiner, F., & Schaufeli, W. B. (2001). The job demands model of burnout. *Journal of Applied Psychology, 86,* 499–512.

Duxbury, L. (2007). The RCMP yesterday, today and tomorrow: An independent report concerning workplace issues at the Royal Canadian Mounted Police.

Duxbury, L., & Higgins, C. (2003). Work–life conflict in Canada in the new millennium: A status report. Retrieved May 16, 2014 from http://publications.gc.ca/collections/Collection/H72-21-186-2003E.pdf.

Duxbury, L., & Higgins, C. (2012). Caring for and about those who serve: Work–life conflict and employee well-being within Canada's Police Departments. Retrieved March 12, 2014, from https://sprott.carleton.ca/wp-content/files/Duxbury-Higgins-Police2012_fullreport.pdf.

Fisher, R., Ury, W. L., & Patton, B. (2011). *Getting to yes: Negotiating agreement without giving in.* New York: Penguin Books.

Folkard, S., & Lomardi, D. A. (2006). Modeling the impact of the components of long work hours on injuries and "accidents." *American Journal of Industrial Medicine, 49(11),* 953–963.

Forastiere, F., Perucci, C. A., Di Pietro, A., Miceli, M., Rapiti, E., Bargagli, A., & Borgia, P. (1994). Mortality among urban policemen in Rome. *American Journal Industrial Medicine, 26,* 785–798.

Gilmartin, K. M. (2002). *Emotional survival for law enforcement: A guide for officers and their families.* Tucson, AZ: E-S Press.

Ibarra, H. (1999). Provisional selves: Experimenting with image and identity in professional adaptation. *Administrative Science Quarterly, 44(4),* 764–791.

Josse, E. (2008). *Le burn-in et le burn-out.* Retrieved September 23, 2017, from www.resilience-psy.com/IMG/pdf/burnin_burnout.pdf.

Maslach, C., Schaufeli, W. B., & Leiter, M. P. (2001). Job burnout. *Annual Review of Psychology, 52,* 397–422.

McCarty, W. P., & Skogan, W. G. (2012). Job-related burnout among civilian and sworn police personnel. *Police Quarterly 16(1),* 66–84.

National Institute of Justice. (2012). *10-hour shifts offer cost savings and other benefits to law enforcement agencies.* Retrieved September 20, 2017, from www.nij.gov/topics/law-enforcement/officer-safety/stress-fatigue/pages/shift-work.aspx.

Navara, K. J., & Nelson, R. J. (2007). The dark side of light at night: Physiological, epidemiological, and ecological consequences. *Journal of Pineal Research, 43,* 215–224.

Netotea, A. (2012). Burnout—An effect of professional stress in the police environment. 2nd *International Conference on Economics, Trade and Development IPEDR, 36,* 38–45. Retrieved September 23, 2017, from www.ipedr.com/vol36/008-ICETD2012-D00028.pdf.

Patton, D., Violanti, J. M., Burke, K., & Gehrke, A. (2009). *Traumatic stress in police officers: A career-length assessment from recruitment to retirement.* Springfield, IL: Charles C. Thomas.

Pavalko, E. K., & Woodbury, S. (2000). Social roles as process: Caregiving careers and women's health. *Journal of Health and Social Behavior, 41,* 91–105. Retrieved from http://dx.doi.org/10.2307/2676362.

Ramey, S. L., Downing, N. R., & Knoblauch, A. (2008). Developing strategic interventions to reduce cardiovascular disease risk among law enforcement officers: the art and science of data triangulation. *AAOHN J, 56*, 54–62.

Reddin, R. A., Van Hasselt, V. B., Baker, M. T., Larned, J. G., & Southgate, L. (n.d.). *Police dispatcher stress and resilience*. Retrieved October 7, 2017, from www.frsn.org/_literature_122271/Police_Dispatcher_Stress_and_Resilience.

Salston, M. D., & Figley, C. R. (2003). Secondary traumatic stress effects of working with survivors of criminal victimization. *Journal of Traumatic Stress, 16(2)*, 167–174.

Seuss, D. (1986). *You're only old once: A book for obsolete children*. New York: Random House Publishing.

Stone, D., Patton, B., & Heen, S. (2010). *Difficult conversations: How to discuss what matters most*. New York: Penguin Books.

Thoits, P. A. (1983). Multiple identities and psychological well-being: A reformulation and test of the social isolation hypothesis. *American Sociological Review, 48*, 174–187. Retrieved from http://dx.doi.org/10.2307/2095103.

Thoits, P. A. (1986). Multiple identities: Examining gender and marital differences in distress. *American Sociological Review, 51*, 259–272. Retrieved from http://dx/doi.org/10.2307/2095520.

Thoits, P. A. (1991). On merging identity theory and stress research. *Social Psychology Quarterly, 54*, 101–112. Retrieved from http://dx.doi.org/10.2307/2786929.

Thoits, P. A. (2003). Personal agency in the accumulation of multiple identity-roles. In P. J. Burke, T. J. Owens, R. Serpe, & P. A. Thoits (Eds.), *Advances in identity theory and research* (pp. 179–194). New York, NY: Kluwer Academic/Plenum.

University at Buffalo. (2008, September 29). Impact of stress on police officers' physical and mental health. *Science Daily*. Retrieved September 19, 2017, from www.sciencedaily.com/releases/2008/09/080926105029.htm.

Vila, B. (2008). Managing police fatigue: A high-wire act. *The RCMP Gazette, 70(3)*, 30–31.

Vila, B. (2009). Sleep deprivation: What does it mean to public safety officers? *National Institute of Justice Journal, 262*, 26–31. Retrieved September 21, 2017, from www.nij.gov/journals/262/pages/sleep-deprivation.aspx.

Violanti, J. M., Burchfiel, C. M., Miller, D. B., Andrew, M. E., Dorn, J., Wactawski-Wende, J., . . . Trevisan, M. (2006). The Buffalo Cardio-Metabolic Occupational Police Stress (BCOPS) pilot study: Methods and participant characteristics. *Annual Epidemiologist, 16*, 148–156.

Building Resilience
Mental Armor for Police Employees

> Man is capable of changing the world for the better if possible, and of changing himself for the better if necessary.
>
> (Viktor Frankl, 2006, p. 131)

The material from this chapter, in fact this book, is based upon foundational as well as emerging research on resilience. It also comes from the experience and wisdom shared with me or observed by me in police officers, dispatchers, call-takers, crime-scene technicians, and family members of police. I feel that I am standing on the shoulders of giants reaching out to you, offering what I have learned over the years from others. The information in this chapter is not unlike the concept of resilience itself. It isn't static. It shifts, grows, and challenges us to adapt. The research and programs presented in this chapter will do the same. For this reason, I am offering both the information, its source, and common trusted sources for information about resilience so you can easily stay up to date and explore topics further, if interested. I hope you will.

There are many ways you can develop resilience. Drs. Steven Southwick and Dennis Charney, experts in resilience, have identified at least ten factors that contribute to resilience: 1) positive attitude; 2) flexible thinking; 3) personal moral compass; 4) having a resilient role model; 5) facing fears; 6) active coping; 7) supportive social network; 8) physical fitness; 9) regular emotional, physical, and cognitive training; and 10) recognize and use your strengths (Southwick & Charney, 2012). Let's take a look at each of these, as applied to police officers, administrators, non-sworn employees, and family members.

POSITIVE ATTITUDE

Positive attitude is realistic optimism, which means that you acknowledge your adversities AND you maintain your faith that, despite this, you WILL prevail. Collins (2014) refers to this as the Stockdale Paradox. The Stockdale Paradox is named after Admiral Jim Stockdale, who was held captive for eight years in the Vietnam War. During this time, he was tortured repeatedly. Stockdale relayed in an interview with Collins "I never doubted not only that I would get out, but also that I would prevail in the end and turn the experience into the defining event of my life, which, in retrospect, I would not trade." Stockdale noticed that being optimistic without also confronting the reality of the situation made matters worse for those imprisoned with him. Stockdale took actions, finding ways to communicate intelligence to his wife in his letters and creating a tapping code to communicate with other prisoners.

> Yet there's no difference between a pessimist who says. 'It's all over, don't bother trying to do anything, forget about voting, it won't make a difference,' and an optimist who says, 'Relax, everything is going to turn out fine.' Either way the results are the same. Nothing gets done.
>
> (Chouinard, 2016, p. 175)

I usually remind my clients of their ability to endure by asking if they've ever NOT survived a day of their life. 100 percent have answered in the affirmative, confirming that, although they may not have come out of their adversity unscathed, they came out. Taylor (1989) proposed the notion of *positive illusions* as being helpful when people face adversity. Positive illusions are a form of self-deception where you're more optimistic about your situation than the situation might warrant. This optimism, when it's mild instead of wildly unrealistic, is beneficial for physical and psychological well-being (Taylor). Taylor's findings were based on interviews with breast cancer patients. Interestingly, when the patients subsequently faced objective evidence of the progression of their illness, they were no worse off for having had these illusory perceptions. In short, you don't have anything to lose by being more optimistic. You do, however, have something to gain.

Evidence suggests that positive emotions directly improve physiological health (Segerstrom, Taylor, Kemeny, & Fahey, 1998). Positive emotions are also believed to indirectly improve health by increasing the likelihood of healthy behaviors. It makes sense, if you think about it. If you feel that there is hope for your situation, you are more likely to take health-enhancing steps to better your situation. You are more apt to seek professional help and take care of yourself. If you don't have hope, you won't likely bother. Positive emotions are also believed to result in more social support and active coping which will, in turn, reduce the occurrence or worsening of other problems that might evolve from the initial problem (Taylor, Kemeny, Reed, Bower, & Gruenwald, 2000). For instance, when police officers are involved in shootings, they might feel as though nobody could understand their situation. As a result, they might withdraw from others, including friends, co-workers, and family. This results in strains in social support and might even reduce their physical activity, as they are no longer meeting friends at the gym. This chain of events leads to a downward spiral in coping and health. Neglected health results in health problems, which get lumped on top of the initial situation—the shooting.

Even if you're not convinced by the evidence of the impact of positive emotions on health, the evidence for the damaging impact of negative emotions on health is quite compelling. Negative emotions increase the stress response, compromising immunity (Herbert & Cohen, 1993), contributing to coronary heart disease (Coombs, 2008). In fact, the link between negative emotions and disease is so strong, there is a body of research, *psychoneuroimmunology*, the study of how emotions influence the immune and nervous systems, that examines these effects.

Some experts in coping have proposed that individuals have what they refer to as hardiness (Kobasa, 1979). A hardy person sees difficulties as a *challenge*, not a *threat*. This is a key distinction. When we think of difficulties as challenges, they are considered surmountable, given the right approach. The intensity of distress when facing the challenge is manageable. When a difficulty is perceived as a threat, intense fear ensues. Instead of approaching the problem, fear would likely cause you to retreat from it. A hardy person also maintains commitment to addressing the difficulty. They are invested in the situation, themselves, and others in the situation too much to give up when the going gets tough. They're more likely to actively approach a problem than retreat from it. Certainly, this is easier to do when you don't consider it a threat. Lastly, hardy people recognize their control in a situation. They believe that they have an influence on outcomes and, therefore, they're willing to take action. The opposite of having a sense of control would be *learned helplessness*, which has been very problematic, leading to depression.

The work of Barbara Fredrickson offers further evidence of a positive attitude as promoting resilience (Fredrickson, 2009). Fredrickson's research suggests we are better able to solve problems when we are in a positive frame of mind because a positive mind frame broadens our thought–action repertoire. Simply put, when we are in a positive frame of mind, we are able to perceive more options to solve a problem. On the other hand, when we're in a negative state of mind, our perception of viable options narrows. Therefore, we end up trying to solve a variety of problems with the same solutions, whether they work or not. The ability of a positive mind to broaden our perception of options, and therefore develop better solutions, is aptly named the Broaden and Build Theory (Fredrickson, 2009). People in a positive mindset perceive more options, are more flexible and open and, in turn, develop more personal resources (Fredrickson, 1998). For instance, the positive emotion of playfulness has been found to lead to more physical resources (Boulton & Smith, 1992), social resources (Aron, Norman, Aron, McKenna, & Heyman, 2000), and intellectual resources (Panksepp, 1998). Can you remember the last time you were playful? People usually think of playfulness as something reserved for children. Adults can be playful without being immature. Playfulness involves a good sense of humor, spontaneity, and lightheartedness, which are anything but immature. Adults are actually too serious, if you ask me.

What is very interesting about Fredrickson's research about mind states and problem-solving is that we can actually *undo* the damaging impacts of a negative state of mind, aptly referred to as the *undoing effect*, by purposefully redirecting our thoughts to the positive. Now don't get me wrong. I'm not suggesting that you become blissfully oblivious to your problems and assume that a solution will miraculously manifest itself. What I am suggesting, and considerable research supports it, is that you are in a much better position to discover a solution with a positive, more expanded frame of mind. According to Fredrickson, negativity causes us to narrow our focus in order to protect ourselves. From an evolutionary perspective, it makes sense to hone in on negative circumstances in order to perceive and deal with a threat to our safety. The problem is that we tend to maintain this narrow focus after the threat has passed or when we misperceived something to be a threat when it actually wasn't.

So how does this undoing work? Researchers believe that positive emotions undo the damaging cardiovascular reaction from negative emotions accompanying a perceived threat (Fredrickson, Mancuso, Branigan, & Tugade, 2000). When you encounter a threat, arousing negative emotions, your body prepares for fight, flight, or freeze, increasing blood flow, respiration, and altering vital functions to prepare you for action. Over time, or with repeated activations, the body gets worn down by this physiological response. Positive emotions are believed to correct this damage (Fredrickson, 2009).

Fredrickson offers a Positivity Self-Test, which only takes two minutes to complete. You can find it at Fredrickson's website www.positivityratio.com. Take the test to see how your positivity measures up. There's a good chance that you aren't overly positive because it's quite well known that police officers can be quite cynical. Kevin Gilmartin (2002), a retired police officer and police expert, talks about it in terms of seeing an ever-expanding circle of assholes. People view themselves, people, and the whole world through their own lenses, which may be rosy or dark. You may have guessed that police officers don't tend to see through rosy lenses. They oftentimes *think* they are looking through clear lenses, with a crystal-clear view of how the world *really* is. In fact, I have heard officers profess many times about how the rest of the world just doesn't know what people are *really* like until they do the job. There is a mistaken belief of being more enlightened about the human condition on the basis of seeing people at their darkest hour. Repeatedly seeing people at their darkest hour doesn't make for a very balanced view of people. Some officers, however, recognize that this lens is actually quite dark and reflects a world and the population in it as evil, crooked, lazy, and stupid, which is NOT reality.

When most people think of positivity, they think that it's about only looking for the good in people and situations. When cynical police officers think of the concept of positivity, they think it's sugar coating reality, which could have dangerous consequences. It's considered foolish and an easy way to become a victim. It's blissful ignorance. Resilient people take the middle ground with their perspective. Resilient people don't blindly, foolishly see good where things are bad. On the contrary, resilient people see the bad and find the good that surrounds it. For instance, when you go from one bad call to the next, you can take one of two primary stances: 1) you can say to yourself "The world is going to hell in a handbasket. Everywhere I go bad people do bad things to stupid or powerless people" or 2) you can say to yourself "The nature of my job is to meet people during their difficult times. For every person that I see who is suffering or is causing suffering, there are many more who are doing fine that I will never meet." Unfortunately, you may be most familiar with the first option. You may have said it to yourself or worked with someone who has. I know I have both said it and heard it from others. What about option 2? Does it ring true? Could it ring true? I'm not sugar coating the situation. I'm not saying things are better than they are.

Promoting positive emotions as a resilience factor is not intended to be a directive to stamp out all negative emotions and plaster a smile on your face. Negative emotions are adaptive in the short term, as they mobilize you to action. It's when these negative emotions continue to disturb you outside of the situation that they become maladaptive, dragging down your ability to be resilient, to see the whole picture, and to bounce back from the adversity you face.

FLEXIBLE THINKING

Flexible thinking relates to being able to roll with the punches. When we fight the inevitable, such as change and failure, it amps up our stress levels and limits our ability to move forward. Shit happens. You may not like it but, if you can't do anything about it, you have to accept that and see if there is anything you can learn from the situation. Many times, things will not go our way and we have to change our thoughts about it. We have to accept it, not like it. People get stuck in thoughts such as "They must be respectful to me" or "The world must be fair" when, in reality, this is not true. Albert Ellis referred to this as "musturbating" in that people rub themselves the wrong way thinking that these "musts" are actually true, or maintaining unrealistic expectations and hopes, despite the evidence to the contrary (Ellis, 1994). Ellis contended that people add to their misery by 1) self-demandingness, 2) other-demandingness, and 3) world-demandingness. We demand that we must perform well, never failing, and always winning the approval and respect of others (self-demandingness). Similarly, we make these impossible demands of others in our lives (other-demandingness). We also mistakenly believe that the world should be fair, hassle-free, and safe (world-demandingness). When it isn't, we wear ourselves out by fighting with this reality. We tell ourselves that we can't stand it and things must change. Actually, what needs to change is our thinking. This kind of thinking is so rigid and filled with falsehoods that it erodes our ability to be resilient. We could also benefit from taking things that are not personal so personally. "Telling yourself that a situation is not personal, pervasive or permanent can be extremely useful" (Sandberg & Grant, 2017).

The alternate to this rigid, damaging way of thinking is flexible thoughts such as "It would be nice if others were respectful of me, but sometimes they're not" and "I would prefer that the world was fair but that's just not the case sometimes." This might seem like semantics to you that won't change your frustration with others and the world, but I would urge you to try it anyway. I have talked to hundreds of police officers (and non-police folks too) who have said that thinking so rigidly has led them to feel trapped, while thinking more flexibly has felt more liberating. When we think about thinking, consider this: 1) Is there objective evidence to support this thought? and 2) Is it helpful to think this way? Even if evidence supports your thought, it doesn't mean that it pays off to constantly entertain the thought. Letting it go doesn't mean that you accept or like it. It means that you accept that, for now, you can't change the situation and you're smart enough to see that and move on to something else you can change.

In Chapter 1, I talked about how you can reframe all the things that are on your plate from *having* to do them to *getting* to do them. This

> Telling yourself that a situation is not personal, pervasive or permanent can be extremely useful.
> (Dr Adam Grant, *Option B: Facing Adversity, Building Resilience, and Finding Joy*, 2017)

Chapter 5
Mental Armor for
Police Employees

reframing recognizes the choice you made in the matter. You *have* to work overtime, because you *chose* to do a job that calls for overtime on a regular basis. You could *choose* to do a different job but you may not be satisfied with what comes with that job, which might include lower pay, less interesting/challenging work, more requirements for education or travel/relocation, etc. The key thing is that the language you use, which is an extension of the way you think about things, makes a difference in your resilience. There are two kinds of language you can use when talking (and thinking) about your situation: 1) the language of agency or 2) the language of defeat. I'll introduce the concepts with an activity. Read aloud the following statements and notice what it feels like emotionally, mentally, and physically.

- I have to do that when I get home tonight.
- I should not be eating chips for dinner.
- I'm so busy today.
- I gotta take my kids to their soccer games on my days off.
- I really should do another workout this week.
- I can't tell him what I think of him.

What did you notice? How do you feel? Notice that I didn't put anything in the list that is unusual. These are everyday thoughts that come to mind. Now, read the following, again noticing how you feel while reading them:

- I choose to do that when I get home.
- I decided that I'm eating chips for dinner.
- I have a full day.
- I get to see my kids play soccer on my days off.
- I want to do another workout this week.
- I choose not to tell him what I think of him.

Now, how do you feel? Any different? Again, you may have gotten stuck on the last statement. It might not feel like a choice to not tell your supervisor or significant other you think poorly of them. But, ultimately, you *do* choose not to tell them based on your valuing of your job, harmony at home, etc. When I've done this activity with groups, following the first group of statements, they reported having a sinking feeling, a sense of defeat and being trapped, powerlessness, irritation, and grumpiness. After the second set of statements, they've reported feeling more capable, positive, intentional, and having more "wiggle" room. Now, imagine that you routinely talk to yourself and others with the language of defeat. How do you think this will affect your mood and the mood of others? What do you suppose would happen if you caught this tendency, switched gears, and talked using a language of agency instead? I'm quite sure your mood would improve. Consider the following story:

> One evening an old Cherokee told his grandson about a battle that goes on inside people. He said, "My son, the battle is between two wolves inside us all. One is evil. It is anger, envy, jealousy, sorrow, regret, greed, arrogance, self-pity, guilt, resentment, inferiority, lies, false pride, superiority, and ego. The other is good . It is joy, peace, love, hope, serenity, humility, kindness, benevolence, empathy, generosity, truth, compassion, and faith." The grandson thought about it for a minute and then asked his grandfather, "Which wolf wins?" The old Cherokee simply replied. "The one you feed."
>
> (Unknown)

This story captures the sentiment of this book, especially this chapter, in terms of how we can make choices that assist us in winning battles we face. It reflects the agency within us all to feed ourselves in a way that contributes to our misery or our resilience. It has implications for the stories we tell ourselves about situations, based upon how we see things. We can tell ourselves stories of betrayal and suffering, of victimhood and defeat. We can try to fight with what is, doggedly maintaining our desire for things to stay the same or be different. In the end, we will be sick and tired from maintaining this rigid thinking. I am not suggesting that you stray from your principles or gulp down your sorrow at having been mistreated. What I am suggesting is that you try to take a step back and consider how helpful your righteousness will be in the end. Resilient individuals feed the wolf of compassion (for self and others), kindness, and hope.

HAVING A PERSONAL MORAL COMPASS

Having a personal moral compass may or may not be related to religious faith. It's about knowing your purpose in life and living according to this purpose. What is your mission in life? Are you living your life in furtherance of this mission? If not, take the first step toward a life that serves your purpose. I know it sounds corny to have a personal mission statement because it makes us think of the mission statements we hear at work that we are expected to buy into despite oftentimes not believing in them. We can't buy into it because there might be a gap between what the organization publicly professes as their mission and the reality of what's actually being promoted. I would argue that sometimes the same holds true for individuals. We sometimes say that family comes first but our actions don't reflect this. Until we are forced to look at our lives and how we are spending our time, most of us are not aware of our personal moral compass. Without this compass, we are left to wander away from what is important to us.

Having a personal moral compass means that our commitment to and participation in activities are guided by intentionality. Have you ever spent an afternoon doing something you didn't enjoy and wondered why you bothered? I know I have. Maybe you're doing something as a favor for a loved one or out of a sense of obligation to another. It's not a catastrophe if you do this from time to time, as long as you are connected to your reasons for doing it. Maybe you're doing it because your relationship with your loved one is important and spending the afternoon digging up a garden is based on your intention to keep your relationship healthy. It's important to not lose sight of that while you're digging. Yet, if you're doing something that you can't connect to a bigger goal (strengthening a relationship, improving your health, etc.), you have to ask yourself why you're doing it. Some people take on activities because they were expected to or because they didn't know how to say "no." Others do it because the activity used to be meaningful or connected to the bigger picture in some way but no longer fits with their current life goals and priorities. It just become a mindless habit.

Other times we do things because we just become altogether disconnected from our purpose, lacking a moral compass to guide our direction. For instance, nowadays in North America the average American adult spends 11 of the 16–18 hours a day that they are awake using some form of electronic media (e.g., smartphones, television, computer, etc.) (Nielsen Report, 2015). Granted, many of us work on computers, but they have become an incredible source of time wasting. Being online is like a black hole. Before you know it, you've wasted away the morning and you no longer have time to go for a run before work. Your compass is nowhere to be found. We sometimes lose sight of what's important to us until a tragedy ensues. When tragedy strikes, we take our life off of auto-pilot for a while, reconsider our daily life choices and how they align with our bigger purpose.

As the best-selling author of The Seven Habits of Highly Effective People, and time management guru, Stephen Covey (2004), put it we must remember "the main thing is to keep the main thing the main thing." Covey also wisely suggested individuals live a life where they make distinctions between doing things that are urgent and doing things that are important. According to Covey, there are four combinations of urgent and important placed into four quadrants where people spend their time. In the first quadrant, people spend their time working on tasks that are both important and urgent. In policing, this quadrant would include priority calls for service where delays in responding have serious consequences. In personal life, it would also include emergencies that have grave consequences such as health emergencies. The next quadrant involves tasks that are important but not urgent. This includes tasks related to relationships, physical, emotional, and financial health. These are very important elements of life that typically are not urgent. For instance, if you don't invest in your health today by exercising, you won't instantly develop diabetes or heart disease. If you don't make a $5 deposit to your retirement account today, you probably won't even notice any difference in your retirement balance. If you miss your kid's football game, there will be others. It's okay. Then, after a while, you find that you haven't helped them with their homework, asked them about their day, taken them to a movie, either. It all adds up for better or for worse. You can accumulate a bunch of missed opportunities to connect with your kid (spouse, friend, parent), or you can accumulate a bunch of good memories where you were maintaining, or even building, a better relationship. Each instance, on its own, is important but rarely urgent. Unfortunately, this makes it very tempting to neglect these important, not urgent, parts of life. Over time, these important parts continue to be ignored in favor of the urgent. This brings me to the next quadrant, the urgent but not important. Many everyday tasks get lumped into this quadrant when people don't identify and be mindful of what's important to them. For instance, we often feel a sense of urgency when demands are made of us by others. It might come in the form of an email, text message, or in-person request. Sometimes we simply react to the demand without thinking about how important it is to us. Maybe we're aware that it isn't important to us but we feel like we have to do it anyway. After all, we can't exactly tell our boss that the task she asked us to do isn't high on our list of priorities. That would fly over like a lead balloon. However, if you find that you are always doing what your boss says to the detriment of your health or relationships, you may have to consider the viability and consequences of this choice. Do you wish to exchange a happy marriage for a happy boss? That's a very personal choice but I would guess that most people wouldn't make that choice. They would rather lose at work than lose their family. Again, some people don't feel they have this choice but others tend to not even notice the trade-off they're making. They're not living according to their moral compass because they are foregoing the important for the urgent or mistaking what is important to someone else as important to themselves. The last quadrant includes tasks that are neither important nor urgent. You might wonder "Who in the heck would spend their time here?" We all do! When we find ourselves burned out from running around putting out fires, some of which are created because we have neglected our health or relationships until matters rise to a crisis level, that we need to retreat. We take comfort in zoning out in front of the television, the computer, or taking naps.

We bounce between these four quadrants, paying attention to what is important when we are focused and intentional and dealing with the urgent, when required. When relationships (quadrant two, important not urgent) are chronically neglected, like a parched houseplant, they tend to die. If you happen to notice that the plant isn't looking so good, you might try to revive it. Yet, even when you try to nourish the plant with water, the water doesn't soak into the soil. Over time, the soil has hardened and won't absorb the water. The same is true of relationships. When you try to revive it with attention and affection, the heart of the other won't receive it because it too has hardened. You keep pouring but it's too late. Therefore, it's so important to be intentional about spending time on what is important to you.

I know emergencies often derail our best intentions to tend to the important things in our life. Yet, if you don't carve out the time for the important, you will actually contribute to ongoing emergencies, such as relationship and health failures. Carving out time for the important means being intentional about how you spend your time. It might be cumbersome at first but you have to continuously ask yourself "Is this important in the big picture of my life?" or "Would I trade this for my relationship? My health?" and act in accordance with your response.

I believe Kevin Gilmartin (2002) alluded to this when he spoke of "usta syndrome." Cops "usta" do this and they "usta" do that but now they don't do much of anything other than work. According to Gilmartin, police become exhausted from riding the roller coaster that is their job. Applying Covey's urgent/important concept to Gilmartin's concepts of roller coasters and "usta syndrome" results in police employees spending their days riding the roller coaster, dealing with urgent and sometimes important matters. This leaves them spent at the end of their shift, retreating from family, friends, and maybe even life in general to zone out, doing things that are neither important nor urgent. They struggle to make even the smallest decision, as they have been making decisions all day and can't muster up the energy to make another one. This leaves them with the kind of life they are not *choosing* to have.

A life not chosen has been given a name: *life by design* versus a *life by default* (Covey, 2004). According to Covey, people who live their life by design don't blindly accept the viewpoints from their childhood. They don't follow the scripts that others have written: "A good officer takes ownership of his beat at all costs," "An officer who shows emotions is pathetic and not cut out for the job," "Couples retreat from conflict to maintain family harmony." Rather, they choose their values, act with intention, and accept responsibility for their behavior. In doing so, they are willing to take reasonable risks for the life they choose because not choosing it defaults to someone else's notions of how they should be living.

> The main thing is to keep the main thing the main thing.
> (Covey, Merrill, & Merrill, 2003, p. 75).

Sometimes, your moral compass is guided by your faith. Police officers have identified their faith as giving them hope for the future and assisting them in preparing it (Conn & Butterfield, 2013). You might rely on your faith to cope with workplace difficulties and connect to your purpose for doing the work, which is usually to help people. You might lean on your faith to make meaning of things that can't readily be explained, or to find comfort during the most uncomfortable times. When you can't determine the meaning, or understand why the suffering has to happen, your faith allows you to be okay with not knowing. "Let go, let God" is a Christian example of this kind of coping. Your faith in a higher power, whoever or whatever that is, may also give you comfort that you are not alone in this world.

HAVING A RESILIENT ROLE MODEL

While presenting on the topic of resilience, I asked a large group of cops to identify their role models. Much to my surprise, they said they could identify who *wasn't* their role model but they couldn't identify who inspired them. Sometimes seeing who we don't want to turn out like is great motivation to take better care of ourselves and our relationships, but it isn't enough. Having a role model, a mentor, if you will, to inspire us improves our resiliency. It also shows us that it is possible to be resilient when we have things in common with our role model. It doesn't seem like a pipe dream to be resilient in our work when we see others who are doing it. Practically, having a role model or mentor also shows us what it looks like to be resilient—how a resilient person makes decisions, takes care of themselves, handles difficulties, and so on.

For me, I have always benefited from having a mentor. Talking with someone that I can identify with and who I respect helps me to keep things in perspective. Seeing someone that I can relate to doing well in life and taking care of him- or herself reminds me that it's possible. Sometimes, it even shows me *how* it is possible. We are social beings and we tend to look at others to determine how we are doing anyway. Unfortunately, we tend to look to people from a distance, making assumptions about them based upon what we already believe to be true. Making these assumptions can be problematic because we may assume that they are doing better than us because we're inept in some way, or because they have some special quality or circumstance that makes it easier for them. These assumptions don't ever get challenged because we don't have all the information. We love to compare our insides to other people's outsides. It keeps it simple, even if we're *simply* miserable. When we make contact with someone who seems to have it together, we learn from them. We may learn that things aren't as smooth as we thought they were from our distant vantage point. We may also learn that this person is managing difficulty in a manner that hadn't occurred to us. This is where the magic happens. We get better at managing difficulties by copying what is working for another. There's no shame in this! In fact, we're wired to do this. We have mirror neurons that cause us to mirror the behaviors of others. If you don't believe me, consider what happens when you watch another person yawn. Mirror neurons and imitating others are evolutionary processes that promote our survival. This is the sentiment behind the adage "There's no need to reinvent the wheel."

Behavioral psychologists used to believe that people learned to do things by their own trial and error, weighing the benefits and costs of performing certain behaviors. In other words, people had to experience their own failures and successes in order to learn from them. We now know that this isn't the case. We are able to learn by observing others' trials and triumphs. We are more apt to learn from those who we consider to be like us in some way and from those who we admire.

The benefits of having a resilient role model are supported by the work of a renowned Stanford psychologist, Albert Bandura. Bandura, the creator of social learning theory, discovered that we develop self-efficacy, our belief that we have the capacity to be effective in performing a task, in part by observing others (Bandura, 1977). We learn from our social interactions. Self-efficacy is not only important when you begin a new behavior, but also helps you stick with it and cope with the inevitable difficulties that occur with learning it. Sticking with it allows you to overcome these difficulties, reinforcing your sense of effectiveness and dismantling unfounded fears about the obstacles you encountered. For example, you may not know how you could possibly juggle the conflicting demands of shiftwork and family. It seems like an impossible task and there's no class on this to give you any guidance. Yet, you noticed that an officer on your shift talks about the family events he attended on his days off. You wonder "How did this guy do it?" because you felt too tired to do much of anything. Ask him how he manages to pull it off! I have spoken with many officers who have gotten quite creative in their management of shiftwork.

You might think that you would be well advised to only look toward more seasoned officers to learn how they are managing the demands of the job. I would caution you not to overlook some of the newer, younger officers. They may have a different mindset and a greater openness to being innovative than someone from an older generation. We know there are very distinct perspective differences in people of different generations in the workplace. You would likely benefit from observing the behaviors of officers from various generations, taking what you need from each person who is able to offer you any example of how to be more resilient.

> These assumptions don't ever get challenged because we don't have all the information. We love to compare our insides to other people's outsides.

FACING FEARS

Encouraging officers to face their fears might seem strange. Every day, officers face fears that would send others running for their lives. Let me be more specific. I am suggesting that in order to be resilient, you must face your personal fears, those difficulties you're having but are pretending don't exist because you don't know what to do about them. Maybe you've noticed that you're not doing well after a call and you've been ignoring some of the signs of this. Perhaps you think that if you pour yourself into your work, or sleep, or pour a few for yourself, that things will work out . . . eventually. That seems to be what others do. So that seems normal, right? It could be that you notice your marriage isn't what it used to be but you pretend that everything is fine. The two of you co-exist, managing the demands of your household, parenting, and so on without addressing the ailing relationship. I can't count how many times people have come to me for therapy who have attempted to wait out their problems only to see the problem spread like a cancer, ruining their health, relationships, and work. Much larger changes are needed to return to a state of health.

> What you resist, persists.

Nobody likes facing their fears. We prefer to play it safe and hope things turn out alright. Sometimes we're not sure what to do. So, we do nothing. Yet, this supposed "nothing" really means that we are choosing to allow more of the same—more PTSD, anxiety, or depression symptoms, more suffering in silence in a marriage that is going down the drain. Running from your problems is a race you will NEVER win. Face your fears instead of being chased down by them. What you resist, persists!

ACTIVE COPING

A related concept, active coping, entails taking measures to manage the stressor you're facing. It involves facing your fear, and then determining what you can do to change the situation. If you can't change the situation, you find ways to deal with it. It might mean asking for help from your support system or reassuring yourself that you can deal with the situation such as: "I can get through this" or "This, like everything else, is temporary."

There are various ways to cope. Which way works best depends on the situation. The two common coping categories are problem-focused and emotion-focused (Lazarus & Folkman, 1984). As you might guess, when you cope in a problem-focused manner, you are using problem-solving strategies. There is an action orientation in policing so this manner of coping is quite common. For instance, if you go to a call where your safety is threatened, you will likely take measures to be safer—take cover, draw your weapon, radio for back up, etc. A personal example would include having a disagreement with your spouse. In an effort to resolve this, you might talk to her/him to determine their perspective or share yours. You might collect information to support your viewpoint or even seek counseling. Coping experts suggest that problem-focused coping makes the most sense when the situation is controllable to some degree. In other words, if you can change matters for the better, it makes sense to do so.

Emotion-focused coping, as you might have guessed, means that you've determined that the situation is beyond your control so you're just trying to manage with your emotional defenses. For instance, when you become overwhelmed by a threat such as the prospect of losing your job or losing your spouse, you may cope by denying or downplaying what is happening. You might console yourself by saying that you didn't like working there anyway. You might villainize the spouse, making it easier to detach from a painful experience. Using these defenses can be good or bad. They're good in that they shield you from the pain of the situation and might allow you to move on more easily. The bad is that, as I have said before, you're essentially avoiding the truth, the heart of the problem. It might be more beneficial to actually face the pain to determine what went wrong so you can learn from it. In this way, perhaps you can avoid it in the future. Again, emotions are little motivators, little life instructors that have information for you, if you'll listen to them.

Emotion-focused coping might be fitting at the onset of a threat to shield you from being overwhelmed. This is what happens during traumatic events; denial, disbelief, or disconnection from what is happening. Afterwards, once you've collected yourself and assembled your resources, then task-focused coping might be most appropriate. You will need to be intentional about caring for yourself, eating well, and facing the aftermath of what happened, including your reactions to it. You're in a better position to take action, supported by others, with more information, more time, and so forth.

SUPPORTIVE SOCIAL NETWORK

I can't say enough about having a strong support network. The more people in it, the merrier, provided that their notion of support is a healthy one. Build a strong support network when things are going well so that, when times are tough, you have many sources of support. Some people can support you emotionally while others offer practical support. Sometimes, you want to talk to someone; get things off your chest. Other times, you just need to get a break from your stressful situation. You've been swimming in it and talked it to death. Maybe you just need to go camping and stare at the fire. One friend may be great at listening while another lifts your spirits by just being there with you.

Try to include people from various parts of your life such as work, family, college, neighborhood, church, and recreational teams. In this way, you will have a wide array of interesting people in your life and diverse sources of support, when needed.

Support systems are important in that they provide affect, affirmation, and aid (Kahn & Antonucci, 2014). When you're facing difficulty, it's nice to know that others are cheering you on, offering emotional support (affect), and admiring your determination. It's also helpful to know that others who truly understand your difficulty can affirm for you that it's a difficult situation. A former co-worker who is dealing with or has dealt with retirement is a better source of affirmation than a well-meaning spouse who has not been in your shoes before. The source of support matters for the kind of support offered. Lastly, aid is an important source of support in that it can be practical aid, helping a person with a task such as retirement paperwork, or it can be informational in that it provides you with what you need to do the task yourself. Again, this form of support might be source-specific in that your child will not likely be a good source of support for the paperwork. A human resource person would be better equipped to offer this form of support while your child would be in a better position to offer emotional support.

Developing social support isn't a matter of just having people, but having the *right* people. If you spend the majority of your time with people who are cynical and miserable, you'll likely be cynical and miserable too. As humans, we're affected by the emotional climate of others through a concept called *emotional contagion*. Our mirror neurons cause us to *reflect* (imitate) the behavior of others. These mirror neurons help us understand the behaviors of others that we're observing. This understanding, in turn, activates our goal-oriented behaviors with this person (Ferrari & Rizzolatti, 2015). For example, we mimic the behaviors and reflect the emotions of others that we observe. If you see someone yawn, you will likely yawn. If you look at your watch, it will cause others to look at their watches as well. We're programmed to do this for our survival. So, it makes good sense to surround yourself with people who will be positive influences on your mood and behavior. Emotional contagion research has shown that happiness actually "spreads" between people (Fowler & Christakis, 2008). Being in the presence of happy people who are smiling and positive reinforces your positive behaviors and social interactions. Even more, happy people are also believed to be more apt to offer practical support which, in turn, enhances the happiness of those receiving this support. If you spend all your time with a friend who's always scowling, you may notice a scowl on your face. Social support is only helpful insofar as it supports your ability to be resilient. If it promotes or maintains a nasty attitude, then it is hardly worth calling it support.

Social support during adversities has also been shown to have buffering effects on the physiological stress response (Ozbay, Johnson, Dimoulas, Morgan, Charney, & Southwick, 2007). This, in turn, prevents physiological damage, enhancing your resilience. Having someone nearby during stressful events has also shown to have physiologically soothing effects. Conversely, studies have shown that the absence of social support has negative physiological consequences when individuals are exposed to stress (Southwick, Vythilingham, & Charney, 2005). This is the idea behind having a "buddy" assigned to an officer involved in a critical police incident. The presence of a peer support team member can relieve some of the stress of the officer who would otherwise be alone during the investigation process.

Yet, there is more to the story than social supports as "buffering agents." Social support persons aren't merely shields from damage that might otherwise occur. That stance seems like a sad minimization of what support people actually do. These people go beyond buffering us from stress to *enable* us to do what we do. They encourage us during our time of difficulty. They make us laugh; they lift our spirits with their presence. They also provide practical support that allows us to have more time and energy to deal with our adversity (cook our meals, watch our kids, make phone calls for us, etc.). Beyond this, "Supporters model coping attitudes and skills, provide incentives for engagement in beneficial activities, and motivate others by showing that difficulties are surmountable by perseverant effort. The enabling function of social support can enhance self-efficacy" (Benight & Bandura, 2004, p. 1134). All of these benefits are assumed on the basis that your support system is in place and is a healthy one.

Social support is the product of its size, how often you interact with supports, and the feeling that you receive comfort from interacting with these folks because you get help that's both practical and informational (Sippel, Pietrzak, Charney, Mayes, & Southwick, 2015). Social support is multilayered, including those closest to you and those a little further out. In other words, they don't have to be your best bud to be supportive of you. Everybody plays their part. Your support is a matter of what you *receive* and *perceive* as beneficial. This is a key distinction. You may receive advice or practical support from others but perceive it as intrusive, unwanted, or provided for the wrong reasons. I have spoken with officers who have relayed feeling more irritated and confused by all the advice they were given following a critical event. They've also told me of times when they felt like their supervisor or a member of the critical incident stress management team was offering them something simply to check a box. They did not *perceive* genuine support from any of these seemingly helpful social supports.

> Supporters model coping attitudes and skills, provide incentives for engagement in beneficial activities, and motivate others by showing that difficulties are surmountable by perseverant effort. The enabling function of social support can enhance self-efficacy.
> (Benight & Bandura, 2004, p. 1134).

Much of the research on social support relates to what's called *social capital*, which refers to not only the support that individuals receive from others but their investment in their social system as well (Norris, Stevens, Pfefferbaum, Wyche, & Pfefferbaum, 2008). Investing in others provides you a "return" insofar as you feel you will receive support from those that you have supported in the past. Therefore, it's important to make periodic deposits into your "friendship bank" and your "family bank," in case you need to make a large withdrawal (in terms of receiving support) later. You're also less likely to lose them if you overdraw your account because you've been a good bank customer up until now. The last thing you need during a difficult time is to not have enough established credit with these folks and lose them when you need them the most.

Investing in others also increases your access to resources because you would have additional potential resources from all the connections your social network has. It's an "I have somebody who knows somebody" kind of situation. For instance, if you were looking for a recommendation for a doctor (babysitter, plumber, etc.), asking friends and family about their connections could yield more options. Additionally, investing in your significant others gives you more meaning and purpose.

Historically, research has been correlational, showing a relationship between social support and resilience where the direction of influence was not clear. Are low levels of social support a risk factor contributing to PTSD? Or does having PTSD cause people to have lower levels of social support? Further complicating matters is the recognition that not all social supports are actually considered helpful. There might be a mismatch between the kind and timing of help to the needs of the individual. Some "help" could even be considered harmful, not helpful. An example of this includes unsolicited advice from a well-meaning friend or co-worker. Again, it's more the *perception* of it as helpful than the actual helpfulness of the support. Being given this advice might add stress to an already complicated decision-making process. Individuals might feel that they have to listen to the advice and then defend their decision not to take it. Other times it's the friend who wants to take the friend out for drinks, when rest or going for a run might be more helpful.

When officers are able to access non-police supports, they have reported that it's helpful because these persons are able to remind them of their non-work selves. They encourage them to play non-work roles by asking them about their family, their hobbies, their interests, all of the parts of who they are outside of being a police officer. They don't simply talk shop with them about their work. They have also reported that support persons tend to encourage their participation in hobbies and inquire of their non-work interests, which, in turn, builds their resilience (Conn & Butterfield, 2013).

Social Systems and Health

Most people understand that people get sick from others who are have a contagious illness. However, research shows that there is a contagion effect for illnesses that are not transmitted biologically (by germs) (Smith & Christakis, 2008). Health-promoting behaviors such as exercising, eating habits, or visiting doctors are "spread" within social systems. Health-hindering behaviors such as smoking, poor diet, and substance abuse are also shared within social systems. Granted, people tend to choose their social networks based upon their lifestyle similarities (e.g., smokers spend time with other smokers, etc.). However, research shows that people are still influenced by lifestyle practices of others who are dissimilar (Sacerdote, 2001). This has important implications for those who are wishing to make resilience-enhancing lifestyle changes.

Barriers to Police Support Systems

As a police officer, you have unique struggles in developing and maintaining social support systems. There are two types of interference: 1) practical and 2) perceptual. Practical interference relates to limited time and scheduling conflicts, while perceptual relates to the feelings of being overwhelmed or stressed by the demands of multiple roles (Duxbury & Higgins, 2001). As discussed in Chapter 4, the practical interference is a schedule mismatch between you and your support systems, making connecting more difficult. Shiftwork and overtime also often interfere with your ability to participate regularly in social events and organized events such as sports teams and interest-related groups. Spending time with family and friends requires active, creative planning and sometimes re-planning due to schedule mismatches. Organized sports or interest-related groups that allow more casual or even drop-in participation might assist with the complications of shiftwork. They exist. It's just a matter of finding ones in your community.

I would add that perceptual interference also includes the belief that officers have that they cannot talk about the traumatic nature of their work with their family and friends for fear of traumatizing them. Instead, they pull away from them, holding their struggles in private. Family and friends may not know why the officer is withdrawing and will draw their own conclusions. This can create rifts between officers and their loved ones, which tend to grow over time.

Another complication is your worry that you'll lose a significant part of your support system if you take stress or administrative leave following a critical police incident. When you're not working, you lose regular access to support when your need for it is probably higher than ever. This is one of many reasons officers (and employees in other fields) fight against taking leave. Your co-workers will continue doing their shifts while you're at home. You'll be out of the loop on what's going on at work, which can be isolating. However, loss of some social supports is easier to manage when your system is more substantial and less tied to a particular place. Having a "social convoy," where your support isn't confined to a place, time, or situation, contributes to your resilience. Social convoy means the persistence of a social support system through time (Kahn & Antonucci, 2014). In other words, these people remain your support system whether or not you're in policing, stay married, or continue to play golf.

The problem is that, over time, in police work, a varied social support network can become quite narrow, including mostly work-related supports. This is due to the aforementioned issues relating to shiftwork, the traumatic nature of the work, and the dominant work-related identity role. Narrowing supports to only work-related support systems is problematic in that it substantially reduces the variation of the kind of support that is available and may even reduce the amount of support available during instances such as departure from work through retirement, stress leave, or administrative leave. Worse yet, it is during these times that support is most needed. Some police officers have avoided retirement because they felt that it would effectively cut them off from their social network. One cannot avoid retirement indefinitely.

Even having non-police support has its own complications. Non-police people also ask you about your work, because they find it interesting and think you might have the inside scoop on what they saw on the news. Even when officers make concerted efforts to participate in social events, and leave their work behind, others may prevent them from playing their non-work roles by identifying and treating them primarily as their police officer role. For instance, police officers who were attempting to play parent roles and organized team sport roles were reminded of their police officer roles by others, which made it harder to participate in these non-work roles (Conn, 2015). Sometimes, it was teammates drinking in public after a game where the police member felt they had to leave the situation, or were otherwise given grief for their duty to uphold the law. It's an awkward situation. You can't be fully part of the team, as others could be.

The police officer role draws attention from others due to the fact that police officers are highly visible with distinctive uniforms, experience media coverage of their work, and are oftentimes portrayed in movies and television. Therefore, the expectations of others who interact with you in social settings may be influenced by these depictions, leading them to reaffirm your functionalistic role of police officer instead of the social role you're trying to play (Seay, 2009). The expectations of others likely contributed to your struggle to transition between these roles, causing you to feel hindered in performing the social roles. When out to dinner with friends, you may have to politely redirect invitations to talk about your work. I had to do this at parties when I was a cop and now as a psychologist. People will catch on, with your persistence, that you're not going to talk about your work when you're not at work.

Community-level support networks are very important sources of resilience or pathology for officers. Police officers working in communities that do not support their work tend to not fare as well as those that receive support. Research with military veterans showed that homecoming stress was more damaging than traumatic stress (King, King, Fairbank, Keane, & Adams, 1998). Currently, in the United States, there are many recent instances of public and media scrutiny relating to police services. Research with Canadian police officers also points to media and public scrutiny as hampering their coping (Conn & Butterfield, 2013). Lots of officers follow social media and news stories relating to their calls. Satisfying their curiosity about what is being said is usually offset by the frustration they feel when they view news or social media. It's a good idea to avoid the sources of non-support. Very rarely do police feel better after reading an opinion piece regarding their work in the local media.

PHYSICAL FITNESS

Recommendations such as eating well, getting plenty of sleep and exercise are oftentimes regarded as common sense and therefore insulting to people's intelligence to recommend. Yet, I don't pretend that some of the best advice is obvious advice. In fact, I would say that it is the obvious stuff that is oftentimes overlooked in favor of the magic pill or the latest trend in what's supposed to be good for you. There's nothing sexy about the next few recommendations. What is new and exciting about it is the abundance of research that shows the benefits of taking care of your health and the consequences of NOT doing it.

Physical fitness is critical to being resilient. Sometimes we don't need to talk about our stressors, we just need to burn off some stress and get some endorphins to feel better. Building physical strength often results in emotional strength, improved clarity, and focus. Taking a break from worrying about our problems, getting out of our head and into our bodies, can be the best thing for us. Being physically fit prevents, or at least delays, the onset of diseases, reducing the occurrences of health-related stressors, while simultaneously making us more resistant to the wear and tear from other life stressors.

There is a strong correlation between aerobic exercise and reductions in anxiety, stress, and depression. In fact, exercise is a common prescription for depression for many reasons. For starters, exercise likely gets the depressed person out of the house, into nature, and engaging with others. When a client with depression comes to see me, the first order of business is to get them out into the world. Clients report feeling much better after a brisk walk, even if they don't feel like doing it in the first place. That's the cruel part of it. People oftentimes *wait* to feel like doing something before doing it. If you wait, that time won't likely arrive on its own, or at least not anytime soon. You sometimes have to push through and then experience the benefit of exercise. When you exercise, you're also more likely to be in the sun, be in nature and be with others. Each of these, in turn, contributes to your resilience as well. The benefits of sunshine are so well documented that you can buy "sunshine" from the pharmacy in a therapeutic light box for mood enhancement. This is commonly used by persons suffering from seasonal depression, when the days are short and cloudy. Participating in exercise also puts you in contact with others. Walking the dog, walking with your significant other, meeting a friend for a run or racquetball game, all contribute to your physical and emotional wellness.

Beyond getting you out into the world, exercise has multiple physiological benefits for your resilience. It promotes better sleep. It boosts your immunity. It promotes circulation, reducing inflammation and stiffness. It helps you maintain a healthy weight and blood sugar levels, preventing disease. You might say that you're often too tired to exercise after a long day, and I get that. The funny thing with exercise is that it tends to *generate* energy. You won't feel you have the energy until about 10 minutes into exercise. Then, presto! You get a new supply! Even low-intensity exercise for a mere 20 minutes has shown to reduce fatigue by 65 percent (Puetz, Flowers, & O'Connor, 2008). We just have to pay attention to our bodies to know if it needs rest instead of exercise. This is tricky. If, after 10 minutes, you don't feel more energy, you might need rest instead.

Diet

People tend to find comfort from stress by eating. If they ate kale when they were stressed, this likely wouldn't be a problem. Yet, they tend to crave comfort foods that aren't good for them, causing a high and then a crash. Afterwards, they feel worse physically and feel guilty for having indulged. Furthermore, sugar in comfort food contributes to inflammation, worsening the stress response, contributing to lethargy, and interfering with cognitive functioning—the opposite of the effect they were seeking. Instead, researchers from the National Institute of

Health suggest foods containing omega-3s such as tuna, flaxseed, or chia (Aubrey, 2014). Pumpkin seeds are another mood booster in that they contain magnesium, which is believed to ward off anxiety, and zinc, which boosts immunity. *The Happiness Diet: A Nutritional Prescription for a Sharp Brain, Balanced Mood, and Lean, Energized Body* is a resource for additional information about foods that defend against stress (Graham & Ramsey, 2012).

When your diet has gone off the rails for a while, you may not be in the physical condition you were in during your academy days. Your vest has become a torture device. So, you decide to lose a few pounds. When people are overweight, they tend to set goals in such a way that they're punitive and defeating. They give themselves grief for having let themselves go and begin putting restrictions on their diet. *I can't have this. I shouldn't have that.* It doesn't sound like a very good motivational speech, if you ask me. Instead, be glad that you're doing something about your health *now*. Say things to yourself that encourage, not discourage, as you would someone you were trying to be supportive of. You wouldn't tell someone you care about "I told you that you were going to get fat if you kept eating like that!" would you? I hope not. Set up exercise and nutrition (I prefer the word nutrition to diet, because "diet" is an emotionally loaded word) goals stated in positive terms—I am going to get in X amount of exercise, X days a week. I am going to eat at least four servings of vegetables and fruits each day and drink at least eight glasses of water. It might seem like stating goals in what you *will do* versus what you *won't do* is simply semantics but it isn't. We are more encouraged, and therefore more likely to do it, when we speak with a positive tone. Furthermore, like the scenario of identifying positive role models to emulate instead of poor role models to *not* be like, when we state goals in positive terms we are giving ourselves more specific direction as to what we will actually do. Besides, it makes sense to add more of what is good for you to the plan than to simply omit what isn't. The food you put in your body makes a huge difference in the way that you feel physically, cognitively, and emotionally.

Sleep

A cornerstone of resilience is sleep. The lack of sleep is so damaging, sleep deprivation has been used as a form of torture. Many shiftworkers don't get enough sleep and it greatly impacts their health. Studies show that more than half of police don't get enough rest. One-third of police officers have obstructive sleep apnea, the most common sleep disorder, which is 44 percent higher than the general population (Vila, 2009). Anytime I do a critical incident debriefing I almost feel silly emphasizing getting good sleep because it seems like such a fundamental life force that I shouldn't have to talk about it. Poor sleep could be due to shiftwork, stress and worry, family demands, or a traumatic event or accumulation of events.

Poor sleep has been associated with poor job performance, accidents, increased alcohol use, and health problems (Neylan et al., 2002). You need rest to restore yourself. When sleep is compromised, YOU are compromised. Sleep deprivation leads to oxidative stress, which is the imbalance of the production and elimination of oxygen and nitrogen (Charles et al, 2008). Oxidative stress contributes to conditions such as Parkinson's disease, liver disease, cystic fibrosis, amytrophic lateral sclerosis, and premature aging (Townsend, Tew, & Tapiero, 2003). These are some pretty scary consequences for missing your shut-eye. So, let's go over some of the police-specific situations that interfere with sleep and talk about what to do about it.

Shiftwork

Shiftwork disorder, a mismatch between the internal sleep–wake cycle and the timing demands of shiftwork, affects many police officers. Unfortunately, its impact extends beyond the shiftwork years, even into retirement, because the body has never readjusted. Research indicates that those who work straight days tend to get more sleep than those who work evenings or overnight shifts. This is, in part, due to the impact of lightness–darkness on the sleep–wake cycle. Those who work night shift are more prone to sleepiness due to the absence of light during their waking hours and the presence of light while trying to sleep. We have a body clock that operates on a 24-hour cycle. Our body adjusts our chemistry at night to induce sleepiness and again in the morning to help us wake up. When you're on shiftwork, this cycle is altered, which is chemically stressful because we're fighting against a natural cycle (Bonifacio, 1991).

There are several things you can do to promote better sleep with shiftwork. If you're having trouble going to sleep or staying asleep taking melatonin at least 30 minutes before going to bed may help, since melatonin promotes sleepiness. Making your sleep area as dark as possible, and getting as much light as possible during your waking hours is also suggested. If you're sleepy before going to work, a 20-minute nap can help.

Stress and Worry

Various personal life stressors such as financial strain, health concerns, or relationship difficulties may also compromise your ability to get good sleep. Thoughts of these difficulties may prevent you from being able to fall asleep or stay asleep. Stress and worry have a way of filling the space your mind leaves at the end of your day when you're trying to get some sleep. Sometimes, you deliberately fill the space, reflecting on the past day or the day to come, worrying about what you need to do, don't want to do, and thinking about how something will turn out. Keep a notebook by your bed to write your concerns down. If you find thoughts interfering with your ability to drift off, write them down, and schedule a time to "worry" about them. I know it sounds strange but it works! Each time the thought comes back, remind yourself that you can't do anything about it at the moment and that you have set aside a time to deal with it later. Then, you actually do what you said you would do: worry about it at the scheduled time. In this way, you are being intentional about trying to construct a plan for what is bothering you. You're not going to be a good problem-solver when you're tired and frustrated. It's not the time to try to solve complex issues. There's something to be said for the adage "I need to sleep on it."

Even if you're not worrying, you may find that your mind still won't shut off to let you drift off to sleep. This happens to a lot of people, especially if you have a fast-paced day (or life!). You're not going to be able to clear your mind and think of nothing so that you can fall asleep. Nobody can just hold a blank mind. Instead, make it a point to put your mind to a boring, non-stimulating train of thoughts. Consider common bedtime rituals such as reading a book to a child or activities associated with sleep like counting sheep. It seems silly but these can work for a busy mind. One advanced version of counting sheep was proposed by a cognitive scientist, Luc Beaudoin (2014), called cognitive shuffling. To do this, think of a five-letter word and spell additional words with the first letter of the word, picturing the image with the word. For instance, for the word "sweet" you think of as many words as possible beginning with the letter "s." Once you have come up with as many words as you can with the first letter, which, by the way, should be emotionally neutral words (not gun, murder, etc.), picture the image that goes with each word. Random worries or thoughts will come to mind while you're doing this and that's okay. "Could I have done something different on that call?" or "Did I give Sparky his medicine?" will still pop in your head. So, when it does, just redirect your attention to the word, letter, or image you were on when the thought appeared. The words and images should be both random and neutral so as to not be too stimulating. Do this over and over and over again, even if your thoughts interrupt you repeatedly. Your focus on the word-naming activity will improve with time and practice. Beaudoin created a smart-phone application to aid insomniacs, mySleepButton, where a pleasant voice reads a list of objects, spaced a few seconds apart so you can picture the image. It gives your brain something to focus on that isn't so stimulating that it interferes with falling asleep. There are several other smartphone applications that can be used to aid with sleep. Some are soothing voices reading stories while others are relaxing sounds to focus on to lull you to sleep.

Family Demands

Having a family may make getting sleep even more difficult. Kids may not understand why mom or dad needs to sleep during the day. I remember waking up to find that my nephew had surrounded my bed with army toys so we could do battle the moment I woke up after my overnight shift. He even snuck outside to knock on my bedroom window because he thought I should be up to play since it was daytime. It may also be difficult for the adults in your life such as significant others, friends, and family to adjust to your need for sleep during the day. You may feel internal or external pressure to forgo sleep so that you don't miss spending time with others who have a normal schedule. Resist this urge! You wouldn't wake your family up at 3 a.m. to watch a movie, would you? Talk to your family and friends about your need for sleep and how it affects your health and safety. Then look for ways to focus on them during your waking hours or on your days off. It might seem that you're missing out. But missing out periodically now due to your need for sleep is far better than completely missing out later when you are suffering from physical health problems related to sleep deprivation or the aftermath of an accident that occurred due to fatigue.

Traumatic Event(s)

Sometimes the intrusive thought that keeps you awake is a memory of a traumatic event you have experienced or witnessed. This occurs because the memory has not been stored in your brain properly due to the overstimulation of your amygdala. The memory will continue to intrude until you take measures to process the event. Essentially, the brain has a natural drive to heal so it keeps reminding you of the event until it "learns" that the event has actually ended.

Traumatic events also lead to having nightmares. Even anticipating you will have a nightmare can make it difficult to fall asleep. It's a good idea to have a plan for dealing with being awakened by a nightmare until you can address the source of nightmares in your waking hours. One strategy which has been gaining support for treatment of chronic nightmares since 2001 is called Imagery Rehearsal Therapy (IRT) (Krokaw et al., 2001). In a nutshell, IRT involves changing the nightmare script. It probably sounds too good to be true but between 70–90 percent of people who have tried IRT have gotten significant relief from their nightmares (Krakow & Zadra, 2010). Not only has it reduced their nightmares, but it's reduced their PTSD symptoms as well. Now that I have your attention, here's what you do. IRT is a three-step process: 1) write down a brief description of a recent nightmare, 2) alter the nightmare narrative in a significant way (e.g., instead of you being fatally wounded, you get hit by a rubber bullet), and 3) rehearse this new nightmare narrative during the day repeatedly.

In this way, you are rewriting the narrative you will have in your dreams. This is an overview of IRT. The full treatment plan also includes learning how underlying stress, anxiety, or PTSD trigger nightmares which, in turn, become a form of "learned insomnia" because the nightmares have become a learned behavior or habit to deal with the underlying trigger. To get full benefits, it's a good idea to work with someone trained in IRT.

You may also benefit from medications that prevent you from dreaming, such as Prazosin. Prazosin is a medication originally used for lowering blood pressure but now is more commonly used has to reduce nightmares for people suffering from PTSD. To be safe, check with your doctor to see what options are best for you. The results for Prazosin and IRT are comparable. However, when you add therapy, particularly cognitive behavioral therapy, to IRT, research shows that you get significantly better sleep quality (Seda, Sanchez-Ortuno, Welsh, Halbower, & Edinger, 2015). Therapy during your waking hours can address the causes of nightmares such as stress, anxiety, and PTSD. A counselor trained in trauma, particularly EMDR and IRT, can assist you with this process and offer additional suggestions for better sleep. EMDR is discussed further in an upcoming section on trauma treatments.

Improving Sleep Hygiene

Getting good sleep means having a good pre-sleep routine. Here are some key suggestions:

- stop consuming caffeine 6 hours before bedtime (this includes dark chocolate!);
- once home, dim lights to prepare the body for sleep;
- avoid or reduce use of lit electronics—smart phones, computers, and televisions since these stimulate the brain, preventing it from going toward slumber mode;
- avoid alcohol (yes, it makes you sleepy at first, but it actually disrupts sleep);
- move slower and avoid work-outs right before sleep (if possible) to avoid stimulating the body;
- have sex—hormones released contribute to sleepiness;
- avoid foods that might contribute to indigestion or heartburn such as spicy foods or high-protein foods that your body will have to expend energy to digest at the expense of your sleep;
- look for foods that convert serotonin into melatonin: corn, broccoli, cucumber, tart cherries, rice, barley and rolled oats, walnuts, peanuts, and sunflower seeds;
- look for foods that are high in four main vitamins and minerals: tryptophan, magnesium, calcium, and B6.

FOODS THAT AID SLEEP

Turkey or chicken
Warm milk
Peanut butter
Bananas
Grains— rice, barley, and rolled oats
Nuts and seeds—walnuts, peanuts, sunflower seeds

FOODS THAT INTERRUPT SLEEP

Caffeine (of course)
Alcohol
Chocolate
Spicy foods
High-fat foods
High-protein foods

You might have a ritual before you go to bed where you make preparations for the next day such as laying out your clothes, packing your lunches for work, or your kids' lunches. You probably want to get this done as quick as possible so you can go to bed. I would advise that you take the extra 5–10 minutes to do it all a little slower so that you are not winding your body up only to try to shut it down for sleep. Getting good sleep shouldn't be a nightmare. Instead, diligent attention to healthy habits can result in sweet dreams.

RESILIENCE TRAINING

A related resilience factor is emotional and cognitive training. Keeping our mind sharp, including our emotional intelligence, helps us problem solve and cope. So, how do you do this? Staying active by engaging in challenging activities across various interests will keep you sharp. It's a "use it or lose it" scenario. Emotional training might include learning to manage strong emotions as they come up. One suggested practice is mindfulness (discussed at length later). For now, emotional training might be learning to *have* the emotion without *becoming* the emotion. In other words, you don't become fused with the emotion itself. It's not "I am angry" but, rather, "I feel angry." In this way, you can learn to manage it rather than be managed by it.

Cognitive training includes strengthening your memory and sharpening various forms of intelligence such as spatial, mathematical, musical, kinesthetic, and complex problem-solving and decision making. You can strengthen your cognitive abilities using games, solving puzzles (jigsaw, word, spatial, logic, riddles, etc.), practicing a physical activity such as martial arts, or learning to play an instrument. You might think many of these are so far removed from coping with trauma in policing that they don't make sense. However, developing your ability to think in different ways will be an incredible asset to you, the person doing the work, which will translate to better coping *with* the work.

USING YOUR STRENGTHS

The last resilience factor suggested by Southwick and Charney (2012) is to recognize and use your strengths. This is a challenge for many since our tendency is to focus on our weaknesses, not our strengths. This is unfortunate, as it limits us instead of inspiring us. Interestingly, you would point out your friends' strengths for them to use to make it through a difficult situation. Why not try this with yourself? Do you have a track record of being creative when helping others get through tough times? Tap into this strength to help you through your current situation. You didn't get into policing without having some people and problem-solving skills. Take it a step further and use your strengths to not just help yourself but to help others. You will likely get more out of helping others than they will.

STRATEGY FOR MAINTAINING WORK–LIFE BALANCE

A very critical component of resilience is balance. I've talked about this throughout the book as a marker of resilience, a non-operational stressor, and as a pitfall in retirement. But it would be important in this chapter on resilience strategies to be specific about how to become aware of your balance (or lack thereof) and how to make improvements. One very simple exercise to become more aware is to do a pie chart on how you are spending your time and how you would *like* to be spending your time. To track your average week, record the percentage of your time that you spend in various life roles: work, spouse/partner, family, social, spiritual, self, community member, etc. Be honest. You're the only one seeing this unless you decide to share it with someone else. Now, in the second circle, record your preferred scenario. Be realistic. It's pointless to say that you want to spend 10 percent of your time at work if you are financially reliant on work. Now, compare your reality to your ideal. Determine which of these categories are most important for you to change that are also within your control right now. There's no point in choosing something you can't change or that isn't that important to you. It'll just be a frustrating exercise. Now, what is one thing you can do THIS WEEK that will get you closer to your ideal? Commit to taking this step, and continue taking this step until your life better resembles your ideal scenario. With each week, choose another, and another. I also recommend returning to this exercise every 4–6 weeks to keep on track. Change requires sustained efforts, monitoring, and adjustments to become lasting habits. Make copies of the next page and repeat the exercise often. You may notice that your priorities change and that's good to be aware of. You may notice that the gap between the current and ideal situation is not narrowing. If this is the case, you need to consider why. Identifying the barriers to change will help you resolve them. Does your loved one protest when you want to spend some time on your personal wellbeing? If so, this needs to be addressed and sooner is better than later. Maybe you can find a way to kill two birds with one stone. If you want to work on your physical health but your family feels you don't spend enough time with them, you can combine the two goals into one activity. When you think of all the things that are "on your plate," can you combine them like you would peas and carrots?

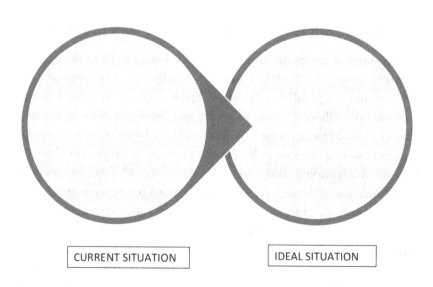

WORK–LIFE BALANCE

CURRENT SITUATION

IDEAL SITUATION

What can I do *this week* to improve my situation?

MINDFULNESS

We live in a world where most of us are plugged in to something. We multitask multiple tasks and are spread so thin you can see right through us. We are anything but mindful. Sometimes this mindlessness is intentional. We don't want to feel what we are feeling or pay attention to the thoughts in our head or the aches in our bodies. We'd rather plug in elsewhere to escape the reality of ourselves and our state of mind. It might be scary to plug into ourselves and become acutely aware of what we are thinking and feeling. We might even fight with it, asking "Why do I feel this way?" "Why can't I just move on?" These are not really questions. They're judgments against ourselves. Allow me to translate. "Why do I feel this way?" typically means "I don't want to feel this way" or "I *shouldn't* feel this way." We are fighting with ourselves. I see it as fighting in quicksand. The more we struggle with what we feel or think, the more tired, desperate, and powerless we feel as we continue sinking. What are we advised to do if we ever find ourselves in quicksand? We are to accept this is where we are and stretch out our arms and legs, widening ourselves across the sand. Okay great. What does this mean when we are talking about feelings and thoughts? It means we don't fight with them. We don't judge them. We accept them. We become open to them (this is the opening of the body across the sand part). We reach out for help.

So, what does all of this have to do with mindfulness? Most people think of mindfulness as some kind of spiritual voodoo for hipsters. On the contrary, it's about practicing non-judgment of the self, giving yourself and others compassion. It's about being open, curious, and present to the moment instead of fighting with it. It's called "practice" because it requires continuous efforts to do it. It's a way of life, not tasks to be completed and things just become better. Recent research has shown the benefit of mindfulness in police and non-sworn police employees (Christopher et al., 2016; Goerling, 2014). Following 8 weeks of mindfulness-based resilience training, which met once a week for 2.5 hours, police employees showed improvements in perceptions of administrative stress, operational stress, sleep, pain management, anger (emotion regulation), reactivity, burnout, resilience, and acting with awareness (Christopher et al., 2016). If you're curious about how to get started, I would urge you to check out www.mindfulbadge.com or pick up a book on mindfulness to see how simple, yet rewarding, it can be.

POLICE ADMINISTRATORS

Police administrators have to take measures to develop their own resilience while promoting organizational policies, procedures, and programs that promote the resilience of their officers. The guidance offered in this chapter for developing resilience clearly applies to the police administrator. Beyond this, police administrators are advised to not deny their need for building resilience because they are not in the field. The non-operational stressors of the work are more widespread and damaging than the danger on the streets. Don't push help in the direction of your officers, to the exclusion of yourself. Your resilience translates to their resilience.

CIVILIAN EMPLOYEES

The recommendations in this final chapter on building resilience apply to sworn and civilian police members. I would add that, for civilian members, it's important to recognize the tendency to downplay your difficulties and, in turn, downplay your need to take steps to relieve the wear and tear from your work. The physical danger for sworn members is not nearly as pervasive as the danger faced by ongoing exposure to traumatic situations, accompanied by limited control, sedentary work, and an unhealthy (sometimes even toxic) work environment. Don't underestimate your need to take care of yourself, value your contributions, and support others in civilian positions.

POLICE FAMILY MEMBERS

The recommendations in this chapter for building resilience also easily apply to police family members. Your resilience is vital to the resilience of the police employee. You are the first line of defense, so to speak, against the impact of chronic exposure to trauma. This also means that you have to fortify yourself to prevent your own suffering. You're also the mirror for the changes your loved one makes. Change is to be expected. People change throughout their lives as they age, become parents, and face loss. The point is to notice when changes reflect growing cynicism, withdrawal, and irritability. Notice these changes in your loved one and in yourself to take constructive action sooner, rather than later.

TOOLS FOR YOUR DUTY BAG

- Positive emotions, flexible thinking, living with intentionality, guidance by role models, facing your fears with active coping, making use of a varied social support, taking care of your physical, emotional, and cognitive health, and making good use of your strengths all contribute to your resilience.

- Think of support wisely and broadly. Make sure it is varied, not tied to a place, time, or situation, is positive and actually helpful. Negative support is not supportive! Talking things through is only one of many kinds of support.

- Invest in your relationship "banks" before you need to make a withdrawal. These investments also increase your valuation.

- Exercise promotes resilience and doesn't simply require energy, it generates energy.

- Set health goals in positive terms- focusing on what you will eat, what you will do, not what you won't.

- Sleep is vital to resilience. Have good sleep habits, write down worries, don't pass up sleep for family activities, and get help for nightmares, if needed.

- Mindfulness practices help police with stress, sleep, burnout, and pain management.

- Administrators, civilian police employees, and family members, recognize how your resilience matters and also increases the resilience of sworn members.

REFERENCES

Aron, A., Norman, C. C., Aron, E. N., McKenna, C., & Heyman, R. E. (2000). Couple's shared participation in novel and arousing activities and experienced relationship quality. *Journal of Personality and Social Psychology, 78*, 273–284.

Aubrey, A. (2014). *Food-mood connection: How you eat can amp up or tamp down stress.* Retrieved October 6, 2017, from www.npr.org/sections/thesalt/2014/07/14/329529110/food-mood-connection-how-you-eat-can-amp-up-or-tamp-down-stress.

Bandura, A. (1977). Self-efficacy: Toward a unifying theory of behavioral change. *Psychological Review, 84(2)*, 191–215.

Beaudoin, L. P. (2014). *The possibility of super-somnolent mentation: A new information-processing approach to sleep-onset acceleration and insomnia exemplified by serial diverse imagining* (MERP Rep. No. 2013–03, 42 p.). Meta-effectiveness Research Project, Simon Fraser University, Faculty of Education, Burnaby, Canada.

Benight, C. C., & Bandura, A. (2004). Social cognitive theory of posttraumatic recovery: The role of perceived self-efficacy. *Behaviour Research and Therapy, 42*, 1129–1148.

Bonifacio, P. (1991). *The psychological effect of police work.* New York: Plenum Press.

Boulton, M. J., & Smith, P. K. (1992). The social nature of play fighting and play chasing: Mechanisms and strategies underlying cooperation and compromise. In J. H. Barkow, L. Cosmides, & J. Tooby (Eds.), *The adapted mind: Evolutionary psychology and the generation of culture* (pp. 429–444). New York: Oxford University Press.

Charles, L. E., Burchfiel, C. M., Fekedulegn, D., Violanti, J. M., Browne, R. W., McCanlies, E., & Andrew, M. E. (2008). Sleep deprivation and oxidative stress: The Buffalo Cardio-Metabolic Occupational Police Stress (BCOPS) study. *The Open Sleep Journal, 1*, 15–25.

Chouinard, Y. (2016). Let my people go surfing: The education of a reluctant businessman including 10 more years of business unusual. New York: Penguin Books.

Christopher, M. S., Goerling, R. J., Rogers, B. S., Hunsinger, M., Baron, G., Bergman, L., & Zava, D. T. (2016). A pilot study evaluating the effectiveness of a mindfulness-based intervention on cortisol awakening response and health outcomes among law enforcement officers. *Journal of Police and Criminal Psychology, 31(1)*, 15–28.

Collins, J. (Producer). (2014). The Stockdale Paradox. The Brutal Facts. [Audio podcast]. Retrieved October 6, 2016, from www.jimcollins.com/media_topics/brutal-facts.html

Conn, S. M. (2015). *What helps, hinders, and might help police officers to maintain a broad identity.* Doctoral dissertation, University of British Columbia, Vancouver, BC, Canada.

Conn, S. M., & Butterfield, L. D. (2013). Coping with secondary traumatic stress by general duty police officers: practical implications. *Canadian Journal of Counselling and Psychotherapy, 47(2)*, 272–298.

Coombs, A. (2008). A matter of the heart. *Nature Medicine, 14(3)*, 231–233.

Covey, S. R. (2004). The 7 habits of highly effective people: Powerful lessons in personal change. New York: Free Press.

Covey, S. R., Merrill, A. R., & Merrill, R. R. (2003). *First things first.* New York: Free Press.

Duxbury, L., & Higgins, C. (2011). Work–life balance in the new millennium: Where are we? Where do we need to go? Retrieved from www.cprn.org on September 25, 2017.

Ellis, A. (1994). Reason and emotion in psychotherapy. A comprehensive method of treating human disturbances. New York: Citadel Publishing.

Ferrari, P. F., & Rizzolatti, G. (2015). *New frontiers in mirror neurons research.* Oxford Scholarship Online. Retrieved October 12, 2016, from www.oxfordscholarship.com.ezproxy.library.ubc.ca/view/10.1093/acprof:oso/9780199686155.001.0001/acprof-9780199686155.

Fowler, J. H., & Christakis, N. A. (2008). Dynamic spread of happiness in a large social network: Longitudinal analysis over 20 years in the Framingham Heart Study. *British Medical Journal, 337*, 1–9.

Fredrickson, B. L. (1998). What good are positive emotions? *Review of General Psychology, 2*, 300–319.

Fredrickson, B. L. (2009). *Positivity: Top notch research reveals the 3-to-1 ratio that will change your life.* New York: Harmony.

Fredrickson, B. L., Mancuso, R. A., Branigan, C., & Tugade, M. (2000). The undoing effect of positive emotions. *Motivation and Emotion, 24(4)*, 237–258.

Gilmartin, K. M. (2002). *Emotional survival for law enforcement: A guide for officers and their families.* Tucson, AZ: E-S Press.

Goerling, R. (2014). The mindfulness difference: Training ahead can help police recover later. *Royal Canadian Mounted Police Gazette, 76(4)*. Retrieved October 14, 2017, from www.rcmp-grc.gc.ca/en/gazette/mindfulness-difference.

Graham, T. G., & Ramsey, D. (2012). *The happiness diet: A nutritional prescription for a sharp brain, balanced mood, and lean, energized body.* New York: Rodale Books.

Herbert, T. B., & Cohen, S. (1993). Depression and immunity: A meta-analytic review. *Psychological Bulletin, 113,* 472–486.

Kahn, R. L., & Antonucci, T. C. (2014). The convoy model: Explaining social relations from a multidisciplinary perspective. *The Gerontologist, 56(5),* 1–11.

King, L. A., King, D. W., Fairbank, J. A., Keane, T. M., & Adams, G. A. (1998). Resilience-recovery factors in post-traumatic stress disorder among female and male veterans: Hardiness, postwar social support and additional stressful life events. *Journal of Personality and Social Psychology, 74,* 420–434.

Kobasa, S. C. (1979). Stressful life events, personality, and health: An inquiry into hardiness. *Journal of Personality and Social Psychology, 37,* 1–11.

Krakow, B., Hollifield, M., Johnston, L., Koss, M., Schrader, R., Warner, T. D. . . . Prince, H. (2001). Imagery rehearsal therapy for chronic nightmares in sexual assault survivors with posttraumatic stress disorder: A randomized controlled trial. *Journal of the American Medical Association, 286,* 537–545.

Krakow, B., & Zadra, A. (2010). Imagery rehearsal therapy: Principles and practice. *Sleep Medicine Clinics, 5(2),* 289–298.

Lazarus, R. S., & Folkman, S. (1984). *Stress, appraisal, and coping.* New York: Springer Publishing.

Neylan, T. C., Metzler, T. J., Best, S. R., Weiss, D. S., Fagan, J. A., Liberman, A., & Marmar, C. R. (2002). Critical incident exposure and sleep quality in police officers. *Psychosomatic Medicine, 64,* 345–352.

Nielsen Report. (2015). *The total audience report: Q4 2014.* Media and Entertainment. Retrieved November 11, 2016, from http://nielsen.com/us/en/insights/reports/2015/the-total-audience-report-q4-2014.html.

Norris, F. H., Stevens, S. P., Pfefferbaum, K. F., Wyche, K. F., & Pfefferbaum, R. L. (2008). Community resilience as a metaphor, theory, set of capacities, and strategy for disaster readiness. *American Journal of Community Psychology, 41,* 127–150.

Ozbay, F., Johnson, D. C., Dimoulas, E., Morgan, C. A., Charney, D., & Southwick, S. (2007). Social support and resilience to stress: From neurobiology to clinical practice. *Psychiatry, 4(5),* 35–40.

Panksepp, J. (1998). Attention deficit hyperactivity disorders, psycho-stimulants, and intolerance of childhood playfulness: A tragedy in the making? *Current Directions in Psychological Science, 7,* 91–98.

Puetz, T. W., Flowers, S. S., & O'Connor, P. J. (2008). A randomized controlled trial of the effect of aerobic exercise training on feelings of energy and fatigue in sedentary young adults with persistent fatigue. *Journal of Psychotherapy and Psychosomatics, 77(3),* 167–174.

Sacerdote, B. (2001). Peer effects with random assignment: Results for Dartmouth roommates. *Quarterly Journal of Economics, 116(2),* 681–704.

Sandberg, S., & Grant, A. (2017). Option B: Facing adversity, building resilience, and finding joy. New York: Penguin Random House.

Seay, S. D. (2009). *Job related stress and the ability to transition among life roles for police officers.* Unpublished master's thesis, San Jose State University, San Jose, CA (UMI No. 1470987).

Seda, G., Sanchez-Ortuno, M. M., Welsh, C. H., Halbower, A. C., & Edinger, J. D. (2015). Comparative meta-analysis of prazosin and imagery rehearsal therapy for nightmare frequency, sleep quality, and posttraumatic stress. *Journal of Clinical Sleep Medicine, 11(1)*, 11–22.

Segerstrom, T., & Kemeny, M. E., & Fahey. (1998). Optimism is associated with mood, coping, and immune change in response to stress. *Journal of Personality and Social Psychology, 74(6)*, 1646–1655.

Sippel, L. M., Pietrzak, R. H., Charney, D. S., Mayes, L. C., & South, S. M. (2015). How does social support enhance resilience in the trauma-exposed individual? *Ecology and Society, 20(4)*.

Smith, K. P., & Christakis, N. A. (2008). Social networks and health. *Annual Review of Sociology, 34*, 405–418.

Southwick, S. M., & Charney, D. S. (2012). Resilience: The science of mastering life's greatest challenges. New York: Cambridge University Press.

Southwick, S. M., Vythilingam, M., & Charney, D. S. (2005). The psychobiology of depression and resilience to stress: Implications for prevention and treatment. *Annual Review of Clinical Psychology, 1*, 255–291.

Taylor, S. E. (1989). *Positive illusions: Creative self-deception and the healthy mind.* New York: Basic Books.

Taylor, S. E., Kemeny, M. E., Reed, G. M., Bower, J. E., & Gruenwald, T. L. (2000). Psychological resources, positive illusions, and health. *The American Psychologist, 55(1)*, 99–109.

Townsend, D. M., Tew, K. D., & Tapiero, H. (2003). The importance of glutathione in human disease *Biomedicine & Pharmacotherapy, 57*, 145–155.

Vila, B. (2009). Sleep deprivation: What does it mean to public safety officers? *National Institute of Justice Journal, 262*, 26–31 Retrieved September 21, 2017, from www.nij.gov/journals/262/pages/sleep-deprivation.aspx.

Help to be Resilient

> Although the world is full of suffering, it is full also of the overcoming of it. My optimism, then, does not rest on the absence of evil, but on a glad belief in the preponderance of good and a willing effort always to cooperate with the good, that it may prevail.
>
> (Keller, 1903, p. 5)

GETTING PROFESSIONAL HELP

If a doctor told you that you had cancer, what is the first thing you think you would do? Tell family members? Contact an oncologist to outline your treatment regime? Would you let your friends, co-workers, and employer know about your health concerns? Now, let's change the situation. You have depression. You have post-traumatic stress disorder. Now what do you do? Would you do the same as you would if you had received a cancer diagnosis? Or would you deny it? Hide it? Try to resolve it on your own? Unfortunately, for many, the stigma of "mental" illness and the associated perceived sense of weakness prevents individuals from seeking the same levels of social support and treatment as they would with a "physical" illness. The distinction made between "mental" and "physical" illness is misguided. The mind and the body are not separate entities. Brain scans of persons with post-traumatic stress disorder are different than those who do not have the disease. The same is true of other supposedly "mental" illnesses. My hope is that, in time, we will stop using that term as it is proven to be inaccurate.

Historically, police are not good at asking for help. This is especially true when it comes to seeking therapy. Even when police go to therapy, they sometimes have a hard time allowing help to be offered. I have worked with first responders who have continued their rescue behavior in session, trying to put my needs ahead of theirs by hesitating to share their darkest secrets out of fear that they would burden or traumatize me. It's heartbreaking when they cannot accept my support and feel compelled to look after me instead of allowing their needs to be met for once. After all, that's what therapy is about! I have also had officers who, on first meeting, have apologized for wearing their duty weapon to the session even though they were on duty, following up with me about an on-duty shooting. Police should never have to apologize for wearing their gun. It IS part of the uniform and they should not have to worry about alarming a mental health professional. (Whether they are a former police officer or not!)

Being a cop-turned-psychologist gives me a unique vantage point to understand both the policing and the counseling professions. I remember the comments made by my fellow officers about not ever wanting to have to see a shrink, not trusting the department shrink, and not wanting to be psychoanalyzed. Most officers' first (and only) encounter with a shrink is at the psychological assessment in the hiring stage or following a critical police incident. So, it's no wonder where all the "shrink" talk comes from. As a psychologist that has done the psychological assessments in the hiring process, I can say it's a very different role and "climate" than the support role I play when I am doing counseling, debriefings, or training. I remember being nervous about having my own psychological evaluation when I was being hired. You don't get feedback. Typically, you have to answer very personal questions and then watch the psych feverishly writing about your response. It doesn't exactly give you a warm, fuzzy feeling for mental health folks. Fortunately, there's another side to the mental health field, where support is the goal. I have seen the positive impact that counseling can have for those who are struggling. I have seen individuals who were at the brink of suicide transform their struggle into a life filled with purpose and contentment. This is why I do my job.

Some people ask why they should go to counseling if the problem they are having can't be changed by talking about it. Yes, counseling isn't going to make management more understanding. It isn't going to do away with shiftwork. It won't likely reduce workplace bullying incidents. Yet, I still say counseling is worthwhile. It can help you adjust to what you cannot change. It can help you redirect your attention to areas of your life that you can control and that bring you joy. It can help you check your assumptions about a situation. Maybe there's another way to see the situation. Who knows? Maybe there IS something you can do about the situation that once felt impossible.

It's amazing how people can come up with small ways to create change when they are given the time and space to talk through it.

Police officers are problem-solvers by nature or at least by experience. So, it seems unnecessary to ask a third party to help them with a problem. It's oftentimes seen as a sign of weakness or being "less-than" in some way. Counselors aren't there to tell people what to do. That assumes that people are feeble-minded and dependent, which doesn't help anyone feel better. Good counselors help their clients build upon their existing strengths. If you're a good problem solver, you should expect this strength to be used in your work, not ignored.

A common tendency for many individuals, especially police, is to avoid talking about something that is upsetting. I have heard people say that talking about something makes it worse, not better. They believe that they are dwelling on their problems or stuck in the past, which seems like pointless torture. Sure, it feels worse at the time to talk about a painful experience than it is to pretend it doesn't exist. But how long do you think you can avoid a painful issue without consequences? I have received MANY emails from cops who have expressed regret for avoiding their painful experiences. The pain caught up to them eventually and had built up to a degree that was over-whelming. I've said it time and again—running from your problems is a race you will never win. It's best to face your difficulty early with the support of a professional and your social support system to prevent, or at least reduce, the negative impact on your functioning. Some people push their support system away over time by coping in unhelpful ways such as abusing drugs and alcohol, withdrawing socially, and verbally and physically abusing those they care about. It becomes a slippery slope from difficulties to despair. Whatever challenges you face, you never have to face them alone.

I've heard horror stories of voyeuristic therapists who wanted more details of the event out of their own curiosity and I've even heard of one who literally fled the room in tears once she heard the details. I don't think this happens very often (I certainly hope not) but it's not a good scenario and contributes to the hesitancy police already have about talking to mental health professionals, as neither reaction is very "professional." Therefore, it's important to choose a culturally competent mental health professional. Looking for help can be overwhelming since there are a lot of options and you want to pick someone you are comfortable with and who is trained to work with your concerns. Do you choose a psychologist, psychiatrist, counselor, or social worker? Someone who works for the department or someone in the community not connected to the organization? It can be con-fusing so I will offer some information to help you make the choice that is best for you and your situation.

First, I'll draw some distinctions between different mental health professionals. Depending on the location, most psychologists have a PhD in counseling or clinical psychology. Both offer talk therapy but a counseling psychologist tends to have more practice with counseling while a clinical one has more training in performing assessments, oftentimes working with more severely disturbed patients in clinical settings such as a hospital or outpatient treatment center. In a couple of states, psychologists can prescribe medication, but most recommend that individuals obtain needed medication from their primary doctor and consult with the doctor to make sure everyone is on the same page with regard to treatment. A psychiatrist is a medical doctor who has had additional training in mental health and can prescribe medication. Some do talk therapy but some don't. Many work in hospital settings with severely mentally ill individuals. A counselor typically has a master's degree in psychology. Although counselors have less formal education, it's important to look at years of practice and additional training. I'd rather see a counselor with some experience under her belt than a brand-new psychologist who lacks life experience. As you may have guessed, social workers have either a master's or doctorate degree in social work. The difference between social work and psychology varies, depending on the person's approach. Social workers tend to look at the bigger picture to determine the need for referrals for community services or programs. Psychologists and counselors focus more on the person's adaptability to his or her circumstances. Working with psychologists and counselors likely involves more talk therapy and treatment than social workers' referrals to community resources. Admittedly, these descriptions are broad overviews and can vary widely from person to person and state to state.

Now that we've cleared up who's who in the mental health world, where do you start looking for these individuals? Sometimes the information may be available at your agency. Three potential sources are your human resources department, extended health care plan provider, or a peer support team (PST) member. The human resources department likely has a list of culturally competent counselors. Usually, PST members make it a point to have this information as well. I've had officers tell me that they didn't want to go through their PST to get connected to help because they worried about confidentiality. They wondered if the co-worker would talk to others or, one day, be their supervisor, which could be a problem if they wanted to promote or go to a specialty assignment. These may be valid concerns, depending on the professionalism of the PST member(s). PST members who abide by PST policy would maintain your confidentiality unless some very specific criteria were met (if you were suicidal, homicidal, committing a crime, etc.). If your confidentiality concerns you, there are means to finding support outside of the department.

Each state has a registration/licensing body for counselors and psychologists. A simple search on the internet using terms such as police, your city name, and counseling can direct you to a professional in your area. Look for professionals who advertise that they specialize in trauma, first responders, and/or military personnel. Review their website, looking at the specialized training they have had as well as what training they offer to first responder organizations. Many mental health professionals will list or even include their research and publications. Reading these should give you a sense of what the person's expertise and interests are. A simple Google search may reveal other news, interviews, and professional activities of the individual. It probably seems silly to suggest this to police. I suspect you'll be doing your homework on the person you plan to trust with your personal business. Folks have told me of doing their research on me. Some mental health professionals will offer phone or in-person consultations for free. In this way, you can get a feel for how it would be to work with them by asking them questions about their approach and experience. Another option for finding a culturally competent mental health professional is contacting a non-profit first responder organizations such as Badge of Life, First Responder Support Network (FRSN), or Safe Call Now. These organizations collect information about police resources, including culturally competent counselors.

NATURE THERAPY—TAKE A HIKE AND TALK IT OUT!

We spend a lot of time sitting. Unless you're on patrol, you may even spend a large part of this time sitting in an office. Sitting is the new smoking. It's not good for you, but everyone seems to be doing it anyway. In the last few years, mental health research has demonstrated the benefits of exercise on mental health issues such as depression, anxiety, and self-esteem (Deslandes, 2014).

The benefit of nature is a hot research topic, as people are spending more time indoors than ever before. Recent research has supported that exercise performed in nature, such as biking, walking, hiking, or running, provides additional benefits such as reductions in stress, improvements in mood and self-esteem (Barton & Pretty, 2010; Maier & Jette, 2016). In fact, Richard Louv coined the term *nature deficit disorder* to refer to the disconnection that people, particularly children, have with the natural world (Louv, 2008). Louv cited the research linking childhood obesity and difficulty with focus to a sedentary, indoor life filled with television and video games. Louv contends that this is not just a problem with children, but includes adults who live in a "wired" world. In our plugged-in world, filled with rings, dings, and tweets, we're more scatter-brained than ever. Research shows that time spent in natural settings also helps to restore our focus (Berman,

Sitting is the new smoking

Chapter 6
Help to be Resilient

Jonides, & Kaplan, 2008; Faber Taylor, Kuo, & Sullivan, 2001). This, of course, means that you're not taking your phone into the woods. Louv offered the following story that captures the calming power of nature:

> A few years ago, I ran across a particularly intriguing photograph on the back page of a magazine. The photo showed a small boy at the ocean's edge. Beyond him you could see a gray sky, a distant island, and a long, even wave approaching. The boy had turned to face the photographer. His eyes were wide with wonder and there was a touch of impishness. His mouth was open in an exclamation of discovery and joy.
>
> Next to the black-and-white image was a short article about the boy, who, it seemed, had a problem. He was hyperactive and found it difficult to pay attention in school. He was disruptive in the classroom and had been expelled. At first, his parents did not know what to do.
>
> And what became of that little boy on the beach, expelled because of his classroom hyperactivity? Fortunately, his parents had already noticed how nature calmed their son and helped him focus. Over the next decade, they seized every opportunity to introduce him to the natural world—to beaches, forests, dunes, the rivers and mountains of the American West.
>
> The photograph was taken in 1907. The little boy turned out fine. His name was Ansel Adams.
>
> (p. 103)

Therapists have been recommending exercise and nature to their clients for years. More recently, exercise and nature have been incorporated into therapy sessions. They are literally practicing what they are preaching WITH their clients instead of TO their clients. If you have been hesitant to try therapy, I'd urge you to give this kind of therapy a try. A simple internet search could help you locate a "green" clinician or group in your area. This practice goes by all kinds of names—nature therapy, green therapy, walk and talk therapy, eco-psychology, to name a few.

TRAUMA TREATMENTS

It's beyond the scope of this book to offer in-depth discussions of trauma treatments available to police employees. I'm introducing a few of them to give you an idea of what is available and what, generally speaking, each of them entails. There are various options, with pretty comparable results, including Eye Movement Desensitization and Reprocessing (EMDR), cognitive behavioral therapy (CBT), prolonged exposure therapy (PE), and neurofeedback.

Eye Movement Desensitization and Reprocessing

EMDR is a treatment for trauma that has been increasingly demonstrated to be helpful for first responders and members of the military. EMDR stands for Eye Movement Desensitization and Reprocessing, which is a mouthful, to say the least. I won't bore you with all the psychobabble behind it, but hope to offer you a useful description of something that might help you or your co-workers one day. I believe that this treatment can significantly reduce the disturbance first responders experience following traumatic events. EMDR is beneficial shortly after the event or even decades later.

EMDR was created by Francine Shapiro in 1987. Its use has increased drastically in the last decade, largely due to the widespread success of its application to military members exposed to traumatic events while at war. It's been found to reduce post-traumatic stress symptoms in first responders, accident and assault victims, as well victims of many other traumatic incidents. To explain how it's believed to work, it would be a good idea to review how the memories of traumatic incidents are stored in the brain. Again, I'll keep the psychobabble to a minimum.

As discussed in Chapter 2, when facing a traumatic event, the information-processing part of the brain, the cortex, is hijacked by the emotion-processing and storing part of the brain, the amygdala. This hijacking interrupts the brain's ability to properly store the event in memory. Instead, the memory is stored as an emotional memory in bits and pieces—a smell, a face, a flash of the scene, etc. Since the story is fragmented, the brain doesn't realize the story has ended and keeps sending the person reminders because it thinks the threat is ongoing. This is the reason you might have flashbacks, nightmares, and other forms of re-experiencing the traumatic event. The brain thinks it's doing you a favor by continually bringing these fragments back to your attention to be dealt with.

EMDR is believed to help the brain put these fragments together. The eye movements, which I won't describe here because they should be facilitated by an EMDR-trained clinician, are believed to stimulate both sides of the brain while you are thinking about the most significant fragment of the trauma and your interpretation of it. Sometimes, clinicians "tap" on opposite sides of the body such as your right and left hand (or right and left knee) instead of using "eye movements" to stimulate both sides of the brain. The image, your thoughts, your emotional reactions, and any physical sensations are all "pulled together" to integrate the event into a whole. You are then able to properly store the whole memory in your brain, adjust your skewed interpretation of it, and, consequently, become desensitized to it. This lowers your disturbance level, sometimes to the degree that it is not disturbing at all. The reprocessing aspect allows you to use the information-processing part of your brain, the cortex, which was hijacked at the time of the event. In this way, you have shifted your understanding of the event, which might include resolving unfair self-judgments that tend to exacerbate traumatic reactions.

An example might make this abstract concept easier to understand. Sometimes officers respond to calls where they're forced to use lethal force against another person. The officer is thrust into a fight, flight, freeze kind of situation and the fight response is instinctively activated. It might happen so fast and be so shocking that the memory does not get stored properly. The officer re-experiences the event with intrusive images, thoughts, and dreams. The officer watches the news, where the person that was shot is being portrayed as "just a teenager with a future cut short." The officer, who has a disintegrated story in her mind, comes to believe "I made a bad choice" or "I'm not cut out for this work" or many variations of these distorted thoughts. Objectively, this belief about herself is not true. She likely instinctively made the best choice from a group of undesirable options. She could shoot or be shot, or let another person be shot. Since EMDR is helping her to integrate the story, filling in the gaps, and weaving a coherent storyline, she can come to this realization. Shooting that person was not a negative reflection of her but, rather, an unfortunate part of her job. She could then recognize that she did the best she could, given her options. If her negative belief about herself was that she wasn't cut out for the work, similarly, she could come to the realization that, again, she performed her job and that being bothered by taking another life actually means that she's not a sociopath. Feeling bad about taking a life does not equate to wrongdoing. In this example, one has nothing to do with the other. The reprocessing component of EMDR helps individuals *feel* this way, not just intellectually understand it.

This process won't make you forget your trauma nor will it make you indifferent to a loss. You may still be sad about a loss, but that would be appropriate. What EMDR does is give you relief from environmental triggers, extreme emotional distress, and inappropriate guilt that might be stemming from the event. EMDR works whether the traumatic event was last week or 25 years ago. I've worked with clients whose traumas were more than 20 years old and they were astonished at how different they felt about the event after just one EMDR session. EMDR is also useful for events besides the large, discrete traumas police officers face on the job. The rising disturbance from accumulations of smaller, ongoing, events can also be alleviated by EMDR. As strange as it sounds, some people experience PTSD symptoms but can't really point to an exact event as the source. That's okay. You don't have to point to a date as a starting point for working through the clutter of fragmented disturbances. There's a way through that where we can begin with the symptoms and track back to the sources, one by one.

You might be thinking that EMDR sounds too good to be true. I get it. I thought the same thing but I have read the research and, more importantly, I have seen how well it works with my own eyes. It's worked remarkably well with clients for a variety of traumatic events. I have even had it myself. Attempts to discredit it only serve to offer more support because it worked too well to not be considered effective. Theories of it being a placebo effect have also been tested and ruled out. Its effects are usually permanent since the memory is believed to be integrated.

If you or someone you know is struggling with a distressing event, I would urge you to read more about EMDR and find an EMDR-trained counselor. You can find a counselor that uses EMDR by checking the EMDR Institute Inc. website: www.emdr.com or the EMDR International Association website: www.emdria.org. I want to emphasize that this is not something that a counselor is doing *to* you. This is something your brain wants to do anyway (hence all the reminders it keeps giving you of the event) and it simply needs some facilitation to complete the process. One session won't do it all but it will make an appreciable difference, motivating you to continue until you can put the event(s) behind you.

Cognitive Behavioral Therapy

CBT involves working with (you guessed it) your thoughts and behaviors. CBT addresses problematic thinking such as self-blame for a traumatic event, unchecked assumptions about yourself, others, or the world, a tendency to discount the positive, and so forth. CBT also addresses the behavioral problems that tend to occur with depression, anxiety, and PTSD such as withdrawal from people, places, and situations, or problematic interpersonal behaviors such as passive or aggressive communication styles. There's a large psychoeducation component, where you will learn about trauma, how it's reinforced by avoidance, and how other ways of thinking and behaving either contribute to or takeaway from healthy functioning. You might think it's common sense but I assure you it isn't. Nobody teaches you this stuff in school, unless you have a counseling psych degree, and very little is provided in the academy.

Prolonged Exposure Therapy

PE is a form of CBT that works to eliminate avoidance as a coping mechanism, since avoidance only worsens PTSD symptoms. PE is a four-step process: 1) psychoeducation about trauma, the trauma response, and PTSD; 2) breathing retraining; 3) in vivo exposure to the situation that is feared but avoided (is now safe); and 4) imaginal exposure to the traumatic event by repeatedly recounting the memory of it (Foa & Rothbaum, 1998). PE begins by normalizing and explaining why you are having your response to trauma. It then helps you manage the anxiety that comes with the traumatic event through breathing exercises. Once you've managed this, you will create a list of situations you have avoided since the trauma and, one by one, with the support of the clinician, you will expose yourself to these situations. This means that you might visit a scene you have avoided, go into a crowd, if you've been avoiding them, and so forth. While in these stressful situations, you'll be practicing the aforementioned breathing exercises so that you are not overwhelmed. This is no picnic but it's incredibly helpful in reducing your anxiety and avoidance. In a later session, you will close your eyes and imagine the event, recounting aloud what is happening. You will repeat this until the "charge" is gone or at least much lower. It doesn't stop there. You will need to do your own exposures (actual and imaginal) outside of session. Just like going to the gym, you can't expect to get lasting results if you put in the time while there and do nothing else the rest of the time.

Neurofeedback

As the name implies, neurofeedback means getting information (feedback) about your brain processes (neuro) so that you can better manage what it's doing. Recent research has demonstrated that neurofeedback is effective in significantly reducing PTSD symptoms in individuals with chronic, treatment-resistant PTSD (Gapen, van der Kolk, Hamlin, Hirschberg, Suvak, & Spinazzola, 2016). Neurofeedback is a non-invasive treatment that teaches the brain to turn off the stress response. Clinicians use an electroencephalogram to detect electrical activity in your brain by attaching electrodes to your scalp. The results are visible on a computer screen. You're able to monitor this activity, receiving visual and auditory feedback, to condition your brain to achieve and maintain calm states. During neurofeedback, you wear headphones, listening to music while watching a screen with moving colorful patterns. When brain wave activities become too intense, you receive feedback through static in the headphones and hesitations in the pattern movement. Through this brain-training, the brain will autocorrect the intensified activity. This results in individuals learning how to achieve these calm states outside of treatment.

GROUP THERAPY

Group therapy can offer benefits not achieved in individual work. For one, being in a group of people who have shared life experiences can be an excellent source of validation and understanding for what you're struggling with. There's unique wisdom that can come from others in your shoes who have found something that has worked for them. Similarly, being in a group can reduce feelings of isolation and the misguided idea that you are uniquely flawed for struggling with your condition. Others in the group can also help you be honest with yourself. I've done some work with peer-driven groups who have implemented a "no bullshit" rule, where you don't get to deny what you're feeling and thinking. This might sound like a bad thing but it's for the best. Well-meaning friends may not give you the cold, hard truth when you need it the most. That might save you some discomfort at the time but will, ultimately, be a disservice to you. I've also done some trauma decompressions, a short-term form of group therapy borrowed from the military, to help individuals work through workplace traumas. I observed, first-hand, the power of having your story witnessed by supportive others. I shared my own story in the first decompression I did and I felt "held" by the support of the group. That's not an everyday experience.

There are several groups available. Some are specific to police, some to first responders, and others are centered around a mental health condition (mood, stress management, PTSD, etc.). Some are time-limited, like a 3-day trauma retreat (an oxymoron, if I've ever heard one) or trauma decompression, a 10-week stress management group, while others are ongoing. Those that are ongoing are typically on a "drop-in" basis. Some require referral or screening to be included, depending on the kind of group it is.

One group that I have been lucky enough to be included in is the West Coast Post-Trauma Retreat (WCPR) for first responders. WCPR is a program of the FRSN. It originated in San Francisco and includes information about trauma reactions, group discussions of first responders' traumas, EMDR treatment by clinicians specializing in first responders (many of which are former/current first responders), and peer-driven support throughout the entire process. This peer-driven support begins before the retreat and continues even after the 6-day retreat concludes. Needed referrals for ongoing support are offered so that first responders do not fall through the cracks of support when they leave. The best part of this program is the inclusion of first responders as peers. These peers are able to share wisdom they have gained in their struggles. They get to give back to others what was previously given to them. Another great thing about this program is the absence of egos and psycho-babble in the people putting this program on. Clinicians and peers are

VOLUNTEERING their time because they are passionate about their mission to support first responders. They're not doing it for the money, the glory, or to stroke their own ego. The folks included in this program are vetted to make sure that those people would be screened out. To find out more about this program or how you might create one of these in your area, read about it at www.frsn.org/retreats/wcpr.

FAMILY THERAPY

Family members also benefit from support from others. In fact, they are usually an afterthought. Therapy with the police member, spouse, and children with a mental health professional might help the system to deal with the demands of police work. Unfortunately, problems can become so entrenched that it takes a third party to intervene. It's hard to see the frame when you're in the picture. A mental health professional can help you see what you're too close to see. My job, as I see it, is to be a mirror to the people I work with. If I see a family member make a face, turn away, or use a "voice" to speak of another family member, it's my responsibility to reflect that observation. They may or may not even realize they're doing it, but the effect is likely the same. Family therapy can also help bring forth the input of quieter family members. Strengthening families with family therapy makes good sense because they all have to bear the load of police work. "If architects want to strengthen a decrepit arch, they increase the load which is laid upon it, for thereby the parts are joined more firmly together" (Viktor Frankl, 2006, p. 105). The same could be said of resilient relationships.

EQUINE THERAPY

> If architects want to strengthen a decrepit arch, they increase the load which is laid upon it, for thereby the parts are joined more firmly together (Viktor Frankl, 2006, p. 105). The same could be said of resilient relationships.

Yes, you read that correctly. Working with horses can be very helpful for PTSD and other mental health issues. Horses react to body language, as they are regarded as a "flight" animal. Walk along with one and you will learn how you're coming across to others. In Equine-Assisted Learning programs, the horse's honest, and immediate response to your subtle body language is translated so that you become more self-aware. You learn how to recognize your anxiety and are given tools to work through it. One program in Alberta, Canada, Can Praxis (http://canpraxis.com) assists military and first responder couples with managing their conflict more effectively. Chiron Center, in southern Oregon, also offers an equine therapy program, Still Standing, for first responders (www.chironcenter.org/still-standing—-chirons-equine-programs.html), building confidence, self-awareness, and communication skills. Beyond the benefits of walking alongside these majestic creatures, you will be in nature. It's a win–win situation.

MEDICAL MARIJUANA

I've been asked my opinion about the use of medical marijuana for PTSD. It might seem strange that a police officer would want to use a substance that they are oftentimes arresting others for using but, when people are struggling, they will try anything they think will help with their condition. Views of marijuana have been changing as well, with it legalized in several states. Therefore, I will briefly discuss the research on this treatment option.

A review of studies from 1980 to 2015 found that the evidence that medical marijuana improves PTSD is very poor (Wilkinson, Radhakrishnan, & D'Souza, 2016). Yet, there is strong evidence for the consequences of chronic cannabinoid exposure such as tolerance, dependence, withdrawal, psychosis, and impairments of attention, memory, IQ, and driving ability (Wilkinson et al., 2016). In short, the evidence for its benefit over its cost just isn't there to recommend it as a treatment for PTSD. There are so many other options that don't have the complications that medicinal marijuana does.

SUPPORT FOR SUBSTANCE ABUSE

Substance use and abuse in the policing profession is a hushed topic. Yet, in 2010, 11 percent of males and 16 percent of female police officers endorsed alcohol use behaviors that were considered "at-risk" by the National Institute on Alcohol Abuse and Alcoholism (Ballenger et al., 2010). For this reason, it's important to talk about what resources are available for this issue. Employee assistance programs (EAPs) offer confidential substance abuse treatment programs, and those attached to police agencies will have training and experience to work with the unique stressors of police work. Police can also receive anonymous support from groups such as Alcoholics Anonymous. Since it's anonymous, you don't have to disclose what you do for a living and you don't have to worry about anyone contacting the department. Clearly, this might not be doable in a small community, where you may be recognized by others. In this instance, an online version of this program might be a better option (www.onlinegroupaa.org). For other substances, Narcotics Anonymous can help. You may have a bias that you will be among the lower rungs of society, with whom you can't relate. Substance abuse isn't restricted to a class of people; to criminals and misfits. Like other mental health issues, substance abuse occurs across all kinds of people for all kinds of reasons.

As an administrator, responsible for the resilience of those under your command, it's important that you consider your part in developing their resilience *before* it's sorely needed. I'll illustrate this point using the Parable of the Waterfall:

Imagine a large river with a high waterfall. At the bottom of this waterfall hundreds of people are working frantically trying to save those who have fallen into the river and have fallen down the waterfall, many of them drowning. As the people along the shore are trying to rescue as many as possible one individual looks up and sees a seemingly never-ending stream of people falling down the waterfall and begins to run upstream. One of other rescuers hollers, "Where are you going? There are so many people that need help here." To which the man replied, "I'm going upstream to find out why so many people are falling into the river.

(Shelden & Macallair, 2008)

A police agency shouldn't wait until multiple officers have crashed at the bottom to take measures toward promoting their mental health. It's hard to get funding for preventative programs because it's hard to measure what you are preventing. Organizations struggle to get funding for programs that don't show measurable improvements. Yet, they can measure the costs of doing nothing. Police agencies can pay through the nose in lost wages for officers who are disabled by a mental health condition. There are three primary initiatives that police agencies have to prevent mental health injuries in police work: critical incident stress management (CISM) teams, psychological first aid (PFA), and PST.

CISM Teams

When people think of CISM teams, they immediately think of debriefings. Yet, the team is much more than simply the debriefing event. They are designed to assist in managing the stress of the event from beginning to end. This means responding to the scene, meeting with affected employees and accompanying them, as needed, during the initial and ongoing investigation. They are there to normalize, educate, support, and prepare individuals for the aftermath of the critical event. They liaise between affected individuals and department or community resources. I was a member of the CISM team and enjoyed my work. I was in a hybrid team, where we were also the peer support that didn't need to be activated by a critical event. I suspect that there are many CISM team members who do the same in their department, even just informally. The International Association of Chiefs of Police (IACP) offers a model policy for CISM practices on their website (www.theiacp.org).

Critical Incident Stress Debriefings

There is a strong debate about the helpfulness of critical incident stress debriefings (CISD). Do they help officers deal with the traumas they are exposed to? Do they make matters worse by re-exposing them to the trauma, including being exposed to the traumatic information from their fellow officers' perspectives? There is research that supports each position: CISD is helpful, is harmful, and makes no difference at all. So, what are we to believe?

Research supports that debriefings facilitate social support with co-workers, normalize traumatic responses with the psycho-educational component, teach officers to manage symptoms that arise, and are well-liked by most officers who participate in them. The criticism of CISD is directed at the increase of vicarious traumatization from being exposed to the stories of others. For some, it seems more like a hindrance to their moving forward because it is more troubling to be forced to talk about and listen to what others experienced. To be confident that you are doing no harm, it might be wise to focus debriefings on aspects that have been consistently demonstrated to be helpful. For instance, research suggests emphasizing the psycho-educational and supportive components while foregoing the discussion of the details of the traumatic event (Regehr, 2001).

John Violanti, a former police officer and expert on mental health issues affecting police, makes a distinction between interventions that are pathogenic and those that are salutogenic. Pathogenic refers to interventions that script police officers into traumatic symptoms because it presupposes a sick role (Violanti, 2001). It says to the officer "You're going to get PTSD if you don't let us help you using these steps" and encourages the officer to take a helpless, passive sick role that requires outside intervention. Nobody in CISM intends or desires to convey this message. CISM members hope to help fellow officers deal with their exposure to trauma, not make them feel they are broken unless they are "fixed" with a debriefing.

On the other hand, salutogenic interventions offered by CISM teams convey a more positive message to officers. This approach recognizes that the vast majority of police officers do not develop PTSD, despite continuous exposure to trauma. Police officers are, on the whole, naturally resilient and capable of being active in their own healing from trauma with the support of family, friends, and professionals. Salutogenic interventions assume officers' potential for growth and healing. As opposed to the pathogenic script, the salutogenic script would be "I can get through this because I have been trained to handle adversity and I have been doing it" or some variation of this. I am not proposing that one repeats this script if it doesn't fit the current situation but, rather, to recognize the individual's strengths and not merely focus on the challenges. If the officer is experiencing trauma symptoms, then these should be acknowledged and the officer should be offered support that normalizes his or her response along with a referral for professional help.

So, how does one offer assistance that embraces the natural resilience of officers and does not write a pathogenic script? It's a matter of how the interventions are executed. Flexibility is favored over rigid adherence to a set of procedures. Optional attendance at debriefings is one recommended way of being flexible. Admittedly, making a debriefing may eliminate the stigma associated with attending because you have to go. Being able to choose to go or not adds an element of pressure for some due to outward appearances. However, the problem with mandatory debriefings is the presumption of the passive sick role of the officers. This is to be avoided, if possible. An additional problem with mandating attendance at debriefings is that it may be perceived as someone merely "checking a box" that they have offered a service without a genuine motive to be helpful. This was the feedback I received in a study of what hindered officers' coping with traumatic stress. The timing of the debriefing can also be problematic, as it might conflict with time off and/or a sleep schedule. Being flexible with the days and times that the debriefing is offered is another way to promote a salutogenic outcome. Offering the debriefing in a flexible manner that respects the desires of the officers to participate and considers their work–sleep schedules demonstrates to officers that the department supports their well-being. If an officer desires to participate, but is not able to make it due to schedule constraints, it's best to follow up with the officer individually. When they fall through the cracks, it undermines the credibility of the CISM program.

Psychological First Aid

PFA can be an alternative or a complement to debriefings. According to the World Health Organization and the National Institute of Mental Health, PFA has demonstrated improvements in the psychological health of both emergency service workers and the general public (National Institute of Mental Health, 2002; World Health Organization, 2011). PFA is an eight-part, strengths-based, modular approach offered in the immediate aftermath of the disaster event. It has been applied by the Red Cross and the World Health Organization for years during disaster and mass casualty events. A Psychological First Aid Field Operations Guide was developed by the National Child Traumatic Stress Network and the National Center for PTSD and is available online at www.ncptsd.va.gov. PFA is designed to reduce your initial distress in the field, foster short- and long-term functioning and coping by increasing your access to care. Unlike debriefings, which occur days later, or defusings, which oftentimes occur off-site, PFA comes to you. There's no delay. Your basic needs are assessed and efforts are made to meet them when and where you need them. One other very significant distinction between PFA and a debriefing is that, with PFA, there is no venting of reactions. In this way, it side-steps one of the criticisms wielded against debriefings (justified or not) that it can cause further traumatization. PFA can take place anywhere: on the scene, at a staging or respite center, Emergency Operation Center, first aid station, emergency room at the hospital, or a family reception or assistance center. It's five guiding principles include promoting a sense of safety, is calming, a sense of self and community efficacy, connectedness, and hope (Hobfoll et al., 2007). PFA is made up of four phases, two of which precede the incident, and the other two follow the incident. The phases are outlined in Table 6.1.

As you can see, as much effort goes into program development as does implementation. It also does a good job of assessing its outcomes and training needs for quality delivery. Within Phase 3, exists the eight core actions of PFA as illustrated in Table 6.2.

TABLE 6.1
Four Phases of Psychological First Aid

Phase 1:
Policies relating to implementation of PFA during an event
Promotion of "buy in."

Phase 2:
Pre-crisis steps include interpersonal and intrapersonal support
Organizational practices that promote connection to others
Training for stress management, disaster drills, work skills training, etc.

Phase 3:
Implementation of PFA following an incident.

Phase 4: Follow-Up (monitoring)
Assessing if additional training, support, or policy modifications needed by monitoring outcomes and soliciting feedback.

TABLE 6.2
Eight Core Actions of Psychological First Aid

1. Contact and Engagement

2. Safety and Comfort

3. Stabilization (if needed)

4. Information Gathering: Needs and Current Concerns

5. Practical Assistance

6. Connection with Social Supports

7. Information on Coping

8. Linkage with Collaborative Services

These core actions are not to be considered a linear, mutually exclusive process. There may be some core actions that are not needed at all, depending on the circumstances. A smartphone application, developed by the National Child Traumatic Stress Network and the National Center for PTSD, allows responding support persons to access the information contained in these core actions, record their activity, provides logs and worksheets, lists "do's and don'ts" for working with people, and tips for provider self-care.

PFA can also be used in a group setting, where it mirrors much of the debriefing protocol, save the thoughts and reactions phases (Everly, Phillips, Kane, & Feldman, 2006). Group PFA includes pre-group activities, six stages of implementation, and post-group activities. Pre-group activities include making sure the group is homogeneous (similar exposures—not mixing people who came much later or had a very different task on the scene), making sure that no one in the group is too psychologically fragile to gain from participating, making sure there are no large conflicts between members in the group, and making sure there are no medical issues that need to be resolved first. The six stages of group-administered PFA shown in Table 6.3 are very similar to group debriefings as listed in Table 6.2.

Following group PFA, Everly and colleagues (2006) recommend five post-group activities: 1) making sure the group is aware of the facilitators' ongoing availability, 2) a debriefing among the facilitators, 3) facilitators recognizing and talking about their own reactions to the trauma and the contents of the group PFA, 4) facilitator self-care, as they oftentimes are so other-directed that this gets missed, and 5) formally or informally evaluating the effectiveness of the group PFA. The benefit of group PFA includes: "learning about self from other

---

TABLE 6.3
Six Stages of Group Psychological First Aid

1. Introduction

a. To group members and leaders

b. Purpose of group

c. Expected duration of group

d. Ground rules

2. Overview/Presentation of Event Details

3. Correction/Clarification of Details

4. Psychoeducation regarding responses

5. Facilitate Group Support

6. Facilitate "Other" Support (family, pastor, therapist, etc.)

group members, catharsis, increased sense of belonging (group cohesion), universality (learning that one's reactions were shared by others), and guidance regarding constructive behavior" (Everly et al., p. 132).

Peer Support Teams

PST may or may not be a part of the CISM team. In my department, we were both. These roles call for different but overlapping skill sets. Peer support members are there to provide guidance and support to fellow officers, non-sworn police employees, and, hopefully, family members and retired officers during any kind of distressing situation. It's the everyday stressors like marital problems, parenting, health issues, substance use or abuse, and work–life balance that erode the resilience of police employees. One shouldn't have to have a critical incident before getting support from the department. In my mind, peer support can prevent issues from rising to critical levels.

Ideally, a peer support member would have life experience to draw from to complement their training. I wouldn't want someone helping me through my difficulties that was simply repeating a script given in a training manual. There's something to be said for the wisdom that comes with experience. This is not to say that peer members need to have experienced every difficulty to get it. That's not even possible (nor advisable). But it's hard to take counsel about parenting difficulties seriously from a person without kids. It's a good idea to have peer members in various assignments in the department to increase the likelihood that they will be able to serve various sworn/non-sworn employees, both in terms of access and relatability. It's also important that ranks also vary within the team, as you wouldn't want a line officer to only have a supervisor to speak with. Although it might not be the officer's supervisor at the time, there's always a chance that the peer member could be a supervisor in the future. You can't always avoid this, but having other support options can lessen this likelihood.

The International Association of Chiefs of Police (2016) has recommendations for forming and operating a PST. Confidentiality is a very important detail in operating a PST. I'd say it is foundational, in that nobody is going to talk about their private matters unless they have assurance that their business isn't going to be shared with others, especially their employer. Confidentiality needs to be written into the peer support manual and limits to confidentiality should be openly shared with officers upon contact, BEFORE any compromising information is shared. That was always my practice as a peer support member and remains so as a mental health professional. A peer support program won't be utilized if police employees don't have faith in its ability to offer competent, confidential support.

Family Members

Family members of police employees are routinely out of sight, out of mind when it comes to organizational support efforts. Yet, weakened family systems mean weakened police employee resilience. It's wise for departments to offer support services to police families. Departments usually offer a family night in the academy, where police families learn how officers are trained, to allay their worries about their safety. Occasionally, they get some training on recognizing symptoms of traumatic reactions and maintaining a family life around shiftwork. After this, unless there is a critical event, the family is usually on its own to figure out the rest. Including family members on the PST allows them to serve other family members during times of need. They also offer police peer members valuable insights into the unique challenges of police families. Family peer members who are trained in stress management, effective communications, traumatic stress, and substance use/abuse can offer family members education and guidance in addressing issues their officers/employees are facing.

Retirees

I've already outlined the benefits of having retirees as a part of the PST to serve other retirees or those nearing retirement. I would add that they likely have much to offer to police employees at any point in their career, so long as they stay current in their understanding of agency policies and practices. They would also do well to understand generational differences in attitudes about work and family. In this way, they can be a relevant resource.

It's beyond the scope of this book to offer guidance on setting up or operating PST. The IACP offers guidelines and police psychologist, Jack Digliani, offers a guidebook, training, and support on establishing and maintaining support teams (www.jackdigliani.com). If you don't already have a team, you don't have to reinvent the wheel in setting one up. Other departments likely have policies and training that can be borrowed and adapted to meet your department's needs.

Chaplaincy Program

Another resource departments offer is the Chaplaincy Program. Chaplains offer support to sworn and non-sworn members, as well as members of the public. Support may or may not be "spiritual." In speaking with chaplains over the years, I've found them to be an excellent resource, regardless of your religion or faith. They usually have training in stress management, traumatic stress, relationship difficulties, and much more. Beyond their training, they tend to have a "servant's heart" in that their main focus is the wellbeing of others. Ideally, they also practice with religious plurality, meaning that they accept all forms of religion. They seek to understand and help by seeing things through the lens of your faith. They're there to be a supportive presence.

> Chaplaincy differs from being a pastor in that it is primarily a ministry of presence. Our role as a chaplain is to serve, not preach. We are a witness to our faith by our doing, caring and loving. When an officer asks why we do what we do, then the door is open to share our faith.
> (International Conference of Police Chaplains, 2017)

If you've hesitated to engage with your department's chaplain, I would urge you to suspend your judgment and get to know him/her. In this way, they're a familiar face, a trusted source of support, that you can lean on when needed in the future.

RESOURCES FOR POLICE FAMILIES

There are some great resources for family members of police officers. There may not be many but the ones that exist come from credible sources. One such resource is Jack Digliani's *Law Enforcement Marriage and Relationship Guidebook. Information for Law Enforcement Officers and Spouses* (2015). In this guidebook (www.jackdigliani.com) Digliani extends his sound advice on living a *life by design* instead of a *life by default* in the relationship. Again, intentionality is required for a resilient relationship. Ellen Kirschman (www.ellenkirschman.com) also offers credible, sound counsel for police families. Dr Kirschman has been a credible (and incredible!) supporter of police and their families for decades.

> We think our job as humans is to avoid pain, our job as parents is to protect our children from pain, and our job as friends is to fix each other's pain. Maybe that's why we all feel like failures so often—because we all have the wrong job description for love.
> Glennon Doyle Melton, Love Warrior

Helping children of police employees to be resilient means helping them understand what their parents do as police officers. This is important but oftentimes overlooked. When I do individual debriefings with a significant other present, they are usually surprised when I suggest they talk to their children about what happened. There's a tendency to think that the kids are too young to know, understand, or be affected. I recommend police officers and their loved ones talk with little ones about the work because they will otherwise form their own opinions of it based upon what they hear from others or see on television. These are hardly reliable sources of information! One resource that might be helpful is the book *My Dad's a Hero . . . My Dad's a Cop* (Aumiller & Goldfarb, 2013). The book includes a guide for how parents can use the book to talk with children about their work. The book outlines both what police officers do on any given day and talks about the psychological aspects of the work in a manner that is appropriate for children.

FINAL THOUGHTS

I hope that you have found strategies that you can use to have a healthy life in policing. More than that, I hope that you believe in your ability to be resilient; to take small actions that, little by little, will move you and those you care about toward the kind of life you choose. I urge you to pick up this book, flip through the Tools for Your Duty Bag sections to remind yourself of what you took away from each chapter. I also hope you will follow up by looking into the resources I have offered and see where those resources take you as well. I've been blessed to be connected with so many individuals and organizations who are passionate about promoting police resilience and hope that you will reach out to them if you need help or if you wish to help your brothers and sisters in blue.

TOOLS FOR YOUR DUTY BAG

▌ Not all mental health professionals are "shrinks! Many are current/former first responders who are culturally competent and can offer many kinds of support.

▌ There are several kinds of treatment that help flashbacks, nightmares, and other PTSD symptoms, as well as other mental health issues.

▌ Get outside in nature to improve mood, anxiety, self-esteem, and overall health.

▌ Departments (should) offer multiple forms of support: EAP, CISM, PST, and PFA.

REFERENCES

Aumiller, G., & Goldfarb, D. (2013). *My dad's a hero. . . My dad's a cop.* New York: Probity Press.

Ballenger, J. F., Best, S. R., Metzler, T. J., Wasserman, D. A., Mohr, D. C., Liberman, A., . . . Marmar, C. R. (2010). Patterns and predictors of alcohol use in male and female urban police officers. *The American Journal on Addictions, 20,* 21–29.

Barton, J., & Pretty, J. (2010). What is the best dose of nature and green exercise for improving mental health? A multi-study analysis. *Environmental Science and Technology, 44(10),* 3947–3955.

Berman, M. G., Jonides, J., & Kaplan, S. (2008). The cognitive benefits of interacting with nature. *Psychological Science, 19(12),* 1207–1212.

Deslandes, A. C. (2014). Exercise and mental health: What did we learn in the last 20 years? *Frontiers in Psychiatry, 5(66),* 1–3.

Everly, G. S., Phillips, S. B., Kane, D., & Feldman, D. (2006). Introduction to and overview of group psychological first aid. *Brief Treatment and Crisis Intervention, 6(2),* 130–136.

Faber Taylor, A., Kuo, F. E., & Sullivan, W. C. (2001). Coping with ADD: The surprising connection to green play settings. *Environment and Behavior, 33(1),* 54–77.

Foa, E. B., & Rothbaum, B. O. (1998). *Treating the trauma of rape: Cognitive-behavioral therapy for PTSD.* New York: Guilford Press.

Frankl, V. (2006). *Man's search for meaning.* Boston, MA: Beacon Press.

Gapen, M., van der Kolk, B. A., Hamlin, E., Hirschberg, L., Suvak, M., & Spinazzola, J. (2016). A pilot study of neurofeedback for chronic PTSD. *Applied Psychophysiology Biofeedback, 40(4).* Retrieved October 14, 2017, from www.traumacenter.org/products/pdf_files/Pilot_Study_Neurofeedback_Chronic_PTSD_G0002.pdf.

Hobfoll, S. E., Watson, P., Bell, C. C., Bryant, R. A., Brymer, M. J., Friedman, M. J., . . . Ursano, R. J.(2007). Five essential elements of immediate and mid-term mass trauma intervention: Empirical evidence. *Psychiatry, 70(4),* 283–315.

International Association of Chiefs of Police. (2016). *Peer support guidelines.* Retrieved October 21, 2017, from www.theiacp.org/portals/0/documents/pdfs/Psych-PeerSupportGuidelines.pdf.

International Conference of Police Chaplains. (2017). *Religious pluralism in the U. S.* Retrieved October 21, 2017, from www.icpc4cops.org/chaplaincy-intro/religious-pluralism.html.

Keller, H. (1903). *Optimism: An essay.* New York: Book Jungle.

Louv, R. (2008). *Last child in the woods: Saving our children from nature-deficit disorder.* New York: Algonquin Books.

Maier, J., & Jetter, S. (2016, May). Promoting nature-based activity for people with mental illness through the us "exercise is medicine" initiative. *American Journal of Public Health, 106(5),* 796–799.

Melton, G. D. (2016). *Love warrior: A memoir.* New York: Flatiron's Books.

National Institute of Mental Health. (2002). *Mental health and mass violence: Evidence based early psychological intervention for victims/survivors of mass violence. A workshop to reach consensus on best practices* (NIH Publication No. 02–5138). Washington, DC: U.S. Government Printing Office.

Regehr, C. (2001). Crisis debriefing groups for emergency responders: Reviewing the evidence. *Brief Treatment and Crisis Intervention, 1(2),* 87–100.

Seda, G., Sanchez-Ortuno, M. M., Welsh, C. H., Halbower, A. C., & Edinger, J. D. (2015). Comparative meta-analysis of prazosin and imagery rehearsal therapy for nightmare frequency, sleep quality, and posttraumatic stress. *Journal of Clinical Sleep Medicine, 11(1),* 11–22.

Shelden, R. G., & Macallair, D. (2008). *Juvenile justice in America: Problems and perspectives.* Long Grove, IL: Waveland Press.

Violanti, J. M. (2001). Post-traumatic stress disorder intervention in law enforcement: Differing perspectives. *The Australasian Journal of Disaster and Trauma Studies, 2.*

Wilkinson, S. T., Radhakrishnan, R., & D'Souza, D. C. (2016). A systemic review of the evidence for medical marijuana in psychiatric indications. *Journal of Clinical Psychiatry, 77*(8), 1050–1064.

World Health Organization. (2011). *Psychological first aid: Guide for field workers*. Retrieved October 15, 2017, from www.who.int/mental_health/publications/guide_field_workers/en/index.html.

Suggested Resources

UNITED STATES

Support Organizations for Police

Cop Line
Website: www.copline.org; phone: 1–800–Cop–Line
A confidential national law enforcement officer hotline that is operated by peer-support counselors on a 24/7 basis.

The Badge of Life
Website: www.badgeoflife.com; contact: Ron Clark at badgeoflife@gmail.com
A non-profit 501(c)3 organization with the mission of lessening the impacts of both stress and trauma upon police officers and retirees. Trauma, in particular, can lead to PTSD and suicide. Badge of Life is also committed to providing accurate statistics and profile information on police suicides in the United States.

International Conference of Police Chaplains
Website: www.icpc4cops.org/; phone: (850) 654–9736
An international, professional membership organization made up of chaplains and liaison officers from different faith groups and law enforcement agencies.

International Critical Incident Stress Foundation
Website: www.icisf.org; phone: (410) 750–9600
The mission of the International Critical Incident Stress Foundation, Inc., is to provide leadership, education, training, consultation, and support services in comprehensive crisis intervention and disaster behavioral health services to the emergency response professions, other organizations, and communities worldwide.

FRSN
Website: www.frsn.org; email: wcpr2001@gmail.com; phone: (415) 721–9789
Provide first responders and their families tools to reduce personal and family stress, encourage appropriate career decisions, and reduce the effects of traumatic incident stress on an individual's life. The key components of FRSN are the 6-day residential treatment for first responders, also known as the WCPR, and the 6-day program for significant others and spouses (SOS).
FRSN is a collaboration of first responder peers (included but not limited to police, fire, corrections, dispatch, and emergency medical services), SOS peers, culturally competent mental health clinicians, and chaplains; all of these individuals volunteer their time.

Safe Call Now

Website: www.safecallnow.org; phone: (206) 459–3020

A confidential crisis hotline, which is operated 24/7 by individuals vetted to support first responders.

Support Organizations for Police Families

The National Alliance for Law Enforcement Support (formerly Wives Behind the Badge)

Website: http://nalestough.org; email: info@nalestough.org; phone: (559) 392–9868

A non-profit organization dedicated to providing resources and emotional support to law enforcement officers and their families, and serving as a positive voice for law enforcement in the community.

National Police Wife Association

Website: http://nationalpolicewivesassociation.org; email: admin@national policewivesassociation.org

A non-profit organization that supports law enforcement spouses and families and provides resources to those new to the law enforcement community. National Police Wife Association is dedicated to helping individuals face the daily struggles of being in a law enforcement relationship.

The Police Wife Life

Website: www.thepolicewifelifeblog.com

Dedicated to supporting law enforcement officers and focused on bringing awareness, as well as creating respect of officers from the public. Additionally, The Police Wife Life is a national online community that offers support to those in law enforcement, spouses, family, or loved ones.

SOS

Website: www.frsn.org/retreats/significant-others-and-spouses; phone: (415) 721–9789

The SOS residential program is for emergency responder partners and spouses who have been affected by their loved one's critical incidents (resulting in secondary or vicarious trauma), but may also be experiencing symptoms of depression or anxiety and need a program to address their needs.

CANADA

Badge of Life Canada

Website: http://badgeoflifecanada.org; email: info@badgeoflifecanada.org

"Badge of Life Canada is a peer-led, charitable volunteer organization committed to supporting police and corrections personnel who are dealing with psychological injuries diagnosed from service. Providing a national online resource hub, fostering the development of peer-led support resources, develop a national training and resource network, and advancing the public's understanding of operational stress injuries, including post-traumatic stress and suicide prevention."

Tema Conter Memorial Trust

Website: www.tema.ca; phone: (888) 288–8036

Canada's leading provider of peer-support, family assistance, and training for public safety and military personnel dealing with Operational Stress and PTSD.

INDEX

US spelling is used throughout.

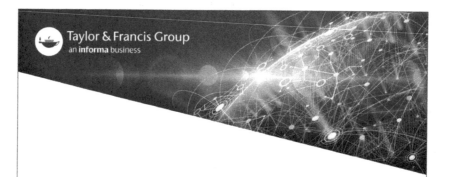